NOT EVEN A GOD CAN SAVE US NOW

McGILL-QUEEN'S STUDIES IN THE HISTORY OF IDEAS
Series Editor: Philip J. Cercone

1 Problems of Cartesianism
Edited by Thomas M. Lennon, John M. Nicholas, and John W. Davis

2 The Development of the Idea of History in Antiquity
Gerald A. Press

3 Claude Buffier and Thomas Reid: Two Common-Sense Philosophers
Louise Marcil-Lacoste

4 Schiller, Hegel, and Marx: State, Society, and the Aesthetic Ideal of Ancient Greece
Philip J. Kain

5 John Case and Aristotelianism in Renaissance England
Charles B. Schmitt

6 Beyond Liberty and Property: The Process of Self-Recognition in Eighteenth-Century Political Thought
J.A.W. Gunn

7 John Toland: His Methods, Manners, and Mind
Stephen H. Daniel

8 Coleridge and the Inspired Word
Anthony John Harding

9 The Jena System, 1804–5: Logic and Metaphysics
G.W.F. Hegel
Translation edited by John W. Burbidge and George di Giovanni
Introduction and notes by H.S. Harris

10 Consent, Coercion, and Limit: The Medieval Origins of Parliamentary Democracy
Arthur P. Monahan

11 Scottish Common Sense in Germany, 1768–1800: A Contribution to the History of Critical Philosophy
Manfred Kuehn

12 Paine and Cobbett: The Transatlantic Connection
David A. Wilson

13 Descartes and the Enlightenment
Peter A. Schouls

14 Greek Scepticism: Anti-Realist Trends in Ancient Thought
Leo Groarke

15 The Irony of Theology and the Nature of Religious Thought
Donald Wiebe

16 Form and Transformation: A Study in the Philosophy of Plotinus
Frederic M. Schroeder

17 From Personal Duties towards Personal Rights: Late Medieval and Early Modern Political Thought, c. 1300–c. 1650
Arthur P. Monahan

18 The Main Philosophical Writings and the Novel *Allwill*
Friedrich Heinrich Jacobi
Translated and edited by George di Giovanni

19 Kierkegaard as Humanist: Discovering My Self
Arnold B. Come

20 Durkheim, Morals, and Modernity
W. Watts Miller

21 The Career of Toleration: John Locke, Jonas Proast, and After
Richard Vernon

22 Dialectic of Love: Platonism in Schiller's Aesthetics
David Pugh

23 History and Memory in Ancient Greece
Gordon Shrimpton

24 Kierkegaard as Theologian: Recovering My Self
Arnold B. Come

25 Enlightenment and Conservatism in Victorian Scotland: The Career of Sir Archibald Alison
Michael Michie

26 The Road to Egdon Heath: The Aesthetics of the Great in Nature
Richard Bevis

27 Jena Romanticism and Its Appropriation of Jakob Böhme: Theosophy – Hagiography – Literature
Paolo Mayer

28 Enlightenment and Community: Lessing, Abbt, Herder, and the Quest for a German Public
Benjamin W. Redekop

29 Jacob Burckhardt and the Crisis of Modernity
John R. Hinde

30 The Distant Relation: Time and Identity in Spanish-American Fiction
Eoin S. Thomson

31 Mr Simson's Knotty Case: Divinity, Politics, and Due Process in Early Eighteenth-Century Scotland
Anne Skoczylas

32 Orthodoxy and Enlightenment: George Campbell in the Eighteenth Century
Jeffrey M. Suderman

33 Contemplation and Incarnation: The Theology of Marie-Dominique Chenu
Christophe F. Potworowski

34 Democratic Legitimacy: Plural Values and Political Power
F.M. Barnard

35 Herder on Nationality, Humanity, and History
F.M. Barnard

36 Labeling People: French Scholars on Society, Race, and Empire, 1815–1849
Martin S. Staum

37 The Subaltern Appeal to Experience: Self-Identity, Late Modernity, and the Politics of Immediacy
Craig Ireland

38 The Invention of Journalism Ethics: The Path to Objectivity and Beyond, Second Edition
Stephen J.A. Ward

39 The Recovery of Wonder: The New Freedom and the Asceticism of Power
Kenneth L. Schmitz

40 Reason and Self-Enactment in History and Politics: Themes and Voices of Modernity
F.M. Barnard

41 The More Moderate Side of Joseph de Maistre: Views on Political Liberty and Political Economy
Cara Camcastle

42 Democratic Society and Human Needs
Jeff Noonan

43 The Circle of Rights Expands: Modern Political Thought after the Reformation, 1521 (Luther) to 1762 (Rousseau)
Arthur P. Monahan

44 The Canadian Founding: John Locke and Parliament
Janet Ajzenstat

45 Finding Freedom: Hegel's Philosophy and the Emancipation of Women
Sara MacDonald

46 When the French Tried to Be British: Party, Opposition, and the Quest for Civil Disagreement, 1814–1848
J.A.W. Gunn

47 Under Conrad's Eyes: The Novel as Criticism
Michael John DiSanto

48 Media, Memory, and the First World War
David Williams

49 An Aristotelian Account of Induction: Creating Something from Nothing
Louis Groarke

50 Social and Political Bonds: A Mosaic of Contrast and Convergence
F.M. Barnard

51 Archives and the Event of God: The Impact of Michel Foucault on Philosophical Theology
David Galston

52 Between the Queen and the Cabby: Olympe de Gouges's Rights of Women
John R. Cole

53 Nature and Nurture in French Social Sciences, 1859–1914 and Beyond
Martin S. Staum

54 Public Passion: Rethinking the Grounds for Political Justice
Rebecca Kingston

55 Rethinking the Political: The Sacred, Aesthetic Politics, and the Collège de Sociologie
Simonetta Falasca-Zamponi

56 Materialist Ethics and Life-Value
Jeff Noonan

57 Hegel's *Phenomenology*: The Dialectical Justification of Philosophy's First Principles
Ardis B. Collins

58 The Social History of Ideas in Quebec, 1760–1896
Yvan Lamonde
Translated by Phyllis Aronoff and Howard Scott

59 Ideas, Concepts, and Reality
John W. Burbidge

60 The Enigma of Perception
D.L.C. Maclachlan

61 Nietzsche's Justice: Naturalism in Search of an Ethics
Peter R. Sedgwick

62 The Idea of Liberty in Canada during the Age of Atlantic Revolutions, 1776–1838
Michel Ducharme
Translated by Peter Feldstein

63 From White to Yellow: The Japanese in European Racial Thought, 1300–1735
Rotem Kowner

64 The Crisis of Modernity
Augusto Del Noce
Edited and translated by Carlo Lancellotti

65 Imprinting Britain: Newspapers, Sociability, and the Shaping of British North America
Michael Eamon

66 The Form of Politics: Aristotle and Plato on Friendship
John von Heyking

67 War as Paradox: Clausewitz and Hegel on Fighting Doctrines and Ethics
Youri Cormier

68 Network Democracy: Conservative Politics and the Violence of the Liberal Age
Jared Giesbrecht

69 A Singular Case: Debating China's Political Economy in the European Enlightenment
Ashley Eva Millar

70 Not Even a God Can Save Us Now: Reading Machiavelli after Heidegger
Brian Harding

NOT EVEN A GOD CAN SAVE US NOW

Reading Machiavelli after Heidegger

Brian Harding

McGill-Queen's University Press
Montreal & Kingston • London • Chicago

ISBN 978-0-7735-5050-6 (cloth)
ISBN 978-0-7735-5051-3 (paper)
ISBN 978-0-7735-5052-0 (ePDF)
ISBN 978-0-7735-5053-7 (ePUB)

Legal deposit second quarter 2017
Bibliothèque nationale du Québec

Printed in Canada on acid-free paper that is 100% ancient forest free (100% post-consumer recycled), processed chlorine free

McGill-Queen's University Press acknowledges the support of the Canada Council for the Arts for our publishing program. We also acknowledge the financial support of the Government of Canada through the Canada Book Fund for our publishing activities.

Library and Archives Canada Cataloguing in Publication

Harding, Brian, 1976–, author
Not even a god can save us now: reading Machiavelli after Heidegger / Brian Harding.

(McGill-Queen's studies in the history of ideas; 70)
Includes bibliographical references and index.
Issued in print and electronic formats.
ISBN 978-0-7735-5050-6 (cloth). – ISBN 978-0-7735-5051-3 (paper). – ISBN 978-0-7735-5052-0 (ePDF). – ISBN 978-0-7735-5053-7 (ePUB)

1. Machiavelli, Niccolò, 1469–1527 – Criticism and interpretation. I. Title. II. Series: McGill-Queen's studies in the history of ideas; 70

JC143.M4H37 2017 320.01 C2016-907952-X
C2016-907953-8

This book was typeset by Marquis Interscript in 10/12 New Baskerville.

Contents

Preface

In the opening chapter of his *Some Lessons on Metaphysics*, the Spanish philosopher José Ortega y Gasset writes that there is an element of dishonesty in teaching and studying philosophy. According to Ortega, the doctrines and theories taught in a philosophy course were developed not impartially or cold-bloodedly but in the heat and sweat of a kind of intellectual desperation: "if they found these truths, it is because they sought them, and if they sought them, it is because they have need of them, because for one reason or another they could not do without them."[1] For Ortega, the philosophers on his syllabus *needed* to develop these theories, and they would have considered their lives a failure if they had failed. The teacher and the student, on the other hand, do not always have that same intensity. The student may be satisfying a prerequisite; the teacher is satisfying the terms of her contract. Both will talk about philosophy in the class but are quite capable of doing it without really caring, of going through the motions. Unlike the writers studied, they can philosophize coolly and impartially. There is a similar phenomenon in writing and publishing. When we write and publish as academic philosophers in the early twenty-first century, we tend to take the stance of the impartial scholar as normative. We present ourselves as going through the motions of analysis and scholarship coolly and objectively with little personally at stake. We hide and don't admit that we wrote what we wrote because we felt the need or desire to do so. Instead, works are justified by appeals to gaps in the literature, a reply to an objection, the importance of publicizing new archival discoveries, and so forth. Rarely do academic philosophers admit that the gap appeared to them (and not others) because for some reason they (and not others) needed it to be filled, or that they formulated a reply to that

1 Ortega y Gasset, *Some Lessons in Metaphysics*, 14.

objection because they needed that reply. I know this is the case because this is what I have done many times in the past.

The aim of this work is, for better or for worse, to put Machiavelli into dialogue with a number of philosophers with whom he is not often associated: in general, what is still called "continental philosophy." In this sense, this work is undoubtedly eccentric. I hope, however, that by creating this admittedly odd conversation, certain issues and questions will come to light that would not have done so otherwise. In a recent study of Peter Abelard by the eminent medievalist John Marenbon, the latter argues that one can distinguish between four ways of approaching a figure in the history of philosophy: one can approach in terms of (1) the philosopher's past, the tradition in which he saw himself working, the predecessors he recognized; (2) the philosopher's present, his interlocutors and colleagues during his life; (3) the philosopher's future (i.e., how his work was received and interpreted by subsequent generations); and finally (4) the philosopher in *our* present (i.e., how the philosopher's work can be understood in the context of contemporary debates and concerns).[2] When it comes to Machiavelli, works addressing (1) to (3) are fairly common, and, while one can sometimes find works that relate Machiavelli's insights to contemporary concerns (nationalism, foreign relations, business ethics), there are none that I know of that address Machiavelli and continental philosophy. This book is largely a contribution to (4); I've long suspected that continental thought would benefit from a splash in the face with cold Machiavellian waters. The major themes of Machiavelli's work – the constellation of civil foundations, violence, religion, and so on – are also major themes running across twentieth-century, and now twenty-first-century, continental thought. If this isn't always apparent to casual readers, we can thank the almost surrealist prose many continental philosophers prefer to employ. In any case, I argue in this book that Machiavelli's chief themes are also present in certain continental philosophers. I do not provide any kind of encyclopaedic treatment of "Machiavelli and Continental Philosophy" but, rather, focus on the resonances of a few key thinkers and key arguments with Machiavelli's work. The three main continental thinkers upon whom I focus (Heidegger, Derrida, and Girard) are not chosen at random or arbitrarily. As will become clear in the text to follow, there is an ongoing confrontation with the works of Heidegger in Derrida and Girard; the debated points in Heidegger – without intending it or knowing it – echo many Machiavellian themes. Since the proof of the pudding is in the eating, I leave the rest for the body of the text. Nevertheless, if

2 Marenbon, *Abelard in Four Dimensions.*

the reader thinks that other philosophers would make better interlocutors for Machiavelli, he or she ought to rely on his/her own insight and write another book rather than complain that fortune did not give her/him the book she/he wanted.

* * *

A word about the structure and organization of this book is in order. While it is broken up into chapters, the chapters themselves are broken up into sections. It may appear to the reader that the transitions between numbered sections are sometimes quite abrupt, especially in the first chapter. For that, I beg the reader's patience and forbearance. My hope is that, even if the transitions seem somewhat abrupt, the overall development of the argument will be clear. If I may venture a self-serving comparison, the reader should take the numbered sections as so many dots in a pointillist painting.

Pieces of the argument in this book have been presented at conferences in Belfast, Houston, Mexico City, New Orleans, and San Antonio. Needless to say, I benefited by the comments and questions from participants at these conferences. J. Aaron Simmons and an anonymous reviewer read the entire manuscript for the press and provided helpful comments and criticisms. While I am confident that there is still material in the book with which they will not agree, I am sure that it is stronger thanks to their efforts. My editor at McGill-Queen's University Press, Mark Abley, was both encouraging and helpful; Joanne Richardson did a wonderful job editing the book. While I am thinking of past debts, it occurs to me that McDwyer's Pub in the Norwood section of the Bronx has closed after over fifty years of service. While I generally resist nostalgia, I make an exception for Washington Heights, Inwood, and the Bronx. When I was a graduate student, McDwyer's Pub (and the other bars on Bainbridge Avenue) became my refuge from both the lonely stress of studies and the expensive silliness of Brooklyn and Manhattan. I would not want to let the passing go unnoticed. Much of my time at McDwyer's was spent with Jeff Hanson and Mike Kelly, and they remain my two principle interlocutors in matters philosophical. I also owe thanks to my colleagues at TWU, my friends (Matt, Kim, and the entire Edgar clan; the Pilkington, Lee, and Chapman families; Rob Guzman, Chris Bartek, Jack O'Connor, Joe Trabbic, the Flannerys of County Mayo, and many others), my brother, sister, parents, in-laws, nieces and nephews, and my children. But I am especially grateful to my wife Felicia, to whom this book is dedicated, for having patiently listened to me ramble on about murder, human sacrifice, and other cheerful topics.

NOT EVEN A GOD CAN SAVE US NOW

1

Reading Machiavelli with Post-Heideggerian Philosophy

WITH A FEW NOTABLE EXCEPTIONS, Machiavelli is rarely discussed in depth by philosophers working in what is commonly called "continental philosophy," but which, with more accuracy, might be called "post-Heideggerian philosophy." While one can find occasional references to him here or there, these remarks are usually superficial gestures towards a generic "Machiavellianism" rather than a careful engagement with the themes of his thought. Likewise, few scholars working on Machiavelli attempt to engage post-Heideggerian philosophy. Both tendencies, I think, are lamentable since many of the problems that engage major figures in the continental tradition also engaged Machiavelli. I have in mind themes including the relationship among violence, religion, and politics; the origin or foundations of authority; the relationship between philosophy and politics; the critique or overcoming of Platonism. This list is not meant to be exhaustive, but it is meant to be suggestive of the fertile yields this cross-pollination of Machiavelli and post-Heideggerian philosophy could produce. In fact, I believe that a careful reading of Machiavelli in dialogue with at least some post-Heideggerian philosophers (Heidegger himself, Jacques Derrida, and René Girard) will shed more light on these themes than either Machiavelli or those post-Heideggerian philosophers could in isolation.

SACRIFICIAL THEMES IN MACHIAVELLI AND OTHERS

"Post-Heideggerian" is an ugly word; in fact, the hyphen is probably the least objectionable part of it. But I use it, despite the infelicitous style, because it does double duty, both designating a time period (commencing in the twentieth century) and indicating a tradition or conversation that takes it inspiration from, or responds to, the work of Heidegger. It might be better to replace it with another phrase, such as "new phenomenology." Simmons and Benson use this term to designate "those French philosophers in the latter half of the twentieth century who all think in the wake of Edmund Husserl and Martin Heidegger."[1] I think we can all agree that "new phenomenology" is more euphonious than "post-Heideggerian." However, I cannot avail myself of the term because it would be a bit misleading in the context of this book since one of the thinkers with whom I concern myself – René Girard – can hardly be considered a phenomenologist, although he does engage Heidegger's work at length, and even occasionally refers to Husserl.[2] So, I am stuck with "post-Heideggerian." Obviously, the philosophers I discuss are not the only post-Heideggerian philosophers in the world. Moreover, it should be obvious from the list of themes in the earlier paragraph that I am not addressing every important theme or argument in Heidegger's thought. Instead, I am only addressing those post-Heideggerian themes that are illuminated by reference to themes in Machiavelli, and only addressing those post-Heideggerian philosophers who I believe address them in an interesting or important way. Whence, while, for example, Jean-Luc Marion is certainly a post-Heideggerian thinker, because his work focuses more on (a) replacing Heidegger's concern with being with a concern with givenness and (b) rethinking subjectivity on the basis of givenness rather than, say, the more Machiavellian theme of the relationship between philosophy and politics, I do not discuss Marion.[3]

So far, I have referred to "Machiavellian themes" and "post-Heideggerian" themes and suggested that there are interesting overlaps between the two. The reader would be right to wonder if there is any deeper unity. That is to say, even if the themes overlap, is there anything that unites all of them, any overarching horizon that enables us to treat them as related to each other? I think that there is such an overarching horizon, and that it is, in a word, sacrifice. While I have more to say about that later, for now let's invoke René Girard's understanding of sacrifice as a kind of communal violence involving a distinction between (a) good sacrificial violence that preserves or founds the community and (b) bad non-sacrificial violence that undermines or threatens the community.

For Girard, the essential moment in the life of a community is the murder or expulsion of the scapegoat. Due to what Girard calls the mimetic

1 Simmons and Benson, *New Phenomenology*, 1.

2 The engagement with Heidegger is discussed later in the book, with appropriate references given at that point; for the brief reference to Husserl, see R. Girard, VS, 200. The reference to Husserl is fairly trivial anyway.

3 For a more inclusive discussion of post-Heideggerian thinkers under the rubric of new phenomenology, see Simmons and Benson, *New Phenomenology*.

nature of desire – that is, that one wants or desires primarily what other people desire – conflict is inevitable among those who live close together. Over time, the various tensions, problems, and rivalries in community build up towards an explosion of violence. If an outlet for this violence is not found, the community will tear itself to pieces. In these paroxysms of mimetic violence, communities spontaneously turn on one person or group of persons as the source of all ills. It is not important, in the final analysis, whether or not this unfortunate person really is guilty – in most cases, he or she is probably not guilty. What is important is that he or she is perceived as such and punished accordingly. This person or persons functions as the scapegoat; he or she is expelled from the community, becoming subject to punishment, exile, and death. Turning against this victim restores the unanimity once shattered by mimetic rivalry. The death of the victim restores calm, at least temporarily (VS 78–9). But because the cure is only temporary, mimetic rivalry will eventually rear its ugly head again. In this case, the community may return to what worked in the past, repeating the murder of the scapegoat in the hopes of forestalling the crisis. This time the killing is a premeditated sacrifice rather than a spontaneous one. This is, according to Girard, the beginning of ritual: "Rite is the re-enactment of mimetic crises in a spirit of voluntary religious and social collaboration, a re-enactment in order to reactivate the scapegoat mechanism for the benefit of society rather than for the detriment of the victim who is perpetually sacrificed" (SG 140). In the sacrificial rite, we find the distinction between good and bad violence (the good violence of sacrifice and the bad violence of communal strife), the selection of a victim, and the direction of good violence towards this victim. Good sacrificial violence functions as a kind of catharsis that relieves some of the pressure and enables the community to (re)constitute itself.

Machiavelli's philosophy arguably orbits around the question of sacrifice; and Heidegger, Derrida, and (of course) Girard all make their own attempts at understanding, interpreting, explaining, and critiquing sacrifice. I am not claiming that Machiavelli self-consciously set sacrifice at the centre of his project. That is to say, while he distinguishes between good and bad violence (as, for example, in his distinction between cruelty well used and badly used), I do not think that he saw that distinction as the core of his thought. But this is, in fact, what I think happens irrespective of his intentions, and I believe that a "sacrificial" reading of Machiavelli can clarify many obscurities in his thought. At the same time, this way of reading Machiavelli offers a number of insights that are useful when engaging with post-Heideggerian philosophy. I will not try to prove either point right now, but hopefully, over the course of the book, the reader will be convinced.

There is a certain amount of decontextualizing at play: rather than reading Machiavelli in terms of his immediate historical context, I am looking centuries ahead of him. If I translate Machiavelli into a new context, it is inevitable that someone will say *traduttore, traditore.* This is the risk one takes whenever one attempts to bring a historical figure to bear on contemporary philosophical debates. One who does so is, essentially, betting that the benefits of translation outweigh the risks; whether or not this is a good bet cannot be determined clearly at the outset. The juxtaposition, for whatever purposes, of Machiavelli with post-Heideggerian philosophy is admittedly weird. Some of the weirdness can be alleviated by drawing a distinction between (a) doing philosophy historically and (b) doing the history of philosophy. This distinction has been explored by Robert Piercey at some length.

According to Piercey, the historical philosopher differs from the historian of philosophy in two ways. First, the historical philosopher is interested not so much in historical questions of sources, biography, and cultural context as she is in how philosophers have responded to an idea or problem. Second, the "idea" the historical philosopher is interested in is not so much a theory as it is the picture of the world that the theory attempts to articulate. Piercey explains this distinction by quoting the words of Gary Gutting: "it is very important to distinguish between the *theory* that provides a specific detailed formulation of a philosophical position such as Platonic realism or Berkeleyean idealism and the general *picture* of reality that such formulations are trying to articulate."[4] As Piercey points out, many philosophers who would reject the details of, for example, Cartesian philosophy are characterized as Cartesians because they accept the general picture that Descartes was trying to articulate. These pictures are not so much principles or fundamental theoretical commitments as they are "dispositions to approach philosophical problems in certain characteristic ways … They are not explanations of phenomena, but injunctions to seek explanations of a certain kind."[5] One could say that the "pictures" in question are tendencies or predilections towards certain kinds of questions and, inevitably, certain kinds of answers. Often the picture functions as the (almost entirely) unnoticed horizon on which the thinker operates. Doing philosophy historically involves tracing the history, or "track record," of these pictures. Understanding the history, or *wirkungsgeschichte,* of these "pictures" offers a different kind of understanding than does that of the inquiry into

4 Gutting, *Pragmatic Liberalism,* 191; quoted in Piercey, *Uses of the Past,* 21 (emphasis in original).

5 Piercey, *Uses of the Past,* 26.

theory: by seeing how these pictures are formulated, developed, challenged, and revised, one can gain insight into their overall strengths and weaknesses. As Piercey continues, he remarks that one who attempts to do philosophy historically will have four tasks: (a) to select the historical figures, (b) to argue for a certain way of viewing these figures, (c) to persuade the audience they are related in some way, and (d) to engage critically with these thinkers.[6] Finally, on the basis of (a) through (d), one should make some kind of general point about the picture in question. The goal, finally, is "to bring about a certain kind of 'seeing as'… the experience of seeing a number of philosophers not just as individuals, but as embodiments of a certain picture."[7] When the historical philosopher is successful, the reader sees his or her subjects in a new way, as part of a new story or narrative. As far as this work goes, I am interested in pictures of the sacrificial distinction between bad and good violence. I find these themes clearly articulated in Machiavelli but more obscurely at work in other more recent thinkers; after recognizing the picture in Machiavelli, it is easier to see it in them. While none of the recent figures I address (e.g., Heidegger, Derrida) would normally be characterized as followers of Machiavelli – to continue with Piercey's terms – this book suggests that they should be "seen as" sharing the same basic picture.

READING MACHIAVELLI BY HIMSELF

Since the bulk of this text is about Machiavelli, it makes sense to say some things about the man himself. Machiavelli's identity is not very much in question: he is the former secretary of the Florentine Republic and the author of some very important and influential books – most notably, *The Prince* in 1513 and *Discourses on Livy* around 1517.[8] Admittedly, this account of his life is only slightly more detailed than Heidegger's famous biography of Aristotle – he was born, he worked, he died – but it serves the purposes of this paragraph well enough, and more details are available to anyone who wants them in the many excellent biographies of

6 Ibid., 34.

7 Ibid., 40.

8 These dates are approximate, and more details about the precise dates of Machiavelli's composition can be found in Black, *Machiavelli*, 89–96 (on *The Prince*); 130–8 (on the *Discourses*). Black does not accept the theory that the writing of the two texts overlapped, but he does argue that they are closely related (132).

Machiavelli.[9] Let us focus on those "important and influential books": what kind of books *are* these books, and what kind of writer *is* Machiavelli?

To provide an answer that may seem straightforward: he is a political philosopher and his major works are books on political philosophy. It is fairly common to describe Machiavelli as a founder of modern political theory. However, when the issue is pressed and one asks about the precise nature of Machiavelli's work one finds much less agreement. The various conflicting interpretations of Machiavelli's work – ranging from Cardinal Pole's claim that *The Prince* destroys civilization to Rousseau's claim that it is a highly moral text[10] – stem, I think, from the multilayered structure of his books. Machiavelli's texts proceed on (at least!) three distinct levels. To take *The Prince* as an example, although I believe similar considerations apply to all his major texts, one can discern (a) a sort of mirror for princes (*specula principum*), albeit an unconventional one; but also (b) the development and application of a political theory, broadly construed; and finally (c) the broader philosophical horizon upon which (a) and (b) stand. The tripartite structure of Machiavelli's texts already makes interpreting him difficult; this is compounded by his habit of saying one thing, only to take it back or qualify it later. He is a slippery fish. Take as an example Machiavelli's discussion of Agathocles in *The Prince*: after describing his cruel and murderous rise to power, Machiavelli says that one cannot call this virtuous behaviour (P VIII). However, by the end of that same chapter, he has argued that Agathocles's cruelty, executed quickly and decisively, is well used and in fact a virtue. He goes so far as to imply that both God and man will forgive cruelty well used. Not surprisingly, a wide variety of hooks and nets have been constructed to try to catch this fish.

For the sake of convenience, I divide the readings into two groups. This division is arbitrary and, in the long run, misleading. But, for the next few pages, it is a useful heuristic device, and I use it here, although I abandon it as soon as it has served its purpose. The first group approaches Machiavelli in terms of larger philosophical questions. Here, the interpretation of Machiavelli is guided by extra-Machiavellian concerns; one might say that the ultimate concern is not to get Machiavelli right but, rather, to use Machiavelli as a way of gaining access to something else, or as a way of framing a question or group of questions. The

9 See, for example, Black, *Machiavelli*; de Grazia, *Machiavelli in Hell*; R. Ridolfi, *Life of Niccolò Machiavelli*; Viroli, *Niccolò's Smile*. This list is hardly exhaustive.

10 Both these judgments and others are discussed in Benner, *Machiavelli's Prince*, xix–xii; Soll, "Reception of *The Prince*," 31–60, offers a more detailed account of the early reception of Machiavelli.

second group approaches Machiavelli largely in terms of Machiavelli himself and his historical context: here the goal is to get Machiavelli right, to discover what he really meant. In this approach, the question of Machiavelli's sources is much more pressing than in the first approach: we want to know what he read, when he read it, and so forth. While each approach can complement the other, there is inevitably a tension between them. Group one tends to complain that group two misses the philosophical significance of Machiavelli, that it can explain his sources and context in detail, but not why anybody should be interested in them; group two tends to complain that group one plays fast and loose with the texts, pulling them out of their historical context and either misunderstanding or wilfully misinterpreting them to make philosophical points.[11] This is not to say that group two does not think we can learn anything from Machiavelli but, rather, that if we are to learn anything from him, we must first carefully attend to the cultural, historical, and literary context.

Turning now to group one, I discuss two representatives: Leo Strauss and Louis Althusser. Both treat Machiavelli as a philosopher of the first order. For those who follow Strauss, Machiavelli's importance consists in a rejection of classical political philosophy and the endorsement of an alternate morality based on that rejection; Machiavelli's break with classical political and moral thought is a philosophical and moral revolution on par with that of Socrates. For Althusser, Machiavelli's devotion to thinking through one concrete political problem – an Italian revolution – marks him as "the greatest materialist philosopher in history."[12] In Althusser's reading, Machiavelli offers "objective knowledge" of politics rather than ideology. The ideology in question is that same great tradition that Strauss saw Machiavelli as breaking with, and, interestingly enough, Althusser – like Strauss on occasion – argues as much from what Machiavelli says as from what he does not say:

Through his silences even more than his words, we may infer which discourses Machiavelli condemns definitively: not only *edifying* religious, moral or aesthetic discourse of the court humanists, and even radical humanists; not only the

11 For a dated but still representative statement of group one's criticisms of group two, see Tarcov, "Quentin Skinner's Method and Machiavelli's *Prince*"; Tarcov's paper has the advantage of offering good summaries – if only to argue against later – of group two's criticisms of group one. More recently, pages 4 to 11 and the endnotes running from pages 188 to 199 in William Parsons, *Machiavelli's Gospel*, offer a thorough discussion of the debate. Parson's allegiance is squarely with what I call group one.

12 Althusser, *Machiavelli and Us*, 103.

> revolutionary sermons of Savonarola; but also the entire tradition of Christian theology and all the political theories of Antiquity. How can we fail to notice that with the exception of Aristotle, cited once in passing, Machiavelli never invokes the great political texts of Plato, Aristotle, the Epicureans, the Stoics and Cicero? He who admired antiquity so much, he whose thoughts were nurtured on examples drawn from the history of Athens, Sparta and Rome, never explained himself on this score except by silence. But at a time when no one discussed politics except in the language of Aristotle, Cicero and Christianity, this silence stood for a declaration of rupture.[13]

While numerous objections have been raised to the Straussian or Althusserian reading of Machiavelli, both remain compelling insofar as they take Machiavelli as a philosopher of the highest order, worthy of comparison with Plato, Aristotle, Marx, and Heidegger. For both Strauss and Althusser, and group one readers of Machiavelli in general, one approaches Machiavelli primarily in terms of philosophical problems or themes rather than his historical context. In both cases, one could plausibly argue that neither Strauss's *Thoughts on Machiavelli* nor Althusser's *Machiavelli and Us* are, in the final analysis, *really* about Machiavelli. One might claim, for example, that Strauss's book is really about the nature of modern thought and how it differs from the classical tradition or that Althusser's is really about developing a historical pedigree for his version of Marxism. In short, both Strauss and Althusser could be described as "doing philosophy historically" rather than as doing the history of philosophy.

In contrast to these readings of Machiavelli, group two is less willing to endorse a radically original Machiavelli but, instead, reads him in the context of a Renaissance republicanism that had been percolating for some time – a movement different from, but no doubt inspired by, the traditions of ancient Rome. Quentin Skinner, Sebastian de Grazia, and Maurizio Viroli (among others) have argued for this position in different, but more or less complimentary, ways. This Machiavelli is typically less radical, less revolutionary, and less subversive than the Machiavelli on offer by group one. Here he emerges as a high-water mark of a longstanding tradition of republican political theory, a figure of immense historical importance, but not as a great philosopher on the order of group one's vision.

13 Ibid., 7–8 (emphasis in original).

FURIOUS WITH *ORLANDO FURIOSO*

Another interpretive wrinkle, especially for the more philosophical readings of Machiavelli preferred by group one, is that Machiavelli never identities himself as a philosopher. His favourite job descriptions were those connected to his diplomatic work for Florence, and, in his literary capacity, he refers to himself as a poet, playwright, and historian. Indeed, in 1517 he complained to Lodovico Alamanni that Ariosto did not include him in the list of major Italian poets in *Orlando Furioso* (L #166). But, it can be objected, the mere fact that *he* didn't identify himself as a philosopher does not mean that he was right to eschew that label and that we should not read him as such. Perhaps, perhaps not. In any case, there has been a great deal of work done on Machiavelli that approaches him as a philosopher. Against this, Maurizio Viroli argues extensively against a philosophical reading of Machiavelli's political writings, contending that they are better understood in terms of rhetoric than of philosophy. He writes: "[Machiavelli] did not intend to found a new science of politics, but to retrieve and refine the conception of political theory as an essentially rhetorical practice."[14] As such, for Viroli, one problem that has long vexed Machiavelli scholars (and that partially motivates Strauss's esoteric reading of Machiavelli), the relationship between *The Prince* and the *Discourses*, simply dissolves. For Viroli, there is no systematic relationship between the two texts: they are just two different works addressed to different audiences. If this is accepted, the problem of explaining or interpreting the various inconsistencies, tensions, and contradictions between his various texts disappears. To readers trained in philosophy (who hear Socrates's debate with Gorgias ringing in their ears whenever "rhetoric" is invoked), such an approach to Machiavelli can be a bitter pill to swallow. Isn't philosophy predicated on the rejection of rhetoric? If Machiavelli merely offers us rhetoric, why should *philosophers* read his works? But the case is not so simple: through the good offices of Cicero, philosophy and rhetoric were reconciled although not identified with each other. And in fact, the rhetoric that Viroli attributes to Machiavelli is that of the Ciceronian, or more generally Roman, *scientia civilis*. This scientia civilis is a rhetoric devoted to the common good of the city, not the individualistic self-aggrandizement of Gorgias or Callicles.

But reading Machiavelli as a rhetorician runs into one of the same problems as does the philosophical reading: he never refers to himself as a rhetorician. This does not, however, mean that he isn't one: it may just

14 Viroli, *Machiavelli*, i.

mean that he did not consider himself a professional rhetorician (i.e., one who makes his living by rhetoric). This would not prevent us from considering that his writings are informed by rhetoric. And Viroli provides ample evidence for such a claim. However, a similar argument can be made for the philosophical reading: he does not refer to himself as a philosopher because he is not professionally engaged in philosophy in the way that he was for his paid work (e.g., historian of Florence). This would not prevent us from considering that at least some of his writings are informed by philosophy. Moreover, the fact that he uses rhetorical devices and structures his writing according to the rules of rhetoric does not exclude the possibility that his rhetoric may be a vehicle for his philosophy. Cicero, after all, wrote according to the rules of Roman rhetoric, but he did not think that this precluded writing philosophy.

EXAMPLES TO IMITATE AND AVOID

Let us return to that wrinkle I mentioned earlier: while Machiavelli did not refer to himself as a philosopher or as a rhetorician, he did identify himself as both a poet and a historian. Certainly, the identification of himself as a poet refers to his poems and his plays, and we can assume at a minimum that the biography of Castruccio Castracani (1518) and the *Florentine Histories* (presented to Pope Clement VII in 1525) provide good grounds for his self-identification as a historian. Did he forget about his works of a few years earlier, *The Prince* and *Discourses on Livy,* when he chose these labels for himself? Or maybe they fit here somehow? A case could be made for including the *Discourses* under the rubric of history since it is (nominally at least) a commentary on the works of Titus Livy. *The Prince* fits less well, but could be shoe-horned into "history" because of the vast number of historical examples. Presumably, when Machiavelli encourages young princes to exclusively study history in P XIV, he does not mean to exclude *The Prince* itself. In fact, in his epistle dedicatory he presents *The Prince* as a digest of what he has learned from his study of ancient history as well as from his own experiences. Let us allow this hypothesis – that Machiavelli counted the *Discourses* and *The Prince* among his historical works – to stand for a bit, so that it can be explored. If they are histories, what kind of histories are they?

In the nineteenth century, Leopold Von Ranke declared that the task of the historian is to describe the past *wie es eigentlich gewesen ist.* The task of the historian is to describe the past as accurately as possible, making use of as much empirical data – both archaeological and archival – as is necessary. On this standard, even Machiavelli's more obviously historical works are not very good. This is not, however, a standard that Machiavelli would have recognized. Renaissance historians had a rather different understanding of the historian's role; like all other aspects of learning, history, humanists argued, should have a moral or didactic component.[15] This humanist imperative is anticipated in the ancient Roman historian whom Machiavelli loved above all others, Titus Livy. In the opening pages of his history of Rome, Titus Livy writes that the reader should pay close attention to "what life and morals were like; through what men and by what policies, in peace and in war, empire was established and enlarged; then let him note how, with the gradual relaxation of discipline, morals first gave way, as it were, then sank lower and lower, and finally began the downward plunge which has brought us to the present time, when we can neither endure our vices nor their cures."[16] The point of history, then, is not the disinterested attempt to see how things really were, but to acquire moral and political knowledge. This is made clearer by Livy a few lines later, when he challenges his readers to "choose for yourself and your own state (*rei publicae*) what to imitate" and to "mark for avoidance what is shameful."[17] History, on Livy's presentation, is didactic and moralizing. Indeed, Livy – like Machiavelli – has been known to distort the facts when such a distortion is more conducive to the moral he wishes to impart to his readers.[18] Likewise, in the beginning of part two of his *Discourses*, Machiavelli writes that he wants to inspire the "spirits of the youths" to prepare themselves to imitate the ancients when they have the opportunity to do so (D II.p1).

So, if *The Prince* and the *Discourses* are histories, it would mean that they are interested in presenting the reader with noble examples to imitate and base ones to avoid. This would complement the rhetorical reading of Machiavelli to the extent that the use of examples is particularly important in rhetorical arguments.[19] If Machiavelli's major works are "histories" in this Livian sense, then he is not so much interested in recitations of facts about the past as he is in inspiring certain actions by motivating certain ways of looking at persons and events. And we have good reason for thinking of (at least) the major works in these terms: Machiavelli

15 For a discussion of Machiavelli's own practice as a historian that points to this element, see Bondanella, "Castruccio Castracani," 302–14.

16 Livy, *Ab Urbe Condita*, I.p9.

17 Ibid., I.p10–11.

18 See the classic discussion in Walsh "Livy's Preface and the Distortion of History." For an interesting case study of Machiavelli's distortion of the historical record, see Viroli, *Machiavelli's God*, 109–44, on his account of Catarina Sforza.

19 The *locus classicus* for the importance of examples in rhetoric is Aristotle, *Rhetoric*, 1393a25–1394a20; but the same point is also made in numerous places by Cicero (e.g., *De Oratore* II.9.36); there is a good discussion of this point in Viroli, *Machiavelli's God*, 124–7.

states repeatedly his hope that his *Discourses on Livy* will show men of his times that imitation of the ancients is possible, and in *The Prince* he urges the study of history and imitation of great princes of the past (D, I.pr and P XIV). At the same time, Machiavelli, as much as Titus Livy before him, has to offer reasons *why* such-and-such an action is noble and another action is base, or why this prince is great and that one is not, if he wishes to be persuasive. This rhetorical history will have to be able to give reasons *why* this or that is to be imitated. A moralizing history cannot be a mere chronology: it must at least *flirt* with philosophy.

OCCASIONS FOR WRITING

While the precise nature of his writings – philosophy, history, or rhetoric – is debatable, his approach to writing is less so. Machiavelli is an occasionalist in that he mainly writes when he has occasion to: a hope for a job, a request from friends, a commission, and so forth. The occasional character of Machiavelli's writings is reminiscent of St Augustine, whose major works were largely interventions in controversies of his day. And another comparison with Augustine is helpful for understanding Machiavelli on this point. While he held strong views on ethics, politics, metaphysics, and epistemology, Augustine never attempted to develop a systematic exposition that existed apart from an opponent: if he wasn't arguing, he wasn't writing. Augustine's individual pieces are coloured as much by the view he is opposing as by his own. This means that students of the Bishop of Hippo have to weigh each of Augustine's claims against his others; the varying weights assigned to various texts have yielded a robust harvest of different kinds of Augustinianisms. At the same time, there are certain themes that are recognizably Augustinian, and there is a kind of family resemblance between the variety of Augustinianism known to the history of philosophy and theology. Likewise, Machiavelli's occasionalism suggests that there will be both a variety of differing Machiavellianism, depending on what texts are emphasized, but also a family resemblance between all these differing takes on his work.

Augustine's disinclination to develop a theological or philosophical system was not the result of a lack of intelligence; rather, it was symptomatic of the intellectual culture of the day. Philosophy and theology were primarily ways of life, not the theoretical discourse of professors, so the important thing is not the articulation (or the clever concealment) of a system or theory, but the cultivation of the good life. Pierre Hadot describes the phenomenon as follows:

> Philosophical discourse takes the form of an appeal, as not only an exercise designed to develop the intelligence of the disciple, but also that of an exercise designed to transform his life. It is in this way that they are no longer constrained only to pedagogy, but the need for psychagogy and for the direction of souls arises, which keeps ancient philosophical discourse from being perfectly systematic. The propositions that they compose do not always express adequately the theoretical thoughts of philosophy, but they are to be understood in the perspective of the effect that they aim to produce in the soul of the auditor.[20]

By "systematic" I do not think Hadot has in mind solely the Hegelianism criticized under that term by Kierkegaard, but any developed theoretical position regarding some issue(s) in philosophy that attempts to be cohesive, comprehensive, and argumentative. By "developed theoretical position" I mean something going beyond a mere preference or even presupposition, I mean a position that both defends itself and attempts to either accommodate or to refute competing positions and whose primary concern is theoretical – the correct and complete understanding of an issue – rather than practical. This does not exclude practical concerns but, rather, subordinates them to theoretical elegance and consistency. By "cohesive" I mean that an attempt is made to ensure that contradictions and tensions between different parts of the overall project are avoided or eliminated. By "comprehensive" I mean that the answer offered attempts to answer the question completely, leaving as little out as possible, including here responses to possible objections. By "argumentative" I mean that this answer is not a matter of unwarranted assertion or narration but is argued for in a philosophical manner recognizable to his or her peers. I take this understanding of "system" to be quite broad, and the use of the term does not imply success at achieving a cohesive, comprehensive, and argumentative answer to a philosophical question – only a good-faith attempt. A philosopher may by systematic but still unsuccessful. Likewise, nothing in my definition of systematic requires that this be done explicitly or otherwise: in short, it is agnostic regarding whether or not a system is esoteric or exoteric. Moreover, I take it that cohesiveness, comprehensiveness, and argumentativeness are equally necessary for a philosophy to be termed systematic. Lacking any one of the three would be enough to keep a thinker from being properly systematic. Likewise, neither cohesiveness, nor comprehensiveness, nor argumentativeness alone is sufficient for a philosophy to be termed systematic.

20 Hadot, "La philosophie antique," 211–12.

According to Hadot, ancient philosophers were not systematic because their goals were primarily practical rather than theoretical: to obtain the good and to live a happy life.[21] This understanding of philosophy mirrors Livy's presentation of history. In both cases, the theoretician's concern with "getting it right" is subordinated to the practical concern of making people good. While Machiavelli admittedly wants his prince to learn how not to be good (P XV), the general point regarding the primarily practical or moral aims of his work, as opposed to theoretical elegance, I believe can stand. Viroli agrees, pointing out that "all his greatest works … were designed to shape souls."[22] To summarize our discussion thus far: beginning with a consideration of Machiavelli as rhetorician, a lack of systematic philosophical pretensions was noted. Turning to his self-identification as a historian, a brief discussion of the practical goals of the Roman historian Livy followed. These practical goals, we should note, are shared by both the ancient philosopher and the Renaissance rhetorician. Thus, the rhetorical, philosophical, and historical readings of Machiavelli can be synthesized: he is a historian in the mode of Titus Livy who uses historical events to comment on his time and to inspire virtue.

The didactic concerns of ancient philosophy did not, however, render them indifferent to truth. Most, if not all, ancient philosophers argued that their school would make one happy and good because their doctrines were true. So the lack of systematic theoretical interests did not yield an indifference to the truth or falsity of doctrines, or render high-level theoretical debate superfluous, but only subordinated this to the more practical concern of living a good life. Likewise, I do not mean to suggest that Machiavelli doesn't care whether or not his account is true, but only that he is more concerned with inspiring his readers to imitate what he finds to be worthy of imitation than he is with developing a systematic theory of nobility or goodness. Moreover, the lack of both self-identification as a philosopher and a systematic philosophy in Machiavelli does not mean that he had no opinions about philosophy, nor even that he has little relevance to philosophy. Certainly, the history of philosophy, especially political philosophy, attests to the relevance of Machiavelli for philosophers even if he didn't label himself one. More importantly, the deeper background to his practical advice and political theory, although relegated to the horizon of this thought and not systematically

21 For a more detailed discussion, with references, of Hadot on this point, see Harding, *Augustine and Roman Virtue*, 23–6.

22 Viroli, *Machiavelli's God*, 106.

developed, is nevertheless (in my view) profound and worthy of consideration. In the same way that scholars have pointed to stoicism as the philosophical horizon upon which Livy's historical narrative plays out, one may ask about the deeper philosophical horizon of Machiavelli's work as a historian.[23] The above discussion of the unsystematic nature of his thought only serves to suggest *how* we should consider them.

But if this is the case, if (a) *The Prince* and the *Discourses* (and so on) are histories in the Livian sense, and (b) there is more psychagogy than systematicity to Machiavelli's writings, what does this mean for students of Machiavelli? How should we consider him? The above reflections suggest a few strategies for reading Machiavelli. First, we have to be aware of the occasional and unsystematic nature of his writings, and we will have to admit that, due to the nature of his writings, there will probably never be a definitive interpretation of Machiavelli. As noted earlier, there is a great deal of disagreement even regarding simple expository questions, such as "What is *The Prince* about" – a problem that is generally not found in more systematic thinkers. While there may be debates regarding details of interpretation, there is no widespread disagreement as to the overall point of Russell's "On Denoting." Second, we should take seriously the moral and didactic aims of his histories. Machiavelli rarely makes explicit his standards for nobility or baseness; I'm not sure if this is because he prefers to let them emerge through the historical narrative or if it is because he has not thought through the deepest implications of his works.[24] In either case, it is my contention that Machiavelli's recommendations rest on a structure that could be described (for reasons that I describe in more detail later) as sacrificial. By sacrifice I have in mind the (a) production of a distinction between legitimate and illegitimate violence, and (b) the deployment of this distinction for the benefit of the community by (c) producing a class of victims against whom the good or legitimate violence can be directed.[25] I do not mean anything "theological" per se: as René Girard points out, nothing in the account of sacrifice just adumbrated requires that the victim be offered up "to some individual of a particularly bloodthirsty temperament" (VS 8).

23 On Livy's stoicism, see P.G. Walsh's classic paper, "Livy and Stoicism."

24 "Rarely" is not the same as never: arguably, P 15–18 offers a criticism of traditional standards of nobility and baseness that is fairly explicit. However, if my reading of Machiavelli is correct, then the deepest basis of these criticisms is not explicitly stated in those passages.

25 This understanding of sacrifice is borrowed more or less wholesale from the work of R. Girard. I discuss it in more detail with appropriate references later in the text.

Sacrifice is not essentially propitiatory, but it is prophylactic: it protects the community from violence by directing violence outward – *away* from the community. Sacrificial violence founds and preserves communities in the face of threats and crisis. In this sense, we find sacrificial themes in not only Machiavelli but also in Heidegger (most clearly, but not exclusively) in his *Introduction to Metaphysics* and in Derrida (again, most clearly, but not exclusively) in his essays "The Force of Law" and "Faith and Knowledge."

2

Sacrifice and the Eternity of the World

IT IS NOT READILY APPARENT that the sacrificial distinction between good and bad violence is at the centre of Machiavelli's thought. He assumes something like this distinction in a variety of places but never explicitly or directly argues for it, and he certainly never discusses opposing views, either that all forms of violence are bad or that all forms of violence are good. Machiavelli's sacrificial distinction remains implicit and unstated, and almost never argued for. I say "almost never" because, while he doesn't take up the issue directly, he often beats around the bush, coming frustratingly close to (a) explicitly stating and endorsing it and (b) rejecting one or more alternatives to it. We can see this dynamic at work in his discussion of the eternity of the world in book II of Machiavelli's *Discourses on Livy*. The endorsement of this thesis functions – as I argue shortly – as a substitute for (b), and the discussion of ancient religion that nearly immediately precedes it comes as close to (a) as we get in Machiavelli. To see how, let us turn to the *Discourses*.

ANCIENT EDUCATION AND THE ETERNITY OF THE WORLD

The discussion of the eternity of the world occurs in chapter 5 of book II of Machiavelli's *Discourses on Livy*. In that chapter, Machiavelli alludes to the fact that some people (philosophers) believe that the world is eternal: "To those philosophers who would have it that the world is eternal, I believe that one could reply that if so much antiquity were true it would be reasonable that there be memory of more than five thousand years – if it were not seen how the memories of time are eliminated by diverse causes, of which part come from men, part from heaven" (D II.5). Nathan Tarcov astutely points out that Machiavelli is arguing *from* the claim that the world is eternal rather than *to* the claim.[1] It is worthwhile presenting Machiavelli's argument more formally since it is fairly convoluted. In the first clause, we find that some philosophers think the world is eternal. Let us call the position that the world is eternal "E." In the second clause, Machiavelli suggests a kind of conditional: "If the world is eternal, then there should be a memory of more than five thousand years." Using "M" to mean "memory of more than five thousand years," we could render the statement as "if E then M." His tone suggests that he is planning a kind of *modus tollens* – "there is not a memory of more than five thousand years, therefore the world is not eternal." But he immediately changes course, explaining why the initial conditional should be rejected: there are explanations of the shortness of historical memory compatible with the eternity of the world. This claim could be interpreted as ~ (if E then M). So, the upshot of Machiavelli's argument in the quoted passage is to (a) introduce the claim that the world is eternal and (b) an objection to that claim so that he can (c) remove the force of the objection. It is less an argument for the eternity of the world than it is a response to those who deny it.

Obviously, there is more to say about the argument and the chapter than this brief sketch can provide, and I will say more later. Prior to launching into that discussion, however, it is worthwhile to pause and set the stage a bit by recounting the development of book II up to that point. In the preface to book II, Machiavelli begins by criticizing the tendency of men to praise ancient times. This tendency, he argues, has various causes. First, he notes that the victors write history, such that one should assume that it has been whitewashed and sanitized to suit their purposes. He argues that the victors exaggerate that which will bring glory and downplay that which will bring infamy. Machiavelli had already alluded to this problem at D I.10, when he noted that it was forbidden to criticize Caesar under the empire. But he also notes, at the same place, that writers got around this prohibition by praising Brutus or criticizing Catalina.[2]

1 Tarcov, "Machiavelli's Critique of Religion," 199. Tarcov's discussion of the argument is, as his title indicates, couched within a broader treatment of Machiavelli's philosophy of religion. In what follows, I push the religious question to the side. I think that Tarcov's position that the discussion of the eternity of the world bears on religious questions is correct, but I want to postpone my treatment of Machiavelli and religion until later.

2 It was pointed out to me by a reviewer that one could wonder if Machiavelli is using ancient Rome as a kind of Brutus, such that his praise of ancient Rome allows him to offer backhanded criticisms of his contemporaries. I think this is probably correct, but to develop the point now would take us too far afield from our present concerns. We will come to the matter of Machiavelli's critique of his contemporaries later.

The sanitizing of history by the victors is never complete and the problem it presents can be overcome with a careful use of the sources. The second cause of misunderstanding of ancient times is psychological. The ancients are long dead and not a threat, arousing neither fear nor envy. This stands in contrast to one's contemporaries. They can do both. If one feared or envied the ancients, those emotional states might inoculate one against the exaggerations of historians; but lacking them, one is easy prey to the error of believing in the superiority of ancient customs. Machiavelli wishes to disabuse his readers of that error.

In the second paragraph of the preface, he attempts just that. Since he cannot make us fear or hate the ancients, he asserts a constant rising and falling of *mores.* The argument here has a somewhat abstract tone, consisting as it does of a number of universally quantified statements. "Human things are always in motion, either they ascend or descend" (D II. P). Because of this up-and-down movement, it is sometimes true that ancient times were better, but it is also sometimes not true. It all depends on the current movement of human things. Despite this movement, however, there is also stability: "I judge the world always to have been in the same mode and there to be as much good as wickedness in it" (D II.P). If we take Machiavelli literally, he seems to be suggesting that, while the sum total of human misery and excellence remains fairly constant, the distribution of that total varies, with some provinces at different times being more or less good. He then offers a historical example to support this abstract account: the journey of virtue from the Assyrians, through Media, to Persia, then Rome. Following the fall of Rome, however, virtue was scattered across the world, no longer residing in one central place but turning up, at various times, in the kingdom of the Franks, the Turks, Germany, and other places.

In the third paragraph Machiavelli returns to his first theme, our inability to correctly judge ancient times. Here the emphasis still falls on the second cause, the emotions; he expands on the causes of fear and envy: "human appetites are insatiable" (D II.pr). Unlimited appetites combined with a limited ability to satisfy them causes us to "blame the present time, praise the past and desire the future." Apparently, one blames the present because one is discontent with what one has and one desires the future in the hopes that later one will have more of what one desires. But can desires cause one to praise the past? Why not just be indifferent to it as something that is out of reach? Machiavelli doesn't provide a clear answer here, but within the general atmosphere of his preface, an answer emerges: the past can provide models of what should be desired and how to get it. Because the figures of the past are long dead, and do not cause either fear or envy, they can be taken as models.

Machiavelli's closing remarks in the preface allude to precisely this point when he says that his goal is to inspire the youth to imitate the examples discussed in his text.

So, the preface to book II, in sum, proposes two main points: our difficulty in understanding the past and the importance of imitating the past once it is properly understood. In chapter 1, he addresses another obstacle to imitating the past: the belief that Rome's success is due to fortune, not virtue, and that therefore it cannot be imitated. Machiavelli will not hear of it: Rome's orders made her victories possible, and if her victories have not been replicated that is because her orders have not been imitated (D II.1).[3] Of course, things are never completely straightforward with Machiavelli, and by the end of the chapter he has admitted that the Romans had some help from fortune, or, more precisely, "very great virtue and prudence mixed with fortune" (D II.1). This fortune, it turns out, is the result of Rome's virtue. She never had the misfortune of having to fight two wars at once because she managed her affairs in such a way that she was never forced to do so. Chapter 1 of book II, in sum, serves to remove one obstacle to imitating the ancients. Chapter 2 turns to the next obstacle: the love of freedom is less strong than it was in ancient days. According to Machiavelli, this difference is rooted in "the difference between our education and the ancient, founded on the difference between our religion and the ancient. For our religion, having shown the truth and the true way, makes us esteem less the honor of the world, whereas the Gentiles, esteeming it very much and having placed the highest good in it, were more ferocious in their actions" (D II.2). I will have more to say about this passage shortly, for now it suffices to adduce "our education" as one of the obstacles to the imitation of the ancients encouraged in the preface to book II. Commenting on this and related passages, John Najemy points to the importance of Machiavelli's term *educazione*:

> *Educazione* is of course much more than education in our sense of the term; it encompasses both education and upbringing, but also a broader process of acculturation by which customs, values, and modes of behavior are instilled in a people. Machiavelli's *educazione* is, I think, close to what we mean by culture. The assertion that the difference between modern and ancient *educazione* is founded, or based, on the difference between modern and ancient *religione* must mean that *religione* is the core of *educazione*.[4]

3 Following Machiavelli, and Italian grammar, I treat "Rome" as a feminine noun and use the corresponding feminine pronoun.

4 Najemy, "Papirius and the Chicken-Men," 667.

Chapters 3 and 4 seem like digressions: they focus on how Rome became great (chapter 3) and how republics in general can expand (chapter 4). Rome became great, Machiavelli argues, through force and love. By love, she allowed foreigners to come and go, and settle, thereby increasing the population of the city; by force, she destroyed her neighbours and forced them to migrate to Rome. Rome forced people to love her. In chapter 4, Machiavelli lists three ways of expanding: first, the Tuscan way of forming leagues; second, the Roman method of developing what could be called "junior partners"; and third, the Athenian way of subjugating others. The third way is the worst, while Machiavelli believes the Tuscan way is the best. Machiavelli's considerations of the relative advantages and disadvantages of the Tuscan and Roman ways lead him to muse on the fate of the Etruscans. The turn towards the eternity of the world is motivated by these considerations:

> And if the imitation of the Romans seems difficult, that of the ancient Tuscans should not seem so, especially to the present Tuscans. For if they could not, for the causes said, make an empire like that of Rome, they could acquire the power in Italy that their mode of proceeding conceded to them. This was secure for a great time, with the highest glory of empire and of arms and special praise for customs and religion. This power and glory were first diminished by the French, then eliminated by the Romans; and were eliminated so much that although two thousand years ago the power of the Tuscans was great, at present there is almost no memory of it. This thing has made me think whence arises this oblivion of things, which will be discoursed of in the following chapter. (D II.4)

The exhortation to imitate Tuscan glory leads Machiavelli to wonder why it was forgotten. This comment on the "oblivion of things" leads to the discussion of the eternity of the world in the next chapter. I began this section by quoting the first few sentences; I will now quote the passage at greater length:

> To those philosophers who would have it that the world is eternal, I believe that one could reply that if so much antiquity were true it would be reasonable that there be memory of more than five thousand years – if it were not seen how the memories of time are eliminated by diverse causes, of which part come from men, part from heaven. Those that come from men are the variations of sects and languages. For when a new sect – that is a new religion – emerges, its first concern is to extinguish the old one to give itself reputation; and when it occurs that the orderers of the new sect are of a different language, they easily eliminate it. (D II.5)

Given the development from the preface through this chapter, the overall context of the discussion of the eternity of the world is the various obstacles to imitating the ancients: the denial of the eternity of the world appears as one of the obstacles Machiavelli wants to overcome. If this is the context of Machiavelli's discussion, what are his sources?

Medieval Latin philosophy was rocked, in the thirteenth and fourteenth centuries especially, by the debate between Averroists (otherwise known to historians as heterodox or radical Aristotelians), Augustinians, and moderate Aristotelians over the purported eternity of the world. The Averroists, generally speaking, argued that philosophers must endorse the eternity of the world; their opponents demurred. Given the relative historical proximity between Machiavelli and Averroism, one might suspect that Machiavelli's discussion of the eternity of the world was informed by the discussions of scholastic authors. Indeed, the claim that Machiavelli's discussion of the eternity of the world is Averroistic is made most notably in Leo Strauss's influential, perceptive, and controversial *Thoughts on Machiavelli*; it is seconded in Harvey Mansfield's commentary on the *Discourse on Livy*.[5] Strauss notes that educated men of Machiavelli's day were widely familiar with the doctrines of Averroës, whence "we must turn to the books of the 'Averroists' in order to complete Machiavelli's intimations."[6] In other words, Latin Averroism will provide the interpretive key for ferreting out the way Machiavelli understands the eternity of the world. For Strauss this means, among other things, the attempt to displace the Christian revelation with a new secular understanding of life and philosophy. However, Strauss doesn't develop his discussion of the doctrine of the eternity of the world, turning instead to Machiavelli's account of the origin of religion.[7] While there is much to learn from Strauss's account, we should note that there are a number of reasons for resisting the association of Machiavelli with Averroism. First, despite the fact that Averroism was not unknown in Italy around the time of Machiavelli, it doesn't seem to have been particularly prominent in Florence. Florence's university mainly focused on humanistic studies (Greek and Latin classics, law and rhetoric) rather than on natural sciences and theology, where Averroism was more often found in Renaissance Italy. Indeed, the Renaissance humanism Machiavelli is more typically associated with had little patience for the

5 Strauss, *Thoughts on Machiavelli*, 202–3; Mansfield, *Machiavelli's New Modes and Orders*, 202–3.

6 Strauss, *Thoughts on Machiavelli*, 203.

7 Ibid., 203–5; Tarcov does something similar in "Machiavelli's Critique of Religion," 199–200.

turgid Latin of scholastic Averroism.[8] But beyond these historical concerns, there are more crucial systematic differences. Latin Averroistic arguments for the eternity of the world were typically based on detailed and, at times, convoluted studies of Aristotle's *Physics* and *Metaphysics*; they do not trade in the kind of arguments Machiavelli uses. Two more plausible sources for Machiavelli's kind of arguments are unlikely bedfellows: Augustine of Hippo and Lucretius. The objection and reply offered by Machiavelli echoes (a) St Augustine of Hippo's debate with the Neo-Platonist Apuleius in book XII of *The City of God* and (b) Lucretius's argument against the eternity of the world in *On the Nature of Things*. Let us look at both possible sources in more detail, beginning with Lucretius.

LUCRETIAN INFLUENCE ON MACHIAVELLI

Alison Brown, whose work in this regard is invaluable, argues that the Lucretian influence on Machiavelli has been highly underestimated. According to Brown, Lucretius comes to Machiavelli through two sources. First, there is the text of *De rerum natura* itself, which Machiavelli transcribed with his own hand. Second, there are the lectures given in the mid-1490s by his senior colleague at the Florentine Chancery, Marcello Adriani.[9] Moreover, when Machiavelli was writing his *Discourses*, scholars – at the University of Pisa and elsewhere –were debating the eternity of the world. We have good reason to believe that Machiavelli was aware of these debates since the provost (Francesco del Nero) was his relation by marriage and his brother's employer. At least one of the participants in that debate was known as a follower of Lucretius.[10] Brown points out that the opening sentence of D II.5 ("To those philosophers who would have it that the world is eternal, I believe that one could reply that if so much antiquity were true it would be reasonable that there be memory of more than five thousand years") echoes Lucretius's reply to philosophers who believed the world was eternal. They also echo the words of Marcello

8 Black, *Machiavelli*, offers a helpful reconstruction of Machiavelli's education derived from his father's diary and other contemporary sources. Black admits that there is little direct evidence that Machiavelli attended Florence's university (18), but he points out that it is unlikely that he would be elected to high office in Florence without the appropriate humanist education (14–20). On Averroism in the Renaissance, see the discussion in Hasse, "Arabic Philosophy and Averroism," 129–30.

9 Brown, *Return of Lucretius*, 68–72. For a broader consideration of the influence of Epicurean philosophy on Machiavelli, see Rahe, "Shadow of Lucretius" and *Against Throne and Altar*, 33–55.

10 Brown, *Return of Lucretius*, 76.

Adriani, a well-known Lucretian in Florence.[11] Nevertheless, despite this obvious echo of Lucretius, it is a view that Machiavelli goes on, in the remainder of the chapter, to reject, offering a variety of reasons why shortness of historical memory is compatible with an eternal world. Even if the chapter begins with an echo of Lucretius, its argument could be taken as anti-Lucretian. But things are not as straightforward as they seem.

We should begin by identifying Lucretius's teaching on the eternity of the world and placing it in the context of his larger philosophical theory. There is more than one way to deny the eternity of the world. One might do so by endorsing a creationist account, wherein at some point God created the world and at some point it will end. Let this be called the theistic denial of the eternity of the world. Lucretius's denial of the eternity of the world is not a theistic denial. Lucretius's poem argues for a kind of philosophical naturalism wherein all phenomena are to be accounted for in terms of the commingling and separation of atoms as they fall through the void. Normally, the atoms should fall through the void in a straight line, never touching one another; but for some mysterious reason that Lucretius never adequately explains (some of his critics refer to it as arbitrary) the atoms occasionally swerve. This swerve interrupts the orderly cascade of atoms, causing countless collisions whereby atoms are joined to each other, forming, over time, larger and larger structures (DRN II. 70–140). Eventually, in something anticipating Darwinian evolution, these random crashes give rise to the world as we know it; indeed, it may even have given rise to a plurality of worlds. In the fifth book, Lucretius turns his attention to cosmogony, arguing that the world (a) had a beginning (DRN V.65–70) and (b) that the world – both heaven and earth – will one day be destroyed (DRN V. 95–100). So, for Lucretius, the world is not eternal in the durational sense. That he holds this position should not be surprising since it is an obvious consequence of his atomic theory: what the swerve brings together it also breaks apart. Nevertheless, while there is manuscript evidence for Machiavelli's interest in Lucretius's infamous swerve, he seems to be mainly concerned with the swerve's implications for freedom of the will rather than with speculative issues of cosmogony.[12] Even his famous marginal comment that "the gods don't care about the affairs of mortals" can be taken in an anthropological sense as indicating the freedom of human beings from divine interference.[13]

11 Ibid., 71.
12 Ibid., 74.
13 Ibid., 75

So, while chapter II.5 begins with an echo of Lucretius, Machiavelli does not endorse the echo. Instead, he attempts to show the compatibility of (a) the shortness of historical memory with (b) the eternity of the world. The compatibility turns on two points: the destruction of civilizations by natural disasters and the destruction of civilizations by the change of sects. I discuss the details of these changes in more detail later; for now it will suffice to note that the bulk of the chapter is devoted to defending the eternity of the world against a Lucretian-sounding objection. However, while the letter of D II.5 runs counter to Lucretius's position, one could argue that the spirit of the chapter is fairly Lucretian. Certainly, natural disasters destroying great civilizations is compatible with Lucretius's atomism, and so, too, is the dim view of sects as conspiring to keep people ignorant of the past so as to solidify their power. Brown suggests this point, arguing that, in D II.5, Machiavelli isn't really interested in the eternity of the world. She writes that "the main point of the chapter [seems to be] an attack on the role of all sects, including Christianity, in destroying evidence of the past."[14] While there are good reasons for taking this to be the main point, I think the point is slightly larger: it is not merely that Christianity destroys evidence of the past, but that Christian education makes imitation of the past more difficult (and undesirable). And a principle part of this education is its appeal to a world beyond this one, and it is to eliminate this appeal that Machiavelli endorses the eternity of the world. Christian education is an obstacle to the imitation of the ancients insofar as it undermines the sacrificial distinction between good and bad violence. Recall that Machiavelli claims (in D. II.2) that the ancient education made men more "ferocious" in the defence of the patria. It justified and encouraged the "good" violence that preserves the community. This is not to deny the influence of Lucretius on Machiavelli – indeed, the spirit of the endorsement of the eternity of the world, if not the letter, is profoundly Lucretian, and there are a great many passages in his writings that can be clarified with reference to Lucretius. And in any case, while Lucretius is clear that the world is not eternal, he is equally clear that the cascade of atoms through the void *is* eternal, and, more important, he emphasizes that there is not another world, a heaven, beyond this one. In short, Lucretius endorses the eternity of the world in a more profound sense: everything is contained within the system of nature; there is no supernatural. To the extent that there are gods in Lucretius's universe, they, too, are products of the cascading atoms. For those on the lookout for such things,

14 Ibid., 77.

Machiavelli's discussion of the eternity of the world can be read as exhibiting a great deal of sympathy for Lucretius's view, without, however, following Lucretius consistently or systematically.[15]

However, even if Machiavelli doesn't follow Lucretius's teaching on the eternity of the world, he does follow him, or at least takes inspiration from him, as far as the sacrificial distinction is concerned. In Ada Palmer's discussion of Machiavelli's marginal notes on his manuscript of Lucretius's poem, it is pointed out that he made a large mark on the passages containing Lucretius's famous "wormwood simile" in book I. There Lucretius remarks that he is presenting his work as a poem to make his doctrines, which are sometimes thought rather dour, more appealing (DRN I.932–48). Wormwood (*Artemisia absinthium*) is a toxic herb that in large doses can lead to seizures or death but that in small doses was used as a medicine. Commenting on this passage, Palmer notes that the wormwood simile suggests that, by carefully calibrating poison, one can do well; or, more generally, that one can do well "through the careful administration of constructive harm."[16] Taken this way, the wormwood simile suggests a kind of sacrificial distinction between a good (constructive and controlled) violence and a bad (destructive and uncontrolled) violence. While in the case of the wormwood simile, the difference is largely one of quantity, it is not hard to generalize the distinction into something more than that. After all, the lesson seems to be that poison, used properly, can cure; why not generalize this to claim that violence, used properly, can benefit? There is not enough evidence to determine whether or not Lucretius is the *only* source for Machiavelli's usage of this distinction, but his marginalia offer prima facie evidence for taking Lucretius as a source for the distinction.

It is fair to say that Machiavelli's interest in the eternity of the world has little or nothing to do with metaphysical cosmology. Instead, as the preceding chapters of the *Discourses* make clear, he is interested in identifying and removing obstacles to the imitation of ancient modes and orders. In that sense, his discussion does not strike me as mirroring Lucretius's concerns. The key elements of chapter II.5 emerge more clearly when juxtaposed not with Lucretius but with the discussion of

15 A similar point is made by Palmer, *Reading Lucretius*, 85–7. Palmer pays particular attention to Machiavelli's annotations to his copy of *De rerum natura*. According to Palmer, these annotations show that, while Machiavelli did not follow every jot and tittle of Lucretius's system, it nevertheless was a "key enabler" of his work (86) insofar as it provided him with an alternate way of thinking about the world, freeing him "from the necessity of believing in Providence" (87).

16 Ibid., 84.

ancient religion in D II.2. The present religion – Christianity – devalues the world by pointing towards something transcending it as our true home; it "dishonors the world," as he says in chapter II. Moreover, it makes us less ferocious in the defence of the patria by undermining the distinction between good and bad violence. While the ancient education taught that it was a good form of violence to avenge one's beatings, the Christian education urges us to turn the other cheek, suggesting that there is no meaningful distinction between good and bad violence. If one wishes, as Machiavelli wishes, to imitate the modes and orders of the ancients, then one must imitate their "education," and this requires that one assumes and acts as if the world is eternal. To see this clearer, I turn to Augustine's discussion of the eternity of the world. Gennaro Sasso says we cannot be certain that Machiavelli read Augustine, but he admits that it is a very strong possibility; in what follows, I assume that Machiavelli is familiar with Augustine's position.[17] Part of the difficulty of discerning Machiavelli's knowledge of Augustine lay in the fact that they had so much in common in terms of their sources. So, to take one example, Machiavelli and Augustine both had an intimate knowledge of Livy and the Roman historians. But their common sources also make the question of direct influence less important than it might seem. Because they are often talking about the same texts, they often end up talking about the same things, even if there was no direct influence. Of course, their respective interpretations – not only of Rome but also of Christianity – are often at odds with each other. Whence, contrasting Machiavelli with Augustine can be illuminating even if one denies any direct relationship between the two men.

AUGUSTINE AND THE ETERNAL WORLD

In the year 410, Alaric's Gothic tribesmen sacked Rome. Refugees flooded into North Africa and some murmured that it was the abandonment of the old gods and the embrace of Christianity that put Rome in this position. The old gods made her strong, while the new God made her weak. This claim took many forms. The more pious of the old believers

17 For Sasso, see his *Machiavelli e gli Antichi e altri*, 256–60. For an argument that claims Machiavelli had an intimate knowledge of Augustine, see Wright, "Machiavelli's *City of God*." More recently, Warner and Scott, "Sin City," argue that Augustine's interpretation of the Roman Republic had a decisive influence on Machiavelli's, if only in the negative sense that Machiavelli reversed all his judgments. Sebastien de Grazia's *Machiavelli in Hell* makes the even stronger claim that Machiavelli's text shows a "Pauline and Augustinian anthropology" (267).

thought that the old gods were themselves punishing Rome for abandoning them; more sophisticated critics of Christianity argued that, while the old beliefs were probably not true, they did inculcate certain civic virtues that made Rome strong. Without supposing that Machiavelli intended to echo pagan criticisms, the similarity between Machiavelli's criticism of Christian education and these more sophisticated opponents of Augustine should be enough to motivate at least a short excursus into Augustine's long book.

The City of God began as a response to these and similar objections, but it quickly metastasized into something much larger.[18] The growth of the text is due, in part, to the loquaciousness of the bishop of Hippo, but it is also due to the sophistication of his opponents. Augustine found himself having to show that Christianity did not sap the loyalty to the patria that the defence of the empire required. This, in turn, led him to criticize various accounts of virtue found in ancient historians, poets, and philosophers. Augustine's critique is multifaceted and hard to summarize, but the gist of it is an attempt to show that ancient virtue was fundamentally incomplete and that Christian virtue is able to supply what it lacking. For Augustine, the incompleteness of ancient virtue was not due to a lack of intelligence on the part of the ancient thinkers but, more profoundly, to the incompleteness of the world. The happiness they were looking for could never and would never be found in the world.[19] This leaves Augustine with a dilemma: either happiness is impossible or it is achieved apart from the world. Not wishing to deny the possibility of happiness, he is forced to argue that happiness is reached only in the next world, in heaven. This leads Augustine to emphasize the essentially temporary character of the world; the success and sufferings of this life are nothing compared with the glory of heaven. Naturally, as part of his argument for the incompleteness of this world, he must address the theory that the world is eternal. In chapter 10 of book XII, Augustine argues against the eternity of the world. He attributes the claim that the world is eternal to Apuleius, a second-century Neoplatonist. Augustine raises a common objection:

But if the human race has always existed, how can those histories be true which tell us who were the first inventors, and what they invented, and who first instituted the liberal studies and other arts, and who first inhabited this or that

18 For a discussion of the various targets of *The City of God*, see Spiegl, "Zur Universalen Theologie Augustins."

19 For a more in-depth development of this point, see Harding, *Augustine and Roman Virtue*, 104–48.

region of the earth, and this island and that? When such men are asked this, they reply as follows: that most, even if not all, of the earth is devastated by floods and conflagrations after certain intervals of time, that the number of men then becomes very small, but that, from their progeny, the population is once more restored to its former size that the things which seem to be newly discovered and originated at such times are in fact only being renewed, having been interrupted and extinguished by such great devastation; and that man could not exist at all, unless produced by an already-existing man. But they say what they think [*putant*] not what they know [*sciunt*].[20]

On Augustine's telling, Apuleius's endorsement of (a) the eternity of the world entails his acceptance of (b) the claim that disasters regularly wipe out civilization and memory, forcing humanity to start over from scratch. The position Augustine attributes to Apuleius anticipates important elements of the argument that Machiavelli advances in D II.5: the world is eternal, despite our short historical memory, because of various disasters and other causes that lead us to forget the past. Augustine's argument against (a) assumes this relationship, and, instead of entering into the kind of metaphysical speculations required to refute (a) directly, he will argue against (b), reasoning that if (b) is denied, then one can no longer hold (a). In short, his argument is a simple *modus tollens*: if (a) then (b); not (b); therefore not (a).

Augustine develops his argument against (b) in chapter 11; he claims that (b) requires one to believe a number of implausible things about human history. His point is that a temporary world with a beginning and eventually an end provides a more plausible view of history than does the one entailed by the eternity of the world. Augustine provides a brief overview of varying historical accounts – Greek, Egyptian, biblical – to show that no respectable historian believes that cataclysms have destroyed all records of previous civilizations. He argues that the claim that such disasters have occurred is an ad hoc device designed to support the eternity of the world in the face of evidence to the contrary. But, Augustine continues, a study of history shows that there is no reason to believe in worldwide civilization-destroying disasters and every reason not to believe them. If we return to chapter 5 of the *Discourses* we can see that Machiavelli responds to this argument in two ways. First, he advances his conspiratorial view of history: the various historical accounts in question give no evidence of more ancient civilizations because they are engaged in a kind of cover-up, conspiring to suppress knowledge of

20 Augustine, *City of God*, XII.10.

previous sects. As with all conspiracy theories, the lack of evidence becomes evidence. Second, Machiavelli points out that some historians – for example, Diodorus of Sicily – disagree with the commonly accepted reckoning. While Machiavelli purports to reject Diodorus's account, he need not endorse it for his argument to work: its existence is enough to provide a counter-example to Augustine's claim that *all* historians agree in tracing civilization back only about five thousand years.

Since nobody can seriously deny the power of plagues, famine, and floods to destroy, Machiavelli spends the bulk of chapter 5 focusing on the claim that the founders of new civilizations conspire to destroy records of the previous ones. The roots of this argument stretch back to book I. In book I of the *Discourses* Machiavelli discusses the ancient theory of a cycle of regimes – that is, that a city will move through successive forms of government. This idea will be familiar to students of Plato's *Republic*, although there is general agreement that Machiavelli's proximate source is Polybius. Machiavelli criticizes the theory for assuming that any given regime will last long enough to complete the cycle: according to Machiavelli, when in the corrupt and weaker moments of the cycle, another stronger regime will conquer or destroy the weaker one (D I.2). In this part of book II, he adds that the victors will often do their best to obfuscate the admirable qualities of the defeated regime. This tendency is more pronounced when the victors are of a different sect than the defeated regime; in those cases, the victorious sect will attempt to eliminate entirely the memory of the old sect. This, in a nutshell, is his explanation of why history doesn't seem cyclical to Augustine: new civilizations conspired to oppress and destroy the records of previous civilizations. The argument for the eternity of the world in Machiavelli is inseparable from violence, as Sasso puts it, "la politica di conquista."[21] This is a point to which I return later.

Expanding on this point, Machiavelli explains that we don't have memory of more than five thousand years of history due to the "variations of sect and language" (D II.5). The first concern of a new religion is to extinguish the memory of the old religion; Machiavelli's evidence for this claim is the behaviour of Christianity vis-à-vis the ancient religions: "it suppressed all its orders and all its ceremonies and eliminated every memory of that ancient theology" (D II.5). Of course, Machiavelli is quick to admit that they were not entirely successful; because early Christians were forced to use Latin, they were unable to completely bury the past. Machiavelli extrapolates from this account the further claim

21 Sasso, *Machiavelli et gli Antichi*, 173.

that all sects act like this: "It is therefore to be believed that what the Christian sect wished to do against the Gentile sect, the Gentile would have done against that which was prior to it" (D II.5). The reader thinks here of the claim, at the end of chapter 4, that the Romans eliminated the power and glory of the Tuscans; this claim is repeated at the end of the chapter 5. Another cause of short memory comes from heaven. By this locution Machiavelli has in mind plagues, floods, and other events we would label as natural disasters. These disasters kill most of the population, leaving behind only coarse mountain men, who have no education and no memory of ancient things. If anyone preserves knowledge of the past, he will manipulate it for his own purposes rather than pass on the truth to others. Here we see a shadow of the concern expressed in the preface to book II that history does not tell us what happened but, rather, what the victors or survivors want us to believe happened. Even the most sympathetic student of Machiavelli should admit that these arguments are weak. The first argument relies on overgeneralization from a limited number of examples; the second requires the assumption that there are no cities at high elevations. In fact, it is hard to imagine that someone as smart as Machiavelli could have been convinced by those arguments. All this is to suggest that whatever is going on in chapter 5, it isn't an argument for the eternity of the world in the strict sense. That is to say, we can't charitably read it as an argument designed to prove to doubters that the world is eternal. As we saw, Machiavelli begins by reporting that some philosophers say the world is eternal, mentions some objections to that claim, and then develops responses to those objections. In short, rather than proving the eternity of the world, chapter 5 takes it for granted and simply addresses one well-known criticisms of the claim. If one was really interested in advancing a thesis regarding metaphysical cosmology, one could hardly do a worse job. So why does Machiavelli choose this route?

SACRIFICES AND "OUR RELIGION"

We can get a better of idea of what Machiavelli is up to by returning to the context of the discussion of the eternity of the world: a discussion of the obstacles that prevent one from imitating antiquity. As we saw, in chapter 2 Machiavelli claims that the Christian religion is responsible for the weakness of the present age vis-à-vis the Romans: "Thinking then whence it can arise that in those ancient times peoples were more lovers of freedom than in these [modern times], I believe it arises from the same cause that make men less strong now, which I believe is the difference between our education and the ancient. For our religion, having shown the truth and the true way, makes us esteem less the honor of the world, whereas the Gentiles, esteeming it very much and having placed the highest good in it, were more ferocious in their actions" (D II.2). After pointing to the difference between ancient and modern education, he then praises the Roman practice of blood sacrifice – and presumably Machiavelli is aware that this included both animal and human victims – in contrast to the bloodless pomp of the Christian liturgy: "This can be inferred from many of their institutions, beginning from the magnificence of their sacrifices as against the humility of ours, where there is some pomp more delicate than magnificent but no ferocious or vigorous action. Neither pomp, nor magnificence of ceremony was lacking there, but the action of the sacrifice, full of blood and ferocity, was added, with a multitude of animals being killed there. This sight, being terrible, rendered men similar to itself" (D II.2). The endorsement of sacrifice should catch our attention; it is quite straightforwardly an endorsement of sacrifice in the usual sense of the term. But by emphasizing the political benefits that accrue to sacrifice Machiavelli also suggests an endorsement of what I have called the sacrificial distinction between good and bad violence. We should note that the ancient sacrifices differ from the modern sacrifices due to the presence of "blood and ferocity" and the killing of animals. In short, the ancient sacrifices exhibited a kind of good, socially beneficial violence. The modern sacrifice – he is probably thinking of the Roman Catholic Mass – is bloodless, having only delicate pomp; it has no violence in it at all. The blood and gore of the ancient sacrifices displayed the socially beneficial effects of certain kinds of violence and, in so doing, reinforced the sacrificial distinction. The delicate pomp of the Mass avoids blood and gore and, in so doing, undermines, or at least fails to reinforce, the sacrificial distinction. Machiavelli describes in more detail the political and moral effects of these bloody sacrifices: the ancients esteemed active and strong men, while "our religion" has us esteem humility and contemplation:

Besides this, the ancient religion did not beatify men if they were not full of worldly glory, as captains of armies and princes of republics. Our religion has glorified humble and contemplative more than active men. It has placed the highest good in humility, abjectness, and contempt of things human; the other placed it in greatness of spirit, strength of body, and all other things capable of making men very strong. And if our religion asks that you have the strength in yourself, it wishes you to be capable more of suffering than of doing something strong. This mode of life thus seems to have rendered the world weak and given it in prey to criminal men, who can manage it securely, seeing that the collectivity of men, so as to go to paradise, think more of enduring their beatings than avenging them. (D II.2)

The sacrificial distinction has the benefit of teaching the Romans that there is a good kind of violence and encouraging them to use it. The captains and princes mentioned above gain glory by putting violence to use for the good of the republic. In contrast, because "our religion" refuses to distinguish between good and bad violence, it teaches good men not to be violent. Violence becomes the sole possession of criminal men who will use it only for their own purposes: when violence is criminalized, then only criminals will be violent.

Machiavelli's Romans, by locating the highest good in the *hic et nunc* rather than in some world transcending paradise, would never have humbly accepted their beatings; the Romans would raise an army, appoint a captain, and seek redress for their grievances. The violence that avenges one's beating is a kind of good violence; the bad violence of the criminal men running the world is, Machiavelli suggests, made possible by the present education's unwillingness to admit that there are legitimate and good forms of violence. Instead, it teaches people to patiently suffer and hope for the next world. Machiavelli closely links the idea that something transcends the world, in this case paradise, with the denial of a difference between good and bad violence. This denial has disastrous consequences; the thesis that the world is eternal, that this is the only world, counter-acts this belief and can contribute to the re-arming of the world. It aids the return to the ancient education and the distinction between good and bad violence that was exhibited in its rituals and that made ancient men "very strong."

As he continues, Machiavelli suggests that this is not the fault of the modern religion itself but, rather, is an interpretation of religion that understands it in terms of idleness (*ozio*) rather than virtue. He doesn't take the time to explain what he means in the *Discourses*, but he returns to this theme in more detail in his dialogue in *The Art of War*. Although *The Art of War* was published in 1521, he began writing it around 1518, only five years after he began the *Discourses*; but beyond this temporal connection between the two works, it is worth noting that the dedicatees of the *Discourses* (Buondelmonti and Rucellai) appear as characters in *The Art of War*. The principle speaker in the text, Fabrizio, complains that Christianity's emphasis on mercy has sapped the strength of fighting men:

The other reason [for the lack of military virtue] is that today's mode of living, on account of the Christian religion, does not impose the necessity to defend oneself that there was in antiquity. For then, men conquered in war were either killed or remained in perpetual slavery, where they lived their lives miserably. Their conquered towns were either dissolved or, their goods taken, the inhabitants were driven out and sent dispersed throughout the world. So those overcome in war suffered every last misery. Frightened by this fear, men kept military training alive and honored whoever was excellent in it. But today this fear is for the most part lost. Of the conquered, few of them are killed; no one is kept in prison for long, because they are freed with ease. (AW II.305–8)

Commenting on this and similar passages, Marsha Colish notes that Machiavelli's claim that Christianity has made people less warlike would have struck his contemporaries as simply bizarre.[22] Instead, she argues that it makes more sense to read these and similar passages as anti-Savanarolan rather than as anti-Christian per se. She provides ample historical and textual justification for this suggestion. Without wanting to dismiss this reading entirely, I think two points are worth making: (a) the distinction between Savanarolan Christianity and other version of Christianity often blurs for Machiavelli, and (b) the passage just quoted doesn't have Machiavelli claiming that Christianity entails pacifism – the context of the passage from *The Art of War* supposes that Christians are engaging in warfare – but only that the Christian method of war isn't as harsh as is that of the ancients. I think Machiavelli's point is not the bizarre claim that Christianity produced a civilization of pacifists but that it produced a civilization less good at violence than the preceding one. Christian civilization uses violence badly. I think there are three closely related points at play here: (a) Christian education refuses to distinguish between good and bad violence; (b) people often fail to live up to Christian ideals and are violent anyway; and (c) when this happens, they are violent without knowing how to be good at violence: it is a sloppy, ill thought out, and slapdash affair. To anticipate a later discussion, Christian princes are taught that violence is not good, and so they do not know how not to be good. So Fabrizio's claim seems to be that, even though they are taught to be peaceful, (a) Christian states fight wars anyway, and (b) this leads to stupid decisions such as (c) letting defeated enemies go free. In contrast, Fabrizio's ancient warriors did not feel bad about violence and made sure that the defeated enemies stayed defeated. The problem here, although it remains unstated, is that Christianity, even when violent, is not sufficiently comfortable with violence to use it correctly.

22 Colish, "Republicanism."

Machiavelli suggests that a Christianity interpreted according to virtue would be more comfortable with violence and use it well: it embraces severe revenge and punishment for one's enemies. Christianity according to virtue would embrace a distinction between good and bad violence that would encourage the inflicting of immeasurable suffering upon one's foes while discouraging other forms of violence, against one's fellows. Christianity interpreted according to virtue yields violent practices indistinguishable from those of the Romans: the political and martial behaviour will be the same.[23] So why doesn't Christianity import those Roman behaviours? As it turns out, ancient virtue didn't exist in a vacuum: the passages just quoted from the *Discourses on Livy* show that, on Machiavelli's reading, the virtue of the Romans is intimately tied to (a) the sacrificial distinction and (b) the vision of the highest good as something present in the eternal and only world. The problem with Christianity, as Machiavelli sees it, is not merely its emphasis on the next world but its refusal to distinguish between good and bad violence; since few people live up to this theological refusal, instead of a world of non-violence one simply gets a world in which violence is poorly used. He holds this refusal, as we see in the passage from the *Discourses* quoted a few pages earlier, responsible for the *ozio* of "our religion," for its glorification of humble, meek, contemplative men.[24]

BACK TO AUGUSTINE

Machiavelli's comments on "the present religion" cannot fail to call to mind ancient pagan criticisms of Christianity. Again, without claiming that Machiavelli had an intimate knowledge of Augustine's texts, due to their common sources the two often end up talking about the same things. A comparison with Augustine can be a useful way to clarify Machiavelli's views. With this in mind, let us return to Augustine. Around the year 411, Marcellinus wrote a letter to Augustine asking him to respond to questions raised by a pagan named Volusianus. Although Marcellinus's letter is lost, we can reconstruct some of Volusianus's criticism by looking at Augustine's reply:

23 See the discussion in Mansfield, *New Modes and Orders*, 194–7, and, from a different perspective, Viroli, *Machiavelli's God*, 185–98.

24 Maddox, "Secular Reformation," 551, notes: "in encouraging a life of private devotion and contemplation, Christianity promoted a pernicious *ozio*, a form of leisure that could be characterized as a detachment from political and social life." This detachment is contrasted with both Ancient Rome and Machiavelli's hope for the future. See, too, Sullivan, *Machiavelli's Three Romes*, 14ff.

> Furthermore – and this is a common allegation – Christ's teaching and preaching must be incompatible with the ethics of citizenship. For he told us – it is agreed – *to return no one evil for evil*, to *offer the other cheek to an assailant*, to *give our cloak to someone demanding a tunic*, and to *go twice the required distance* with someone who wants to requisition us. He alleges that all these commands are contrary to the ethics of citizenship. Who would allow an enemy to steal something from him? Who would be unwilling to inflict evil, in the form of a just war, as a recompense for the ravaging of a Roman province? ... It is obvious that under the Christian emperors the empire is in a very bad way, even though they have on the whole observed the Christian religion.[25]

Based on this reply, it appears that Volusianus had the following concern: Christian moral teaching is incompatible with the sort of distinctions between good and bad violence required for the maintenance of the empire in peace and security. The passages in italics suggest that all forms of violence are to be avoided, such that the distinction between good and bad violence collapses into an undifferentiated mass of prohibited violence. But, Volusianus seems to reason, the functioning of the empire requires that good violence be used to limit bad violence. The demands of Christianity are at odds with the demands of governance and citizenship. Moreover, it is clear from other exchanges between Augustine and his pagan interlocutors that, on their reading at least, the principle cause of these errors is the preference for a homeland in heaven over that on earth. In another exchange of letters, the pagan Nectarius complains that he doesn't understand why the Christian desire for heaven trumps one's duties to the patria.[26] Indeed, he argues – in a fashion reminiscent of the dream of Scipio – that it is only by serving the earthly patria that one can please the gods. The desire for a world beyond this one seems, to Nectarius, to water down one's commitment to this world: in seeking for that which is above one inevitably neglects the patria.

An obvious objection to the presentation of Augustine in the preceding paragraphs can be raised with reference to his discussion of just war in book XIX of *The City of God*. How can I maintain that Augustine denies the sacrificial distinction between good and bad violence when he is apparently willing to make a parallel distinction between just and unjust wars? This objection, however, is based on a misreading of Augustine's position. Replying to it will serve double duty, since by better understanding Augustine's position we will also better understand the importance

25 Augustine of Hippo, Epistle 136 (emphasis in original).
26 Ibid., Epistle 103.

of Machiavelli. In chapter 7 of book XIX, Augustine notes that sometimes the duty of waging war is thrust upon a wise man because of the evils of his opponent. An enemy that is burning farms, killing children, raping women, and so on forces the wise prince to oppose him with arms. This defensive action is what Augustine calls just war. While this is the case, it is not a happy war. Augustine insists that the prince is miserable while waging this war; in fact, the discussion of just war occurs as part of a larger discussion of how and why one will never be happy in this world. As book XIX continues, it becomes clear that the results of the just war are not entirely desirable. Assuming the wise prince triumphs over his opponent, the peace achieved is only a pale imitation of the true peace found in the city of God. The just warrior achieves a kind of peace, a peace in which the threats of the enemy have been averted, but not the true peace of the kingdom of God. One can compare the "just war" of book XIX with Augustine's discussion of pagan virtue elsewhere in *The City of God*: although pagan virtues are not true virtues, they are nevertheless preferable to more unconstrained pagan vices – Cato is preferable to Nero – likewise, the peace of the just war is not a true peace, but it is preferable to unconstrained violence. Indeed, it is seldom noted that the discussion of just war in book XIX occurs in the context of a discussion of the inability of pagan virtue to produce happiness. The overarching point, for Augustine, is that neither pagan virtue nor just wars offers true virtue and true peace; the virtuous pagan and the just warrior are both, in the last analysis, miserable. The true good and true peace will only be found apart from this world, in the heavenly Jerusalem to come.[27] All this is to say that, for Augustine, the sacrificial distinction doesn't hold: even the just war is not good but simply less bad. This is not the case of happy warriors but of miserable warriors given no choice but to do battle; the result of the war, at best, is only a pale imitation of true peace. The highest praise, in *The City of God*, is not assigned to the just warrior who acts violently to produce a kind of peace but, rather, to the martyr who refuses all acts of violence for the sake of the heavenly Kingdom.

Augustine's account of just war in book XIX is aware of the sacrificial distinction between good and bad violence but relativizes and ultimately rejects it by subordinating the peace produced by the just warrior to the true peace of the heavenly Jerusalem. The rejection of the sacrificial distinction is closely tied to the rejection of the claim that the highest good can be achieved in this world. The overarching point of book XIX, if not

27 For a discussion of the unhappiness of the just warrior, and the broader context of Augustine's discussion, see Harding, *Augustine and Roman Virtue*, 130–9.

the entirety of *The City of God*, is that (a) the highest good is not found in this world and that (b) the Roman distinction between good and bad violence rests on this mistaken and short-sighted commitment to this transitory world. With this in mind, we can return to Machiavelli: his interest in the eternity of the world is the photographic negative of that of Augustine. If Augustine's position is that the sacrificial distinction ought to be rejected because the world is not eternal, then Machiavelli's is that the sacrificial distinction ought to be endorsed because the world is eternal. Affirming the eternity of the world grounds the appeal to the sacrificial distinction between good and bad violence.

As already suggested, the problem motivating Machiavelli's discussion of the eternity of the world is not so much a metaphysical problem as it is a moral problem of misplaced priorities. The Augustinian education prioritizes the city of God over the city of man and refuses the sacrificial distinction with deleterious results: *ozio*, weakness, corruption, and forth. The importance of the thesis that the world is eternal is not found in metaphysical subtleties but in the suggestion that this world is the *only* world that matters; everything is immanent, nothing is transcendent. This reverses *The City of God*: if Augustine would point us towards the heavenly city as our true home, Machiavelli points us back towards Rome as our only home and urges us to use good violence to defend it. And, Machiavelli suggests, this good violence can make us happy, or at least does not make us miserable.

In fact, many Renaissance historians contrasted the doctrine of the eternity of the world to "providentialist" accounts of history inspired by Orosius and Augustine.[28] The eternity of the world meant not merely that it was not created but also that history was not guided by the hand of providence; the anti-providentialist use of the eternal world thesis also serves to harmonize the "Augustinian" reading of the argument with the "Lucretian" one. Note that, according to Brown, one of the main lessons Machiavelli takes from Lucretius's atomism is precisely that there is no providential hand guiding history: in one of his marginal notes to his copy of DRN, Machiavelli writes "the gods don't care about moral affairs."[29] Arguably, this rejection of providentialist accounts of history is part of the true knowledge of history Machiavelli offers us in the preface

28 Connell, "Eternity of the World." He concludes his paper: "What has been suggested here is that the freeing of historical narrative from medieval providentialism was assisted by the presence of ideas both ancient and current concerning the eternity of the world."

29 Brown, *Return of Lucretius*, 75.

to his *Discourses*: there is no place else to go, we cannot fall expecting providence to pick us up (see P XXIV).

The careful reader will have noted that I have two slightly different arguments running parallel in the above section. On the one hand, there is the discussion of the eternity of the world and the importance Machiavelli places on locating the highest good in this world; on the other hand, there is the argument about Machiavelli's preference for the distinction between good and bad violence and his suggestion that one cause of Christian *ozio* is the unwillingness to make this distinction. These two lines intersect insofar as the assertion of the eternity of the world grounds Machiavelli's reintroduction of the sacrificial distinction between good and bad violence. So long as the Christian believer keeps her eyes set on heaven, Augustinians (in the broadest sense of the term) will be able to persuade her to reject the sacrificial distinction Machiavelli wants to make; the doctrine of the eternity of the world persuades her to take her eyes off of heaven and makes the acceptance of that distinction possible. Beyond that point, Machiavelli's account in D II.5 suggests that Christendom is itself a product of the violence it objects to: Christendom founds itself by destroying the records of prior civilizations. The Christian sect appears as a kind of paradox and a failure: it did not entirely succeed in its attempts to destroy records of the past. Christendom, from the very beginning, did not use violence effectively.

TAKING ONE'S EYES OFF OF HEAVEN

There is a strong tendency, exacerbated by the recent publication of his black-notebooks, to read Heidegger as if he were the Red Skull (and the critic Captain America). This is especially the case when one is looking at the more practical or political aspects of his thought; and given Heidegger's own politics, this is easy enough to do. However, in looking at the sacrificial distinction in Heidegger, as I begin to do now, I do not want to reduce my reading to another attempt to catch him and foil his evil plans. Instead, I am more interested in Heidegger because of his influence on subsequent generations of philosophers. With that in mind, numerous scholars have noticed and commented upon the emergence of sacrifice in the thought of Martin Heidegger, particularly in the 1930s. Perhaps Robert Bernasconi provides the best summary of this research:

> Soon after writing *Being and Time*, Heidegger clearly embraced the language of sacrifice. According to "The Origin of the Work of Art," "the essential sacrifice is one of the ways in which truth establishes itself in beings, alongside the founding of a political state, the thinking of being, and, of course, the work of art." In the

post-script to "What is Metaphysics" (1943), Heidegger gave a very abstract account of sacrifice as answering to the need for the preservation of the truth of being by the human essence expending itself. However, prior to both those tests, in the Winter Semester of 1934–35, in lectures on Hölderlin's poems *Germanien* and *Der Rhein,* Heidegger took a concrete approach to sacrifice: he described how for individual soldiers on the front line, the nearness of death and the readiness to sacrifice creates the space for community. Sacrifice thus plays a foundational role for Heidegger's account of a people (*Volk*) as opposed to a mere conglomeration as "the they" (*das Man*) is. This is all the more striking given that Heidegger, in the previous semester, Summer 1934, had given a rich account of the Volk in terms of the existentials of *Being and Time* ... Furthermore, Heidegger does not limit himself to describing the role of sacrifice in shaping a people, he actively promoted it. In a speech he delivered to the students at the beginning of the same semester, he called for the courage to sacrifice in the cause of the state: "in you there must increasingly develop the courage of your sacrifice for the salvation (*Rettung*) of the essence of our people (*Volk*) with their state (*Statt*) and for the direction of its innermost force."[30]

However, we should not be misled into thinking that the sacrificial distinction only appears with the word "sacrifice"; Machiavelli rarely uses the term, but it is (I contend) an essential part of his thought. However, here Heidegger is gracious enough to use the term "sacrifice" to describe a good type of violence that founds and preserves a people against threats. While this vocabulary appears in the 1930s, the concept of a good violence antedates the texts and vocabulary of the 1930s. In *Being and Time* we find the sacrificial distinction presented in an ontological (as opposed to merely ontic) register in Heidegger's defence of his project. He describes the existential analysis on offer in *Being and Time* as "doing violence" to the claims of everydayness; later he laments that "common sense" objects to his circle as "violent" because it attempts to go beyond common sense understandings (BT 359/311 and 363/315). Presumably existential analysis performs a good kind of violence: "Existential analysis, therefore, constantly has the character of doing violence [*Gewaltsamkeit*], whether to the claims of the everyday interpretation, or to its complacency and its tranquillized obviousness" (BT 359/311). This violence, we are reassured later, is never done arbitrarily but is based on "a necessity grounded in the facts" (BT 374/327). The violence of existential analysis is for good cause. If indeed *Being and Time* offers us a kind of good violence, where is the bad violence it opposes?

30 Bernasconi, "Useless Sacrifice," 168.

This question is answered easily enough: tradition, the history of ontology. According to Heidegger, the history of ontology "blocks our access" to primordial sources; as such, "we are to destroy the traditional content of ancient ontology until we arrive at those primordial experiences" (BT 44/22).[31] The destruction and violence of existential ontology is meant to counter-act or displace the violence of the history of metaphysics and to found – or refound – philosophy on proper existential grounds. To be sure, Heidegger's language of "violence" and "destroying" is metaphorical, but these are Heidegger's metaphors and we should take them at least as seriously as he seems to take them. The spiritual (*geistige*) violence of existential ontology is, according to Heidegger's own presentation, inseparable from the phenomenologist's attentiveness to being-in-the-world and eschewal of traditional metaphysical interpretations of being, particularly those that would analyze being with reference to something transcending the world. In his own way, Heidegger urges his readers to take their eyes off of heaven.

In *Being and Time* Heidegger famously defines the human being, Dasein, as being-in-the-world, reminding the readers that it is a "unitary phenomenon" but nonetheless susceptible to being investigated piecemeal. Heidegger himself suggests dividing the investigation three ways, focusing on the world, the entity in the world, and on being-in (BT 79). As part of his discussion of world, Heidegger marks four common uses of the term:

a) World as an ontical concept that signifies the totality of entities present-to-hand
b) World as an ontological term, signifying the being of those present-to-hand entities
c) World as that wherein a Dasein lives
d) World as the ontological-existential concept of worldhood

Heidegger restricts his use to the third (BT 93). In (c), he tells us that world is a "pre-ontological exisential signification." So, in (c) the world is simply where we live. But this is merely an ontic point; the deeper ontological and existential counterpart to world is worldhood. We later see that worldhood and Dasein are bound together such that, without a proper understanding of being-in-the-world, we will not understand the

31 Of course, Heidegger takes pains to emphasize that his projected destruction of the tradition is not purely negative: he hopes that by destroying it, he can rediscover what remained un-thought in the tradition. One is tempted to say that he has to destroy the village to save it.

worldhood of the world and vice versa. The upshot of this is that Dasein must always be in a world and that the world of Dasein is the only world; a phenomenology beginning from Dasein (and, for Heidegger, there is no place else to begin) cannot transcend the world for that would be to deny the basic ontological "fact" of Dasein – that is, that he is being-in-the-world. We cannot take our eyes off the world insofar as all explanation must be immanent to the world. As Jean-Yves Lacoste puts it, for Heideggerian philosophy, "the world is phenomenologically insuperable" (EA 10). This is, of course, not to say that Dasein is trapped in the world the way a fish is trapped in an aquarium but, rather, that whatever appears does so against the world as a horizon of meaning. It is part of Lacoste's project to challenge this, and I have more to say about that later.[32] For now, I want to focus on the effects of Heidegger's position. We may venture to list two. First, as Lacoste notes on the same page just cited, it means that one must accept the logic of worldly immanence. Given that one cannot surmount the world, one only has access to things within the world. Like Machiavelli, Heidegger allows no recourse to the supernatural or supermundane.

This brings us to the second point: anything that purports to transcend the world must be (violently) reinterpreted as immanent to the world. We must take our eyes off of heaven: for Heidegger, theology can only deal with man's experience of faith, not God himself (PT 48–9). To see the novelty of this approach, one should note that Thomas Aquinas argues precisely the opposite: the subject matter of sacred doctrine is God himself (*Summa Theologiae* Q1, a7). Indeed, Heidegger seems to have precisely Thomas's definition of theology in mind when he writes "Theology is not speculative knowledge of God" (PT 48). Theology, in Heidegger's hands, is transformed from a speculative science of something that transcends the world into the cartography of a way of being in the world that does not (cannot) transcend the world. Here we should remind ourselves of Heidegger's insistence upon the methodological atheism of philosophy: "Christian philosophy" is impossible, a squared circle (PT 53; IM 8–9). Likewise, Heidegger suggests that to affirm that God created the world is to close off the question of being (IM 8–9) before it is even asked.

In an unjustly neglected discussion of the relevance of Heidegger's thought for Christian theology, Hans Jonas remarks that Heidegger's central concern, being, is "the quintessence of this world, it is *saeculum.*"[33]

32 For a general overview of Lacoste's project, see Schrijvers, "Jean-Yves Lacoste."

33 Jonas, "Heidegger and Theology," 248.

In subordinating theology to Dasein, and Dasein to time as the horizon for the appearance of being, Heidegger subordinates theology to the *saeculum.* Indeed, later in the same essay Jonas argues that the acceptance of Heidegger's thought by theologians entails the acceptance of the doctrine – still heretical in most Christian confessions – of permanent ongoing public revelation. According to Jonas a consistently Heideggerian theology must interpret the events of the Old and New Testaments merely as phases or moments in the history of being rather than as definitive revelations by something or someone beyond being.[34] As Jonas points out, religious friends of Heidegger's philosophy can plausibly claim that his later work is not atheistic, but they neglect to note that it is "worse than that": it is pagan, it does not think a religiously neutral world but deifies the world.[35] Lacoste makes a similar point when, in his discussion of the Heideggerian fourfold (*Geviert*), he notes that, "in the field of experiences the Geviert attempts to thematize, mortals become acquainted with an immanent sacred, but not a transcendent God" (EA 18).

RIGHTLY PASSING FOR AN ATHEIST

Derrida is often quoted as having said that he "rightly passes for an atheist" and, while many readers interpret the "passing" to suggest that he only pretends to be an atheist, I suspect that the key word is "rightly." One should note at the outset two major trends in reading Derrida: Martin Hägglund's "radically atheistic" reading and John Caputo's "religion without religion" reading. I think that my claims regarding Derrida (in this section at least) are innocuous enough to mesh with either reading.[36] Derrida's programmatic 1967 text *Of Grammatology* famously asserts that there is nothing outside of the text (OG 158). But what is the text? It is, as it turns out, a world that cannot be overcome: "the writer writes in a language and in a logic whose proper system, laws and life, his discourse, by definition, cannot dominate absolutely" (OG 158). The text becomes an eternal world insofar as it is unsurpassable. "There has never been anything but writing" (OG 159) and thus it will always be, *in saecula saeculorum.* The writer (and, as Derrida says, "we are not only

34 Ibid., 254–5.

35 Ibid., 249.

36 As near as I can tell, Caputo's principle objections to Hägglund are (a) the claim that Hägglund misreads Caputo's work, including both his original thought and his exegesis of Derrida, and (b) that Hägglund doesn't understand theology as well as he thinks; needless to say, (a) and (b) are closely related. See Caputo, "Return of Anti-Religion."

thinking of the writer in literature") is inescapably bound to the text, he may push its boundaries, he may challenge and rearrange the structures within the text, but he cannot get out of it (OG 160). This is because there is no transcendental signified – that is, something outside of the text that would organize and structure the meanings within the text. He describes the claim that there is nothing outside the text as the "axial proposition" guiding *Of Grammatology* (OG 163). This claim can be read either epistemologically or ontologically, but it is perhaps best read as a synthesis of the two, whereby the epistemological reading is a consequence of the ontological one.

The easiest way to see what I have in mind is to look at Derrida's roots in structuralism. According to structuralist linguistics, a sign signifies a signified, but the signifying power of the sign is rooted in its difference from other signs and not the signified. For classical structuralism, such as that of de Saussure, language is "a system of interdependent terms in which the value of each term results *solely* from the simultaneous presence of the others."[37] Although de Saussure doesn't emphasize it, the definition just offered reduces the importance of the signified; one of Derrida's principle changes is to make explicit the denial of the existence of the signified. This has the effect, for Derrida, of enabling one to think of language as a system of free floating signs that are not attached or "nailed down" by being linked to a signified. The denial of a reference entails the "endless play of signifiers," of which the early Derrida made so much: in short order this denial of reference was expanded to include an explicit denial of any kind of "transcendental signified" that would function to put a stop to the play of language; this includes but is not limited to God (OG 13). Later, Derrida claims: "One could call *play* the absence of the transcendental signified as limitlessness of play, that is to say as the destruction of ontotheology and the metaphysics of presence" (OG 50). Derrida is quite explicit that the denial of a transcendental signifier means that there is nothing outside of the text to organize or interpret it: not being or any other transcendental origin to the world (OG 51). The world is nothing but play, nothing but the free floating of signifiers without any natural or necessary connection to anything beyond or before the world that would organize them.

It seems to me that in *Of Grammatology* Derrida offers two closely related arguments: first, there is the programmatic argument that if texts can be shown to "auto-deconstruct" themselves, then there is a free play of signifiers; second, if there is this free play, then there is no

37 de Saussure, *Course in General Linguistics*, 114. Emphasis mine.

transcendental signified. Evidence for the first conditional is developed in his readings of Rousseau and Levi-Strauss. The upshot of the two arguments is that there is no transcendental signified organizing and establishing meaning. The world is, in and of itself, meaningless. All meaning is created by human beings rather than discovered: there are neither Platonic forms nor religious divinities that would nail down the play of signification and determine meaning once and for all. In Derrida's world (much like in Machiavelli's) the world cannot be surpassed because there is no meaning, no transcendental signified, outside of it.

Derrida is, or was, fond of pulling images and terms from the nooks and crannies of the history of philosophy. One borrowing that is particularly important for us, for two reasons, is his appeal to Lucretius's infamous swerve (*clinamen*) in his short essay "My Chances." Derrida's appeal to Lucretius serves to link his thought closer to that of Machiavelli, who, as we saw, is also influenced by Lucretius. Derrida also suggests an Epicurean reading of Heidegger in this essay. It is not hard to see parallels between the swerve and key Derridean notions. Commenting on just this point, Christopher Johnson writes:

> Already there is a clear structural similarity between Lucretius' theory of the *clinamen* and Derrida's conception of "the trace" and the "écart." In addition to the preconditions of descent and chance, there is the micrological character of the *clinamen*: Lucretius himself indicates that it is the *nec plus quam minimum*. What is more, although of minimum dimension the *clinamen* is of maximal consequence, since it is the cause and condition of the world we inhabit … Finally, like the trace, the *clinamen* is not a thing or an object, it is, properly speaking, nothing. More precisely, it is a movement, or an atom of movement (but not an atom), and is itself imperceptible. In Derridean terms, it might be described as pure spacing.[38]

I think that there is a larger point beyond the "clear structural similarity" to which Johnson points; or, to put it another way, the structural similarities rest on broader "metaphysical" similarities. As we noted, Derrida's early battle cry was "There is nothing outside the text," and by "text" he meant, ultimately, the world. There is no transcendental signified structuring or governing the world. The universe of Lucretius, like that of Derrida, is one without anything outside of it to structure and order it. There are only atoms swerving and crashing – playing – as they fall through the void. Derrida's appeal to Lucretius's swerve suggests that he

38 Johnson, *System and Writing*, 134.

saw things in much the same way. Indeed, in the essay Derrida's only criticism of Lucretius is (not surprisingly) that he thinks the atomist failed to think the swerve radically enough – Derrida is inclined to "think the *clinamen* [swerve] beginning with the divisibility of the mark." (MC 360). Which is to say, while Lucretius (arguably) envisions two logically (if not temporally) distinct stages – (a) the orderly cascade of atoms through the void and (b) the swerve – Derrida prefers to begin with the swerve itself, prioritizing it ahead of the orderly fall. If the atoms are a "text," then it is one that is always deconstructing itself, always already disordered. In all this, Derrida extends but does not deny the atomism of Lucretius.

Regarding Heidegger, Derrida notes that the emphasis on falling that we find in Lucretian atomism is found in the analytic of Dasein as well. According to Lucretius, the swerve introduces chance into the cascade of atoms; the world as we experience it is the result of this swerve. Derrida argues that the structure of Dasein replicates the Lucretian cosmos: "[Heidegger's] *Geworfenheit* or being-thrown is not an empirical character among others, and it has an essential relation to dispersion and dissemination (*Zerstreuung*) as the structure of Dasein … Dasein is *itself thrown*, originally abandoned to fall and decline or, we could say, to chance (*Verfallen*). Dasein's chances are first of all and also it falls … Heidegger no doubt specifies this: the decline *(Verfallenheit*) of Dasein should not be interpreted as the 'fall' (*Fall*) outside an original, purer and more elevated state" (MC 352–3). Derrida writes that one is struck by "certain analogies" with Epicureanism. He seems to have in mind primarily the role of chance and the idea of a fall that is constitutive rather than punitive. Derrida admits that all this is highly schematic and more suggestive than probative. Nevertheless, beneath the convoluted prose that Derrida is known for lies an important point: that Heidegger's account of things is not as far as one might expect from that of Lucretius and other Epicureans. Heidegger is hardly an Epicurean, but Derrida suggests that he has Epicurean tendencies, reproducing the swerving falling atoms in the falling thrownness of Dasein into the world. Since, as we saw earlier, Heidegger conceives of the world primarily in terms of meaning, rather than things, the fall of Dasein is arguably as constitutive of the Heideggerian world as the fall of atoms is of the Lucretian one.

Returning to Derrida, I argue that his appeal to Lucretius reinforces his fundamental positions, which are that (a) there is nothing outside the text and (b) whatever order or structure the text has is arbitrary and subject to deconstruction. Well, one might ask: What about the Other? Doesn't the later Derrida modify this position precisely through his emphasis on hospitality, on messianism, on religion? In short, isn't the Other, as Other, "outside the text"? This is a vexed question, and a great deal of scholarship has been devoted to sorting out precisely these issues; it is in these later texts that partisans of the religious reading of Derrida find a great deal of support. But, whatever religion one may find in the religious Derrida, it is not a religion involving anything that transcends the world: the other is not an angel; the other is a human (or maybe animal) other. The ethic of hospitality merely structures or restructures the text in which one lives, it does not remove one from the text nor does it open up to something outside the text. Even justice is within the text. Indeed, Derrida's famous claim that justice cannot be deconstructed (FOL 243) cannot be interpreted as placing justice outside the text without undermining his entire philosophical project. Justice would then become a transcendental signified, and a pretty traditional one at that! Instead, justice is inside the text, as a peculiar way of relating to the text in which one finds oneself: justice is the act of deconstructing, or (if you prefer) one deconstructs in the name of justice. This can be taken either uncharitably as a pretty self-serving definition of deconstruction ("if you are against deconstruction, you are against justice!") or more charitably as indicating that, since any given structure is arbitrary and to that extent violent, it is complicit with injustice. Deconstructing those structures is justice to the extent that it attempts to rectify the prior violence. Taken in context, Derrida's claim is fairly clear on this point: "Justice itself, if such a thing exists, outside or beyond law, is not deconstructible. No more than deconstruction itself, if such a thing exists. *Deconstruction is justice.* It is perhaps because law is constructible … and so deconstructible and, better yet, that it makes deconstruction possible, or at least the exercise of a deconstruction that, fundamentally, always proceeds to questions of law and to the subject of law" (FOL 243, emphasis in original). It seems clear to me that deconstruction-as-justice is presented as nothing more than a critique of law-as-construction. Since the law puts force behind an arbitrary structure, the deconstruction of law works against that violence. To be sure, Derrida goes on to associate justice with the singular and the incalculable, and law with the reverse (FOL 244), but this series of (binary) oppositions only reiterates the general deconstructive principle of noting binary oppositions and reversing their prioritization in a legal or political context: if the law privileges the universal and the calculative, and marginalizes the singular and incalculable, deconstruction will reverse it. However, as Derrida is the first to point out (and some Derrideans are the first to forget), the new structures that we arrive at by deconstructing the old ones will themselves be unjust, and they, too, will be subject to deconstruction at a future date.[39] If and when a time comes when the singular and incalculable is privileged over the law, the deconstructionist should support the law.

Arguably, the "justice" enacted by deconstructing violent structures repeats the sacrificial distinction between good and bad violence: here the good violence of deconstruction responds to the bad violence of arbitrary structures. Indeed, in *Of Grammatology* Derrida speaks of a "necessary violence" that responds to the violence of phono-logo-centrism (OG 18). Derrida dodges the conclusion that deconstruction distinguishes between good and bad violence and practises good violence by arguing that structures are always already deconstructing themselves in the play of signifiers. Whence, the deconstructionist is not forcing the texts apart, but only pointing out what is already happening. This image of deconstructionist-as-spectator stands in tension with the image of deconstructionist-as-activist that Derrida also sometimes embraces. Whether or not this tension is resolvable is, for our purposes, less important than its mere existence: it suggests both the presence of the sacrificial distinction in Derrida's work and the effort (conscious or not) to suppress precisely this distinction.

39 This point is made with particular force in Hägglund, "Necessity of Discrimination."

3

Truth and Sacrifice in Machiavelli

MACHIAVELLI'S UNDERSTANDING OF TRUTH is found in one of the most famous passages in *The Prince*, his declaration of independence from the preceding tradition. In many cases, this is taken as a manifesto of a political realist and left at that. However, there is much more going on here than such a reading implies; among other things, this passage clarifies Machiavelli's understanding of sacrifice. As such, a closer inspection of the famous passage – the first paragraph of chapter 15 – is called for:

> It remains now to see what the modes and government of a prince should be with subjects and with friends. And because I know that many have written of this, I fear that in writing of it again, I may be held presumptuous, especially since in disputing this matter I depart from the orders of others. But since my intent is to write something useful to whomever understands it, it has appeared to me more fitting to go directly to the effectual truth of the thing than to the imagination of it. And many have imagined republics and principalities that have never been seen or known to exist in truth; for it is so far from how one lives to how one should live that he who lets go of what is done for what should be done learns his ruin rather than his preservation. For a man who wants to make a profession of good in all regards must come to ruin among so many who are not good. Hence it is necessary to a prince, if he wants to maintain himself, to learn to be able not to be good, and to use this and not use it according to necessity. (P XV)

It is worth noting that the discussion of truth in this paragraph is bookended on either side by moral or political questions – that is, how to treat friends on the one hand and how to not be good on the other. This moral context provides important clues to interpreting the middle sections of this paragraph, and I return to them shortly. First, however, I want to work out a preliminary interpretation of the notion of truth in the middle sentences. Once that is done, I return the role played by the moral context of the passage.

The key phrase is *la verità effettuale della cosa.* Leaving aside for now Machiavelli's important adjective, *effettuale*, we can note at once that he ties the truth (*la verità*) closely to the thing (*la cosa*). The turn towards the things – *zur sache selbst!* – is central to Machiavelli's presentation of his advice in this chapter and to his entire philosophy. The preceding tradition, according to him, had never directly confronted the things themselves; instead, the tradition interpreted these things in terms of an imagined transcendence, for example, platonic forms or divine ideas. This, in part, is what Machiavelli has in mind when he complains that individual things were interpreted through the lens of imagined republics and principalities. As the phrase suggests, imagined republics (as far as Machiavelli is concerned) are not real. The preceding tradition misinterpreted the things in the world themselves by interpreting them in terms of fictional transcendence rather than in terms of the immanence of *la cosa.* In tying the truth to a particular thing Machiavelli refuses to understand truth in terms of universal forms or essences and, instead, focuses on particular truths about particular things. On this reading, Machiavelli appears to be a kind of nominalist, denying the existence of transcendent universal entities so as to focus on the particular sensory things at hand.

REPUBLICS NEITHER SEEN NOR KNOWN TO BE

However, there is more in the phrase *la verità effettuale della cosa* than merely a nominalist rejection of "Platonism" so as to address the things themselves. The orientation towards the things of this world is radicalized when we focus on Machiavelli's adjective *effettuale.* The most straightforward translation would be "real" or "effective," suggesting that Machiavelli simply thinks that we should base our actions on what princes actually do rather than on what soft-hearted idealists think they should do. Some commentators have demurred and felt the need, rightly so, to provide a longer exegesis. In her recent commentary on *The Prince* Erica Benner argues that we ought not to simply identify *la verità effettuale* with what is normally done by princes insofar as Machiavelli is not very impressed by what princes normally do.[1] Indeed, to follow the practices of Italian princes would be terrible advice: what Italian princes actually do is a big part of the problem *The Prince* is supposed to solve! Part of the

1 Benner, *Machiavelli's Prince*, 183–4.

problem with the Italian princes is that they are a product of "the present religion" and its education. This education, recall, refused the kind of distinction between good and bad violence that promotes (in Machiavelli's reasoning) the effective violence of the ancient Romans, leaving only the ineffective violence of an uncoordinated tantrum in its place.

So, we have to look elsewhere for the meaning of the term. Sebastian de Grazia points out that, although Machiavelli did not coin the word *effettuale*, he is one of the first Italian writers to use it. He glosses it as "eminently useful" – suggesting that, for Machiavelli, the truth is primarily something to be used rather than contemplated;[2] in this he is in agreement with Leo Paul de Alvarez's commentary on the word in his translation of *The Prince*.[3] We may add to this the comment of William J. Connell that "*effettuale* is an unexceptional rendering of the Latin *efficiens*," suggesting that the key idea is the separation of truth from final causality.[4] On this reading, Machiavelli can be taken as anticipating modern conceptions of truth more commonly associated with Descartes's claim that there is no need to discuss final causality in the natural sciences. Harvey Mansfield takes a more radical reading of the phrase. In his introduction to his translation of *The Prince* he says the turn towards effectual truth contains an "assault on all morality and political science, both Christian and classical, as understood in Machiavelli's time."[5] Mansfield takes this to indicate the absence of anything like medieval natural law in Machiavelli's thought. I think he is right about this, but would add that, insofar as medieval accounts of natural law rely upon a world-transcending God that creates and orders the world, including the provision of normative moral standards, a thorough rejection of medieval natural law requires the rejection of transcendence.[6] Claude Lefort makes a similar point when he claims that Machiavelli's discussion of truth is, ultimately, a critique of philosophy and its pretension to find a truth apart from the world.[7] Viroli understands *la verità effettuale* rhetorically: "to pursue the effective truth of the matter means to pursue the truth which permits one to attain the desired result – that is, as Machiavelli

2 de Grazia, *Machiavelli in Hell*, 280.

3 De Alvarez, Translation and note on Machiavelli, *The Prince*, 94–5.

4 Connell, "Eternity of the World," n.p.

5 Mansfield, *Machiavelli's Virtue* and the introduction to his translation of *The Prince*, cited in this text as P.

6 See, for at least one instance of this claim, Aquinas, *Summa Theologiae*, Q41, a4. Obviously, classical natural right theories would not have the same dependence on God as medieval natural law theories.

7 Lefort, *Writing*, 133–4.

says in the same sentence, what is useful [*utile*] for the prince. He is committed, in other words, to the truth of the orator not the truth of the scientist."[8] Viroli understands rhetoric primarily in terms of deliberation and persuasion, so that effectual truth is that which aids in deliberations about desired ends and the construction of persuasive arguments that will advance him towards those ends. The truth is, in this formulation, dependent upon the prince's desires: different means will appear as effective depending on the prince's ends. These disparate approaches to Machiavelli, it is worth noting, all agree in (a) focusing on his presentation of truth in terms of something useful or practical as opposed to theoretical or contemplative and (b) being focused on and rooted in this world, not something transcending it.

Worldly success is the mark of truth. This is why in *Discourses on Livy* Machiavelli writes that witnesses to a decision are able to determine whether the opinions undergirding it are true or false by looking to whether or not the plan succeeds and why he later associates divergence from the truth with the weakness of a lord (D II.22 and III.27). Returning to our passage from *The Prince*, Machiavelli's next sentence develops this concept of truth by denying that "imaginary republics" that are neither seen (*visti*) nor known to be (*conocsciuti esse*) can be associated with truth (*vero*). Machiavelli rejects imaginary republics because they – in the most literal sense possible – cannot be seen with the eyes. This is Machiavelli's evidence for the unreality of these imagined republics: they have never been seen. To be real is to be sensible, or, more generally, to be a phenomenon, to appear. Invisible republics and principalities are false or imagined because they are not phenomenal. This takes us beyond nominalism since nominalists – as the example of William of Ockham reminds us – are perfectly capable of believing in non-sensible realities, provided they are understood as singular rather than as universal entities. Indeed, Ockham and other scholastic nominalists were quite capable of accepting the existence of non-sensible and world-transcending truths – for example, truths about God. As a matter of fact, a common complaint about medieval nominalism from philosophers of Thomistic persuasions is that the nominalist God is too transcendent! In any case, in exclusively associating the sensible with knowledge and truth, Machiavelli is rejecting the various accounts of truth that locate it somewhere outside of the world (in the forms, in God, in whatever). If we are looking for philosophical antecedents for Machiavelli's view, we find them in – not surprisingly – Lucretius and the Epicurean tradition. In contrast to most

8 Viroli, *Machiavelli*, 82.

other ancient philosophers, the Epicureans were radically empiricist. Cicero glosses the Epicurean position as follows: "[Epicurus] thinks that this truth is perceived by the senses, as fire is perceived to be hot, snow white and honey sweet. In none of these examples is there any call for proof by sophisticated reasoning; it is enough simply to point them out."[9] Whether or not Machiavelli was familiar with Cicero's exposition of Epicureanism, he could have found the same doctrine in Lucretius. While it might be going too far to characterize the rejection of imagined republics and principalities of chapter 15 as purely Lucretian, it is fair to say that it is entirely compatible with the doctrines of Lucretius.

Looking forward from Machiavelli to our own time, he can also be read as denying or undoing precisely the move that Heidegger associated with the inauguration of metaphysics: Plato's subordination of the sensible individual to the world-transcending forms. In Machiavelli's case, he thinks that the focus on imaginary republics gets in the way of properly understanding the things of this world. The partisan of imaginary republics and principalities believes, after all, that truth is found there, in a super-sensory and transcendent imaginary republic. So (for example) the Augustinian maintains that, despite the fact that I was born in the Bronx, my *true home* is the invisible city of God, and understanding this point will be key for properly understanding anything else about my life. For Machiavelli, knowledge can never be acquired through reflection on imagined republics; instead, we acquire knowledge, as he intimates in the epistle dedicatory to *The Prince*, from history and experience. These two things are, after all, the sources of everything he knows (P, epistle dedicatory). If history and experience are the source of all that he knows, then knowledge is limited to what is immanent in the world. What is experience if not sensory knowledge of worldly things? And what is history if not the record of events in this world? Chapter 15 of *The Prince* suggests three things. First, that there is no super-sensory or transcendent standard of truth and goodness; second, the illusory belief in super-sensory or transcendent truths prevents people from understanding the world; third, by trying to live in accordance with a imagined truth one will always be defeated by princes who do not.

MACHIAVELLI'S PERVERSE UNCONCEALMENT

Having mentioned Heidegger, let us focus on him for a bit. In a series of essays launched in the wake of *Being and Time*, Heidegger presents the

9 Cicero, *On Moral Ends*, I.30.

history of philosophy in terms of a primordial experience of truth as *alethea* (unveiling or unhiddenness) followed by the forgetting and covering over of this experience with truth as the correctness of a proposition, *orthotes* (PDT 176; OET 128–9).[10] Truth as *orthotes*, in turn, gives birth to the metaphysics of presence. The metaphysics of presence develops into the technological experience of beings as mere resources (*bestanden*) rather than as the dynamic and mysterious unveilings of being. According to Heidegger's work of 1930, "Plato's Doctrine of Truth," the beginning of this shift can be found in Plato's analogy of the cave. There, Plato reduces the sensible world to the lower levels of the cave, while the world-transcending forms or ideas found after the escape from the cave are present as true and permanent:

> But Plato, overwhelmed as it were by the essence of εἶδος, understood it in turn as something independently present and therefore as something common (*χοινόν*) to the individual "beings" that "stand in appearance." In this way individuals, as subordinate to the *ἰδέα* as that which properly is, were displaced into the role of non-beings. (PDT 210)

The subordination of the of individuals to the idea (*ἰδέα*), Heidegger argues, changes the meaning of truth, such that truth is no longer understood as unveiling but instead as the "correctness of apprehending and asserting" (PDT 177). In his 1939 essay on Aristotle's *Physics*, Heidegger expands on this point. There he argues for a connection between *phusis* and *alethea*, and, as such, Plato's doctrine of truth indicates a fundamentally new stance towards *phusis*: it subordinates nature to the idea such that *phusis* is no longer understood as a possible source of truth in its own right (ECPA 230). Truth is not found *in* nature but in the idea above and beyond nature. In contrast to Platonism, the understanding of truth as alethea that Heidegger endorses binds truth to the appearances of beings in the world.

Heidegger's rejection of *orthotes* in favour of *alethea* reconfirms his commitment to the primacy of the world as articulated years earlier in *Being and Time*. Plato makes it clear that the task of the philosopher is to ascend from the world of opinion and sensation – which includes *phusis* – to the world-transcending ideas if knowledge of being is to be

10 To be sure, the faultiness of Heidegger's philology is by now nearly universally acknowledged; however, Heidegger's deeper point about the priority of ἀλήθεια arguably stands independent of philology. See Carmen, "Heidegger on Correspondence and Correctness," 106–8.

acquired.[11] So, for Heidegger, Plato's new theory of truth includes a devaluation of the natural world that strips it of its former role as the unveiling of being and instead understands being in terms of a transcendent idea. This can be seen clearly in Plato's "sequel" to *The Republic*, *The Timaeus*.[12] The demiurge's construction of nature is accomplished, Plato says, with reference to the forms: the demiurge looks to the forms as guides and paradigms (TIM 28a-b). As such, the world is only the derivative product of the demiurge's craft, incapable of revealing the secrets of being. Not surprisingly, Heidegger objects to the demiurgic creation account in *The Timaeus*. Indeed, *The Timaeus* goes on to use the platonic devaluation of appearance in the Cave analogy to argue for the non-eternity of the world: "It [the world] has come to be. For it is both visible and tangible and has a body – and all such things are perceptible. And, as we have shown, perceptible things are grasped by opinion, which involve sense perception. As such, they are things that come to be, things that are begotten."[13] In sum, in Platonism, the world is not eternal and truth is found outside the world.

The world, for Machiavelli, is not subordinated to the idea. But why does he resist the Platonic subordination? The answer to this question lies in the adjective "imagined": the truth is not subordinated to the idea because the idea does not exist outside the imagination of philosophers – ideas are only as real as unicorns and golden mountains. We can note here that Machiavelli's interpretation of universals as figments of one's imagination reproduces the nominalist position that universals are found only in the mind rather than in things. In nominalist semantics universal terms referred confusedly to numerous particulars rather than to really existing universals: universals existed only as universal thoughts, ideas, imaginations, not in reality. I am not claiming that Machiavelli was a student of nominalist semantics – I doubt he would have had much patience for the subtle logical distinctions upon which nominalism thrived – but we can surely note the affinities. Of course, Machiavelli's position cannot be reduced to nominalism. As I noted earlier, scholastic nominalism emphasized the transcendence of God in a way that Machiavelli never does and never could. His nominalism is coloured by his commitment to an eternal world. This world is eternal, there is nothing transcending it; claims to the contrary are only delusions. Sebastian de Grazia insightfully notes that, in this sentence, Machiavelli moves

11 Plato, *The Republic*, 518b–d.

12 For evidence that Plato intended *The Timaeus* to function as a sequel to *The Republic*, see Plato, *The Timaeus*, 17c–19b.

13 Ibid., 28b–c.

from speaking of *la verità effetuale* to a more generic "trueness" – by dropping the adjective here, Machiavelli indicates that the effectual truth is the only kind of truth.[14] The only truth is the truth of this world, the visible world, the eternal world. As such, his rejection of imagined republics is not simply a statement of political strategy but a rejection of what Heidegger called "metaphysics" – that is, truth as *orthotes.* Moreover, in rejecting idealized republics and turning to what appears before him, he turns his attention from eternal permanence towards the empirically visible, towards what can be seen. It is a kind of *alethea* that rejects the Platonism of *orthotes* and sees truth as eminently sensible. One might be tempted to characterize Machiavelli's as a perverse *alethea,* contrasting *virtú* with *gelassenheit,* but there is a closer connection between truth and violence in Heidegger than his notion of *gelassenheit* suggests, as we see later when we turn to his *Introduction to Metaphysics.* Anticipating that discussion, we can point again to the well-known philosophical machismo of Heidegger's discourses: one constantly "destroys," "overcomes," and so forth.

THE EXPULSION OF THE TRANSCENDENT

Machiavelli's argument rests on an assumed premise: that these so-called "invisible republics" are, in fact, invisible. There is no argument for his claim that nobody has had any experience of these republics. I have the suspicion that Heidegger makes a similar move – arguably, he assumes that the Platonic ideas cannot unveil themselves as a kind of *alethea*; that the ascent to the forms is entirely propositional rather than mystical – but I won't pursue this point here. The turn towards history and experience that Machiavelli announces in his epistle dedicatory to *The Prince,* and which is reinforced in this section, carries with it certain exclusions. Not every historical event is admitted into what Machiavelli calls history, and not every vision is admitted into the visible. Not every appearance gets to count as an appearance. An older gentleman in the far west of Ireland once told me he had heard the Banshee's cry shortly before someone died; most readers of this book would automatically assume that he had heard no such thing. Some people have claimed to see heaven in mystical visions, but we Machiavellians maintain that it is not visible: Machiavelli takes it as axiomatic that Savonarola didn't talk to God (D I.11). In short, "the invisible" in Machiavelli is not determined in a

14 De Grazia, *Machiavelli in Hell,* 280.

strictly empirical way but, rather, according to a standard provided by his commitment to the eternity of the world: anything that might suggest that the world is not eternal is either excluded or reinterpreted in a way compatible with the eternity of the world. The eternity of the world creates a kind of policing of the visible that limits entry into the visible to certain kinds of things and excludes others. Any appearance or experience that might suggest that the world is not eternal is barred from entry. That way of phrasing it, however, is not entirely accurate: the policing of the visible does not exclude new things that are trying to enter the visible and be taken into account by a philosophy that hitherto had not done so. Machiavelli's policing is more akin to that of bouncers than to that border guards. The point of the policing is to eject or expel troublemakers who were already inside, not to prevent the entry of troublemakers from outside. This is indicated in Machiavelli's emphasis on his novelty: if what was being excluded in Machiavelli's account was not already inside, his turn away from invisible republics would be nothing new. Machiavelli is doing something novel insofar as what he terms "invisible" or "imagined" used to be considered as very visible or real: the bouncers are kicking out long-time residents. In pointing to Machiavelli's policing, I am not saying that that we are obliged to believe everything we are told about world-transcending experiences but, rather, that Machiavelli requires us to believe nothing. His commitment to an eternal world excludes it *tout court.*

The expulsion of the transcendent is an important move in Machiavelli's philosophy. It is not unimportant that he opens chapter 15 with a discussion of the novelty of his doctrines, and it is this expulsion in particular that constitutes his novelty. This double movement of expulsion and constitution is reminiscent of René Girard's account of the scapegoating mechanism, and, because of this, it is possible to give a Girardian reading to this and related passages in Machiavelli's writings.[15] The crisis is Italy's supine state. We saw in the passages discussed earlier that Machiavelli thinks that the Christian denial of the eternity of the world is at the root of Italy's problems. Christianity is to blame for the weakness of Italy and the failures of previous writers on political matters. Having identified the invisible republics of Christianity as the source of the crisis, Machiavelli expels it, creating a new philosophical tradition on the basis of this expulsion, an expulsion his successors will then ritually

15 The general outlines of a Girardian approach to Machiavelli are developed in Wydra, "Human Nature and Politics."

repeat every so often: Hume on miracles, Nietzsche on the death of God, and so on and so on.[16]

However, there are two possible objections to this reading. First, Girardian expulsions are supposed to be violent and bloody affairs, involving (as he likes to put it) collective murder or lynching. Nothing of the kind happens in *The Prince*; instead we just have words on a page (although the words sometimes describe pretty gory things). However, this objection rests on an overly narrow reading of Girard: while he finds lynching to be the most common scapegoating mechanism, especially in archaic societies, he admits that there are other, less dramatic, methods available. In modern thought he detects "a kind of gigantic intellectual expulsion of the whole Judeo-Christian tradition" (THSFW, 262). Machiavelli expels Judeo-Christian transcendence from his thought as the source of innumerable problems without seriously engaging it to see if those things appear as problems from within that tradition. For it is one thing to say that Christian education has discouraged violence and thereby made people less capable of using it effectively (which Machiavelli does say); it is another to say that this is a problem that discredits Christianity rather than being what might be termed user error. For one might agree with him about the fact while disagreeing with the evaluation thereof. And whether or not avenging one's beating is good or bad will depend, as we saw, on whether or not the world is eternal. Machiavelli's discussion of Christianity is determined and guided by his commitment to sacrifice and the eternity of the world. All the parts of Christianity that depend upon transcendence are either reinterpreted (this is, as we shall see, part of what Machiavelli means when he speaks of reinterpreting Christianity according to virtue) or ignored altogether to create a kind of sacrificial Christianity. We return to this point later; this much suffices to dispatch the first objection.

Turning now to the second objection: if one is giving a Girardian reading of Machiavelli's expulsions, then one must include the next move in Girard's account – the sanctification of the scapegoat. According to Girard, once the expulsion of the scapegoat has done its work, the remaining community thinks better of him. In a mysterious way, they see the scapegoat as not just the cause of the problem but also as the solution: in the story of Oedipus, the man who left Thebes in shame is

16 One might object to this reading by saying: "Well, the armies conquering Italy were Christian armies too, so Machiavelli couldn't really think that the Christian denial of the eternity of the world is to blame." But this misses the point of scapegoating: of course that denial isn't to blame for the crisis, but the scapegoater doesn't realize this. On the self-deception involved in scapegoating, see Girard, SG, 1–11.

divinized at Colonus (vs 85–6). If the Girardian parallels are to hold, then the transcendent should not merely be expelled from Machiavelli's politics but also be held up in esteem, admired in its absence. But just as the scapegoat returns transformed (as in the story of Oedipus), so, too, does Machiavelli's scapegoat. If Christianity is blamed for the crisis, it is also held out as a possible solution to it, if only it could be interpreted in terms of virtue. Indeed, how many times has one heard or read that Christianity would be a great source of social progress if only we could remove the deleterious influence of Paul, or Augustine, or Thomas, or Luther and Calvin, or Trent, or the Pope, or the fundamentalist? This is a basically Machiavellian ritual, rejecting Christianity as it is while hoping for a better, transformed Christianity according to virtue that will help bring about desired social change. Machiavelli's Christianity according to virtue is a doppelganger of Christian belief that looks very much like the original but is something entirely different.[17] I return to this point later. For now, I note two points: first, in turning towards experience or visibility, Machiavelli is actually turning towards certain kinds of experience, certain kinds of vision, and excluding others; second, this move can be interpreted as a kind of scapegoating expulsion of the experiences that purport to point towards a good apart from this, the eternal world.

EFFECTING THE TRUTH

The Machiavellian vision of the eternity of the world in the *Discourses* is mirrored in *The Prince*'s rejection of imagined republics and principalities. He does not create the space for a new science of politics that exists apart from metaphysics (in the broadest sense of the term) but instead – and this is crucial for the remainder of the text – introduces a new metaphysics of immanence to support the new science. This new metaphysics, in turn, is constituted by the expulsion of the old metaphysics. Our question becomes: What is this metaphysics? It is helpful to return to Heidegger's discussion of the relationship between one's understanding of truth (as *alethea* or as *orthotes*) and how one understands nature

17 This, I take it, is the point that Vickie Sullivan wants to make in *Three Romes.* While I differ with Sullivan's analysis of particular passages in Machiavelli, I think that she is generally correct in her assessment that Machiavelli is hostile towards traditional Christianity but finds some uses for modified "temporal" Christianity. I depart from Sullivan's general point insofar as I would locate the difference between Machiavellian Christianity and traditional Christianity in terms of the question of sacrifice. While Machiavelli's thought is, I am arguing, basically sacrificial, Christianity (in theory if not always in practice) is anti-sacrificial.

(*phusis*): different doctrines of truth imply different understandings of nature. Heidegger argues that Plato's doctrine of truth led to a fundamentally new stance towards *phusis*: nature is now subordinated to the idea and no longer a possible source of truth in its own right (ECPA 230). Truth is not found *in* nature, but in the idea transcending nature. If Heidegger is right about this (and I am stipulating for the sake of argument that he is) then we can learn something about Machiavelli by asking if and how his new doctrine of truth yields a new approach to nature. As Mansfield suggests, Machiavelli's new doctrine of truth entails the rejection a transcendent structure or meaning with which human beings are morally obliged to be in accord. The world is eternal and the world is merely what appears in it with no super-structure of meaning attached. There is no transcendental signified in Machiavelli: this is rejected when he rejects imaginary republics. That is to say, for Machiavelli as for Derrida, there is no preordained structure to which the world or our actions in it should conform; instead, whatever structures we find are purely human affairs, internal to the world. If there is a difference between Derrida and Machiavelli on this score, it is only that Machiavelli more highly estimates the ability of princes to restrict the play of signification.

One objection to Machiavelli's understanding of truth as effectual truth is fairly straightforward: truth is not a matter for the prince to determine but, rather, is already out there in the facts of the world. One might kick a rock, proclaiming, "I refute Machiavelli thus!" But I think that this misses the point. Machiavelli never suggests that there are not certain empirical facts, or even necessities, that the prince must take into account. However, I do think that he strongly wants to maintain that these facts are under-determined and open to a multiplicity of possible interpretations, without a transcendental signified specifying the correct one(s). The prince determines, or attempts to determine, the correct interpretation of the fact. But, recalling Viroli's claim that "to pursue the effective truth of the matter means to pursue the truth which permits one to attain the desired result,"[18] we should add that the correct interpretation depends on the goals of the prince. If we take the heaviness of a rock as a fact, whether or not that heaviness is good or bad will depend on the prince's goal. But beyond this, for Machiavelli, a successful prince will be able to both interpret facts and influence what the facts actually are. The prince makes empirical facts to the extent that he is capable of influencing events and outcomes in the world: if he is strong enough to

18 Viroli, *Machiavelli*, 82.

move the rock, he may do so and thereby change the fact. In digging dams and ditches (P XXV) the prince's exercise of virtue not merely defends him against fortune but changes the facts regarding topography. To clarify, let us introduce a distinction between two kinds of statements: empirical statements and metaphysical statements. Empirical statements can be said to be the kind of statements the truth or falsity of which can be determined by the senses – for example, that the brown cat is on the blue mat – in a fairly straightforward way. The truth or falsity of metaphysical statements, on the other hand, cannot be determined in the same way – is the brown cat essentially a cat, but not essentially brown? And *should* the cat be on the mat? The answers to these questions, I take it for granted, are not visible. Sensation shows where the cat is, but not where it should be; it shows me the brown cat, but not the distinction between substance and accidents. One should note that one function of a metaphysical statement is to interpret empirical statements. Machiavelli's rejection of imagined republics does not claim that there are no true empirical statements, but it does claim that there are no privileged metaphysical statements that definitively interpret the empirical; instead, the interpretations are due to the princely imposition of modes and orders.

IMAGINED REPUBLICS AND REAL PRINCES

If appeals to imagined republics and principalities – to transcendent realities – have no basis in reality, if they are false and fictitious, where then do they come from? Machiavelli's answer is quite simple: the modes and orders of the prince. The prince, as we learn in chapter 6 of *The Prince*, introduces new modes and orders. In my view, the introduction of new modes and orders is most profitably read alongside the doctrine of effectual truth. In introducing modes and orders the prince produces a discourse or text that includes metaphysical claims (invisible republics) that interpret the empirical truths of the world in this or that manner. One might easily give this a Heideggerian spin, with reference to the discussion of essential violence in *Introduction to Metaphysics*: the Machiavellian prince, like the Heideggerian poet or thinker, orders and discloses being in such a way that human beings can enter into it (IM 175). Of course, there are limitations to this analogy that I will spell out in later. For now, however, I want to highlight the analogy so that the reader will keep in mind the broader significance of our discussion of Machiavelli. In the face of the overwhelming presence of nature, the prince's modes and orders offer his subjects an interpretation or organization of nature. The discussion in chapter 6 of *The Prince* is the seed of an idea that comes to full bloom in *Discourses on Livy*, in which Machiavelli asserts that, "since the inhabitants were sparse in the beginning of the world, they lived dispersed for a time like beasts; then, as generations multiplied, they gathered together, and to be able to defend themselves better, they began to look to whoever among them was more robust and of greater heart, and they made him a head, as it were and obeyed him. From this arose knowledge of things honest and good, differing from pernicious and bad." (D I.2) In this (very Lucretian) passage we see that initially human beings lived in a manner akin to beasts: without understanding, without insight, without morals. However, over time they began to form communities with one person at the head. It is through the work of this person that the overwhelming confusion that plagued them is reduced to order; this "disciplining and disposing" (IM 175) of the overwhelming marks the beginning of history, for both Heidegger and Machiavelli.

The ordering of how the world is disclosed to us, I take it, is what Machiavelli has in mind when he refers to the modes and orders introduced by the new prince in chapter 6 of *The Prince.* The greatest princes (Moses, Cyrus, Theseus, and Romulus) did not simply order governments but ordered or reordered societies or cultures, including – as the case of Moses makes clear – beliefs about things that transcend the world and yet guide one's experience of the world. In this sense, I think that Machiavelli's assimilation of Moses's introduction of modes and orders to that of the other three princes is the most important part of chapter 6. It explains how or why people in an eternal world come to believe in something transcending it by placing the source of those beliefs in the modes and orders of the prince. Transcendence is an illusion created by the prince's modes and orders. In the *Discourses* Machiavelli writes, "since he wished *his laws and orders* to forward, Moses was forced to kill infinite men" (D III.30, emphasis mine). The source of the law, it seems, is the arm of Moses not the finger of God. The effect here is an immanentizing of Mosaic Law. Interpreting Mosaic Law in terms of our discussion of chapter 15 of *The Prince* indicates that (a) Moses presented it as coming from God and that (b) the Israelites believed it came from God but that (c) it actually came from Moses, in the same way that the modes and orders of, for example, Rome came from Romulus. This claim can be further developed if one accepts the claim, recently propounded by Mark Jurdjevic, that Machiavelli's presentation of Moses is influence by his meditations on Savonarola. In 1498, Machiavelli wrote a commentary on some of Savonarola's sermons at the request of Ricciadro Bechi. The sermons he heard were on Moses. In those sermons Savonarola emphasized Moses's willingness to employ violence in leading Israel out of Egypt and his (Savonarola's) willingness to do the same. And while there are good reasons for supposing that Savonarola provided Machiavelli with a lifetime of material upon which to reflect, for us, the important point is that Machiavelli's account of the sermon famously refers to Savonarola as a liar. I take this to indicate, at least, that he did not accept Savonarola's pretensions to speak with God, but it also suggests that he doesn't accept Moses's either. His treatment of Numa, in *Discourses* I.11, reinforces this reading: there he praises Numa's duplicity in founding Roman religion – Numa pretended to speak with a nymph.[19] I have more to say regarding Numa later, but for now it suffices to note Machiavelli's explicit denial that either Numa or Savonarola spoke with divine beings.

The (effectual) truth of metaphysical statements depends on the prince, not the world. But the prince does not create the truth entirely *ex nihilo*. He owes the world the opportunity to impose an interpretation upon it: first, things are unveiled as brute facts; second, the prince interprets those facts in the way he sees fit. If there were no shellfish, they could not be unclean. In this case, the metaphysical statements of imagined republics are promulgated by princes when they impose modes and orders on the people that influence how they interpret visible things: for example, that it was wrong to eat shellfish.

This – as we will see later – is what Machiavelli sees Numa to have done with the Romans. And to do both these things, the prince may have to learn how to not be good. So, the moral context of the opening paragraph to chapter 15 makes it clear that Machiavelli is primarily concerned with disputing the traditional view of transcendence; he is not interested in denying the brute facts of nature, but only in their being interpreted in terms of a transcendent reality. This insight is an essential one for Machiavelli since it is what makes his own project possible. If he did not assume that the modes and orders he inherited were the arbitrary impositions of dead princes, he would not attempt to replace them with his own. If he thought that the tradition preceding him was correctly developing a true doctrine concerning those things unseen, he would err gravely in departing from those orders. Machiavelli's oft-proclaimed novelty is inseparable from his rejection of imagined republics and principalities and the view that traditional metaphysical or moral doctrines are merely the calcified modes and orders of dead princes. The constructed and arbitrary nature of traditional metaphysical and moral discourse (they are simply the modes and orders of a prince or

19 The discussion of Machiavelli and Savonarola above is based on and indebted to the much longer account in the first chapter of Jurdjevic, *Great and Wretched City*, 16–52.

princes) shows why those discourses can be deconstructed. Machiavelli is not claiming that there are not certain determinate states of affairs that human beings can notice and to which they can adapt themselves – as if the world were simply the prince's daydream to be put together as he likes – but, rather, that there is no transcendent signified (metaphysical, moral, or whatever) that determines the correct interpretation of the world. In the absence of any imagined republic the prince may impose whatever modes and orders seem appropriate to him. Machiavelli reveals both the constructability and deconstructability of any discourse, including and especially religious discourse. Machiavellian deconstruction is not identical to Derridean deconstruction in all aspects, but they are kindred spirits (they both rightly pass for atheists) as both require the rejection of imagined republics – and what else is Derrida's injunction to do without recourse to a (non-existent) transcendental signified? – because they, in the last analysis, purport to transcend the only world we have. Later, however, we will have cause to wonder whether Derrida is entirely consistent in his rejection of imagined republics.

One important upshot of Machiavelli's account of truth is found in chapter 22 of *The Prince.* There he is ostensibly discussing the relationship between the prince and his secretaries. Throughout this discussion, however, he refers to the "brains" (*cervelli*) of the prince and the advisor.[20] Accordingly, Machiavelli argues that one can judge a prince by how well he chooses his advisors – "the first conjecture that is to be made of the brain of a lord is to see the men he has around him" – and offers advice for how a prince may choose a good advisor. In this discussion we learn, for example, that:

> There are three kinds of brains: one that understands by itself, another that discerns what others understand, the third that understands neither by itself nor through others; the first is most excellent, the second excellent, and the third, useless. (P XXII)

This reference to brains, rather than to the more abstract terms preferred by philosophers – for example, mind, soul – is closely linked, I think, to the dismissal of imagined republics in chapter 15. The brain is visible in a way that the mind or soul are not. There is, contained in this linkage, a key to Machiavelli's anthropology. The mind, the soul, and so forth are among those invisible truths that are excluded with the

20 In P 18, Machiavelli also states that princes that can get "around men's brains with their astuteness."

rejection of imagined republics; the human being is strictly and simply visible. Understanding, to the extent that the brain accomplishes it, appears as a strictly material process, explicable (in principle, if not actually) in terms of the brain and the nervous system.[21] If human intellectual powers are reducible to the functioning of their visible brain, then the visible truths about the human being will exhaustively explain or interpret humanity.

Machiavelli shows an interest in truth only insofar as it is useful for some end; against the classical and medieval vision of *scientia* as a contemplation of super-sensory and transcendent truths, Machiavelli focuses on the practical uses of knowledge because there is nothing to transcendent to contemplate. In his *Discourses*, Machiavelli asserts that all sciences require practice: there is no such thing as a purely theoretical science (D III.39). If we return to the first sentence of chapter 15 of *The Prince*, we see that Machiavelli's goal is not to write something merely for the sake of contemplation but, rather, to produce *una cosa utile a chi la intende*: a useful thing for he who understands. The goal of truth is its effect: truth must be a useful thing for the person who compels the unveiling. For this reason, Machiavelli bases his doctrines on how one lives (*vive*) rather than on how one ought to live (*vivere*). In choosing the third person singular, rather than the infinitive, Machiavelli reinforces his previous rejection of imagined republics: infinitives remain vague and uncertain – that is, universal – while the conjugated verb finds a determinate meaning by being attached to a particular agent in a particular tense.[22] Moreover, one can only see how individuals actually live – one can observe their behaviour – but one cannot see, and will never see, how they *should* live. By rejecting imagined republics and accounts of "how one ought to live" Machiavelli rejects both traditional philosophy and theology as a grounding for politics, principally because they involve the discovery of eternal and universal verities rather than the particular products of human action. Both the theoretical city of the

21 Brown, *Return of Lucretius*, 82, writes that the soul played no part in Machiavelli's physiology. The replacement of souls with brains is, it is worth noting, consistent with the atomist doctrines of Lucretius. Palmer, in *Reading Lucretius*, notes that Machiavelli's notes on his copy of Lucretius's poem showed particular interest in Lucretius's arguments for the physical or tactile nature of "thought, emotion and sensation" (83).

22 In syllogistic logic, infinitives are interpreted as A-propositions – that is, universal affirmative propositions. So the phrase "To run is healthy" is interpreted as meaning "All running is healthy." Renaissance humanism eschewed logic because of the barbarous style of scholastic logic as well as its distance from practical affairs, but it did not challenge the system of logic as such.

philosophers and the heavenly city of the theologians are rejected in favour of immanent cities.

TO LEARN TO BE ABLE NOT TO BE GOOD

Let us now (finally!) return to the moral context of the opening paragraph of chapter 15 of *The Prince.* Recall that the discussion of truth is bookended by moral concerns: the opening sentence concerns how one should treat one's friends, and the concluding remarks note that one should learn how not to be good: "For a man who wants to make a profession of good in all regards must come to ruin among so many who are not good. Hence it is necessary to a prince, if he wants to maintain himself, to learn to be able not to be good, and to use this and not use it according to necessity" (P XV). This passage is inseparable from the middle sentences' discussions of the effectual truth; in fact, "to learn to be able not to be good" may be the most effectual truth. The key to unlocking this passage is the word "good." What does Machiavelli mean by "good"? It should be clear from the forgoing that he does not mean "good" in the sense of conformity with a moral code derived from God or nature; instead, he seems to mean what people "profess" or say is good. In terms borrowed from the *Discourses* we may say that "good" here indicates what our current – Christian – education teaches people to take as good. If so, then learning to be able not to be good means learning the distinction between good and bad violence and learning to embrace good violence, even though the embrace of any kind of violence runs contrary to Christian education. Of course, Machiavelli knows that Christendom has never been pacifist, but it has been worse: it has been ineffectually violent. By refusing to make the distinction between good and bad violence (in the name of high ideals) but failing to live up to their refusal, Christian princes blunder from one escapade to the other, from one instance of incompetent violence to the other. Learning not to be good means learning the distinction between good and bad violence. If one accepts the distinction, then one can learn how to use good violence effectively when necessary. The ability to be "not good" means (at least, if not entirely) that one knows (a) that there is a difference between good violence and bad violence and (b) how to use good violence for the benefit of one's state. Of course, one might prefer to avoid violence altogether, and those who profess to be good claim to detest violence, but since they never live up to the profession of goodness, one must use violence. The difference between the one who has learned what Machiavelli teaches and the one who has not is *not* whether or not they are violent *but* whether or not they know how to use violence effectively.

If one learns to be not-good, one has, in effect, learned the sacrificial distinction between good and bad forms of violence. It may seem that this has few, if any, connections with the more abstract metaphysical, Heideggerian remarks on the effectual truth that came just a few pages earlier. However, this is not the case. Recall that the Augustinian rejection of the sacrificial distinction rests on an appeal to the world that transcended the visible one and yet provides the only proper way of interpreting this one. It is only by means of the city of God that the city of man can be understood; according to Augustine, it is only by understanding the city of God that one can finally understand the deepest and most profound truths about our life and world, and this city of God desires mercy, not sacrifice. All of this is rejected in the rejection of imagined republics. The prince's imposition of meaning and order on an otherwise chaotic world, either through the proclamation of imagined republics or the promulgation of laws, is, as we see in more detail later, inseparable from a good kind of violence – the founding violence of the armed prophet.

FORWARD TO THE BEGINNING

If my interpretation is correct, then Machiavelli is saying that philosophical and theological interpretations of transcendence are neither discovered nor revealed, but created by princes. Machiavelli addresses this issue late in his *Discourses on Livy*: in particular, chapters 43 and 46 of book III. He begins chapter 43 by noting that the passions of human beings – among other things, their natural desire to acquire – does not change much over time. However, despite the seeming permanence of human passions, one notes also the contrary: that people in different times and places seem to act quite differently from each other. This is due to the varying "forms of education" and "modes of life" in which differing peoples engage. These forms and modes are (as we saw elsewhere) imposed by the prince or other political leaders. In chapter 46 he develops these ideas in a passage worth quoting at length:

> It appears that not only does one city have certain modes and institutions diverse from one another, and procreates men either harder or more effeminate, but in the same city one sees such a difference to exist from one family to another … These things cannot arise solely from the bloodline, because that must vary through the diversity of marriage, but it necessarily comes from the diverse education of one family from another. For it is very important that a boy of tender years begin to hear good or bad said of a thing, for it must of necessity make an impression on him, which afterwards regulates the mode of proceeding in all the times of his life. (D III.46)

These two chapters give us a précis of how Machiavelli sees the modes and orders initially set down by the ruler and passed down, over the years, decades, and centuries, such that they infect the thoughts and influence the behaviour of those born many years later. One is never outside the text. That which the armed prophet forced his followers to believe and do many years ago, the citizen generations later believes and does voluntarily because he was raised to do so.

The connection between tradition and the founding violence of the armed prophet is made clearer early in the opening chapter of book III. Machiavelli admits that tradition is not a perpetual motion machine; it needs to be periodically recharged. The question then becomes, how do we do this? Machiavelli's answer is clear: one renews tradition by returning to the great beginnings in a repetition of the original founding. This is because "all the beginnings of sects, republics and kingdoms must have some goodness in them" (D III.1). Machiavelli's claim that all beginnings have some good in them finds an echo in Heidegger's *Introduction to Metaphysics* when he claims that all beginnings are "great" (IM 17). In Heidegger's case, "The great begins great, sustains itself only through the free recurrence of greatness, and if it is great, also comes to an end in greatness." The great end seems inexplicable – if something is great, why would it end – until we note that he earlier spoke of greatness in the sense of "the enormity of total annihilation." A great end, in Heidegger's sense, is compatible with a decline and fall in Machiavelli's sense; and in both cases the end is deferred by a return to the great and good at the beginning. Machiavelli's reasoning seems to be that if a city lacked goodness, it would have been destroyed at the beginning. It is this goodness that enabled the acquisition of "their first reputation and first increase" (D. III.1)

Republics return to their beginnings either through "extrinsic accident or intrinsic prudence" (D. III.1). Machiavelli gives two examples of this kind of repetition. Both kinds repeat the fearful conditions of the founding, the first unwillingly and the second intentionally. To describe the first, Machiavelli refers to the sack of Rome by the Gauls as narrated in the fifth book of Livy. The beating delivered to the Romans by the Gauls showed the Romans the extent to which they had departed from the modes and orders of their founders. Describing the second kind of return to beginnings – the one motivated by intrinsic prudence – Machiavelli writes:

> Those who governed Florence from 1434 up to 1494 used to say, to this purpose, that it is necessary to regain the state every five years; otherwise it was difficult to maintain it. They called regaining the state putting that terror and that fear in

men that had been there in taking it, since in that time they had beaten down those who, according to that mode of life, had worked for ill. But as the memory of that beating is eliminated, men began to dare to try new things and to say evil; and so it is necessary to provide for it, drawing [the state] back towards its beginnings. (D III.1)

There is a crucial difference between the two modes. The first mode, exemplified by the attack of the Gauls on Rome, is uncontrollable. One would not recommend that a leader rely on enemy attacks to drag the people back to their noble beginnings. On the other hand, the Florentine practice offers a kind of controlled violence that beats the people just enough to remind them of greater beatings in the past. Here, to maintain the state it was necessary every so often (under controlled conditions) to recreate the fear and terror associated with the founding of the state. Creating and maintaining tradition is, on this reading, inherently violent. Commenting on this and similar passages, Vicki Sullivan writes of the "life-giving properties of spectacular executions."[23] This is a wonderful phrase. It (a) expresses Machiavelli's view of the important role that executions play in politics but also, (b) without meaning to, gets at precisely the point Girard wants to make about scapegoating and (c) suggests an application of Girard's thought to Machiavelli's executions. In Sullivan's view, Machiavelli recommends that these executions be directed primarily against young and ambitious men – that is, those most likely to challenge republican modes and orders. On my reading, Machiavellian executions could target men like that but need not be limited to them. These executions are sacrificial rather than punitive and do not simply eliminate specific threats. Machiavellian sacrifice renews the modes and orders, or what Girard would call the system of differences, that order the city.

The movement Machiavelli describes (i.e., regaining the state every five years) can be read as a kind of Girardian ritual: the spontaneous violence that led to the foundation of the state has to be repeated every so often as a kind ritualized and planned violence to maintain the state. Indeed, there is a kind of ritual of cruelty in tradition as Machiavelli describes it. This insight confirms a crucial point hinted at earlier: it is not entirely correct to say that Machiavelli offers us a secular politics, or a politics free from ideological and religious constrains.[24] Instead, we

23 Sullivan, *Machiavelli's Three Romes*, 157.

24 This is not to say I totally reject Maddox's thesis in "The Secular Reformation" that Machiavelli contributed to a secular reformation ("the secularization of all religious matters that impinge on the business of the state" [Maddox, "Secular Reformation," 540]) but

must say that (in René Girard's understanding at least) Machiavelli offers us a new religion. In saying this I am not speaking to Machiavelli's explicit religious intentions (if he indeed had any) but pointing to his reproduction of the structure of archaic religions. In "regaining the state" the terror of the beginning is intentionally reproduced in a limited and more manageable fashion, to keep at bay a total return to the terror of the beginning – that is, lawlessness and disorder. In short: the good violence of execution keeps the bad violence of lawlessness away. Whether he intends these passages to have a religious meaning or not, what Machiavelli describes as a political act mirrors exactly Girard's presentation of archaic religious rituals: a re-enactment of the punishment of the scapegoat that serves to avoid a return to the condition that led to the original scapegoating. According to Girard: "Rite is the re-enactment of mimetic crises in a spirit of voluntary religious and social collaboration, a re-enactment in order to reactivate the scapegoat mechanism for the benefit of society rather than for the detriment of the victim who is perpetually sacrificed" (SG 140).

This, says Girard, is the origin of religious ritual, and in this sense, the practice adduced here by Machiavelli is religious. In *Things Hidden since the Foundations of the World*, Girard argues that "religion is nothing other than this immense effort to keep the peace. *The Sacred is violence*, but if religious man worships violence it is only insofar as the worship of violence is supposed to bring peace; religion is entirely concerned with peace, but the means it has of bringing it about are never free of sacrificial violence" (THSFW 32, emphasis in original). One could replace the word "religion" with "politics" and have a fairly accurate summary of Machiavelli: politics is nothing other than this immense effort to keep the peace. The political is violence, but if Machiavellian politics worships violence it is only to the extent that the worship of violence is supposed to bring peace; politics is entirely concerned with peace, but the means it has of bringing it about are never free of sacrificial violence. This is not accidental; rather, it is evidence for the claim that Machiavelli, like Jonas's Heidegger, does not offer us something religiously neutral but, instead, a whole new religion.

This being the case, it should not be surprising that Machiavelli turns then to religious examples of the return to founding moments, this one (apparently) less violent: the reforms of Sts Francis and Dominic. These

only that this secularization is not theologically neutral, despite its claims to the contrary. Instead, I would want to maintain that Machiavelli reproduces religious structures but puts them at the service of the state; religion appears as subservient to the state only after it has reinterpreted the state in terms of the eternal world.

two saints, according to Machiavelli, saved Christianity by returning to the example of its founder. The effect of this reform, however, has been negative: it has allowed the prelates and princes of the church, says Machiavelli, to continue to be terrible rulers and leaders. While the two saints saved the church, it is not clear that Machiavelli thinks we are better off with it saved: it seemed to ensure that the corrupt went unpunished. "They [Francis and Dominic] give them [the people] to understand that it is evil to say evil of evil and good to live under obedience to them and, if they make an error, leave them for God to punish" (D III.1). What are we to make of this? It seems that Machiavelli wants to distinguish between those traditions that can and should be rescued by a return to origins, on the one hand, and traditions that should be allowed to die off, on the other. It is clear, to me at any rate, that he ranks traditional Christianity in the latter. I return to this point later. For now, I want to point out, in light of the reference to Girard's work above, that Girard claims that the sacrificial death of Christ as narrated in the Gospels is unlike those of other ancient texts. Mythic texts – for example, the Oedipus cycle – assume the guilt of the victim; the Passion narratives constantly assert the innocence of the scapegoat. The Passion unveils the hidden workings of the scapegoat mechanism, disrupting the power of sacrifice (THSFW 172–4). The Passion narrative is an anti-sacrificial text. To the extent that Machiavelli appeals to the power of sacrificial acts in his account of tradition, he must find a way to underplay, or evacuate entirely, the unmasking effects of the Passion. Is this what the discussion of Francis and Dominic is supposed to do? Machiavelli writes that, by imitating the "life of Christ… [they] brought back into the minds of men what had already been eliminated there" (D III.1). Machiavelli is lamentably vague as to the details of what is restored to men's minds, except to say that the effect of Francis and Dominic is to focus the people's attention on the next world, where God will punish wrong-doers, over and against this world, where one must avenge one's own beatings. If we call to mind the comparison between Roman and Christian education in the opening of book II, it seems clear that the two great saints reinforce and revivify the difference between Christian and Roman education. In short, Francis and Dominic err by rejecting, and teaching others to reject, the sacrificial distinction between good and bad violence. The criticisms of Francis and Dominic suggest that the revivification of this tradition was not beneficial in the same way as was the Florentine example. In fact, it seems downright unhelpful since Francis and Dominic made the people more comfortable in their chains rather than freeing them. If one does not benefit by a return to the founding of the tradition, then one could argue it is not a good tradition, not a tradition worth rescuing. Also, if returning to the foundation is not helpful, then the initial founding was equally (or more) unhelpful. If Francis and Dominic ultimately provided a disservice to the people by returning to the origins of Christianity, then we might conclude that the founding of Christianity was a lamentable disservice. Or, to be more precise, conclude that the original Christian rejection of the sacrificial distinction between good and bad violence was a lamentable disservice – as we noted, Machiavelli still holds out the possibility of a reformed sacrificial Christianity that is more comfortable with and proficient at using violence.

One could say, therefore, that Machiavelli divides traditions into two kinds: beneficial and harmful. This distinction corresponds to, but is not identical with, the sacrificial distinction. The beneficial traditions should be maintained by returning occasionally to their origins via good violence, while the harmful ones should be allowed to run out of steam; rejuvenating harmful tradition only prolongs the problems. Note that both involve a kind of violence. The beneficial tradition is founded and preserved by violence, while the harmful tradition seems complicit with violent oppression. This association of tradition with violence and oppression – interpretative or physical – anticipates Derrida's approaches to tradition. Deconstruction rests on the premise that traditional discourses are founded on a hidden violence that it is the task of the philosopher to dig up and hold up for our inspection, making the violence – interpretive or otherwise – known to all. I've noted already some kinship between Machiavelli and deconstructive analysis, mainly insofar as both agree that there is no transcendental signified and that tradition is inseparable from violence. While I think that the parallels between a Machiavellian and a deconstructionist view of tradition are many, they depart at a central point: for Derrida, the goal in unmasking the violence in tradition is to minimize it as much as possible; for Machiavelli, it is to better understand how to use the interplay between violence and tradition for one own ends.

FISH AND GUESTS STINK AFTER THREE DAYS

There is another, closely related point, that is worth dwelling on. Hospitality emerges as a major theme in the later works of Derrida. I can't hope to unravel the complex web that Derrida weaves in his various discussions of hospitality in the space devoted to the issue, but it is worth noting a few points. In general, Derrida's interest in hospitality is linked to his interest in forgiveness (in fact, both are discussed at length in "Hospitality") and, in general, to ethics understood in a broadly Levinasian sense of openness to, or right relations with, the other. In his eulogy for Levinas, Derrida goes so far as to characterize hospitality as the "whole of ethics" (AEL 50). If Derrida means "ethics" in the Levinasian sense, then one can describe hospitality as a kind of radical openness to the other – an openness so radical that, in Derrida's eyes, it becomes almost impossible. In one treatment of the topic, Derrida writes that "hospitality – if there is any –must, would have to, open itself to an other that is not mine, my hôte, my other, not even my neighbor or my brother" (H 363). This radical openness, for Derrida (as for Levinas), is fundamental and opposes hospitality to violence. And, as usual, John Caputo provides a useful summary of the key idea and it is worth quoting him at length. We join him as he is introducing some of the questions Derrida is concerned with when discussing hospitality:

> How to welcome the other into my home, how to be a good "host," which means how to make the other at home while still retaining the home as mine, since inviting the other to stay in someone else's home is not what we mean by hospitality or the gift. Hospitality, as Penelope learned while Odysseus was off on his travels, means to put your home at risk, which simultaneously requires both having a home and risking it. Derrida's growing discourse on hospitality reflects the Jewish and Levinasian provenance of Deconstruction, for hospitality is the most ancient biblical virtue of all. In a desert world, the world of nomads, the primordial and life giving virtue was to offer respite to the stranger, the traveler, the migrant, whose survival turns on the expectation of hospitality, who cannot so much as set out without anticipating hospitality, without *trusting* in hospitality.[25]

The aspect of *risk* that Caputo emphasizes here is important. For Derrida, to be hospitable is to take a grave risk – the other that one welcomes may bring dangers with them; they may, like Penelope's suitors, stay on as enemies within the gates, eating her substance and plotting to kill her son, Telemachus. Derrida's point, however, is that it is a risk that one is obliged to take without taking it into account. Once one weighs the risks, one has exchanged hospitality for economy.[26] In short, for Derrida, hospitality is risky. To be hospitable is to take a risk. Whatever the merits of this position, we can see some of the distance between Machiavelli and Derrida by examining Machiavelli's account of hospitality and risk.

In brief, Machiavelli suggests that hospitality should not be considered as taking an uncalculated risk but as a calculation made to avoid or

25 Caputo, *More Radical Hermeneutics*, 57 (emphasis in original).
26 For an argument along these lines, see Derrida, GD, 111–12.

minimize risk. There is a crucial passage from his *Discourses on Livy* that reads as follows: "Duke Valentino had taken Faenza and made Bologna bow to his terms. Then, wishing to return to Rome through Tuscany, he sent his man to Florence to ask passage for himself and his army ... In this one [the Florentines] did not follow the Roman mode, for since the Duke was well-armed and the Florentines so unarmed that they could not prevent him from passing through, it was much more to their honor that he should appear to pass by their will rather than by force" (D I.38). In this passage, the Florentines refuse to welcome Duke Valentino (Cesare Borgia) to their lands. Machiavelli's criticism lies in the claim that, since they could not stop him, they should have been hospitable towards him. I believe that this passage, and others like it, offers a radically different view of hospitality than that developed by Derrida and Caputo, and that juxtaposing the two offers a number of interesting results.

The passage from Machiavelli suggests that, rather than being a risk, hospitality is a strategy for reducing risk: one welcomes the stranger, giving him or her what he or she wants, in the hopes that, by doing so, one will preserve the peace and one's own authority or state. Hospitality is not a radical openness to the other but, rather, precisely the opposite: it is a kind of strategic closedness to the other that attempts to manage and minimize the effects of his arrival. It is not the antithesis of violence or totality but, rather, a strategy for preserving totality rooted in violence. Of course, one can readily point out that the Derridean and Machiavellian examples are quite different: one a stranger wandering through the desert, the other a bloody-minded prince leading an army. On this basis one could object that the desert stranger seems quite harmless and would be easy to expel from the camp or tribe if necessary. Whence, in letting the stranger enter as a friend, one is taking a greater risk than in keeping him out, and, insofar as this is the case, hospitality is a risk. This approach, which seems in keeping with the views of Derrida and Caputo, is perhaps too sentimental and naive. In the pre-modern context (mainly the Old Testament), from which Derrida and Caputo like to draw examples of hospitality, a solitary stranger *could* bring danger to the camp; he or she might be capable of destroying it if insulted, if not through force of arms, then through curses, magic, or other supernatural powers. For example, in Greece, the stranger might call on Zeus Xenios as the avenger of strangers or, even worse (from the point of view of the inhospitable), the stranger might by Zeus Xenios in disguise.[27] Inhospitality in the latter case could have devastating consequences.

27 On Zeus Xenios, see Dowden, *Zeus*, 78–80.

If we keep this point at the forefront of our minds, one of Derrida's preferred examples of hospitality-as-risk can be readily interpreted as hospitality-as-risk-reduction. I have in mind here Genesis 17–18. There a visitor shows up unannounced at Abram's tents and is received with great welcome. Derrida writes: "This is indeed hospitality *par excellence* in which the visitor radically overwhelms the self of the 'visited' and the *chez-soi* of the host" (H 372). God overwhelms Abram by changing his name to Abraham and promising him a multitude of descendants. The important point for Derrida is not the interpretation of the passage typically given by theologians but, rather, the fact that the passage indicates something like the phenomenological structure of radical hospitality: hospitality not only welcomes the other, but transforms or interrupts the host. The move from Abram to Abraham is easily interpreted as a kind of Levinasian movement from the illusion of self-possession and autarchy to the more profound realization – due to the presences of the other – of heteronomy, and I think this is what Derrida finds exemplary in this text. Derrida's account of hospitality trades on a sentimental way of imagining the scene: the stranger is always taken as weaker and in need of help. This is also true in the passage cited above from Caputo. While both Caputo and Derrida admit that there is always risk in hospitality, hospitality as they present it precedes risk, and it is in a sense risk that depends on hospitality. If one is not hospitable, then one is not taking a risk. The "risk" is the lamentable consequence of our obligation to be hospitable. In contrast, Machiavelli sees risk as preceding hospitality, not resulting from it, and interprets hospitality as one possible way of managing the risk. So, for Derrida, the stranger is not dangerous unless and until I am hospitable; for Machiavelli, the stranger is dangerous independently of my choices, and the choice to be hospitable or inhospitable is a way of dealing with that risk.[28]

28 Another possible motivation for hospitality, which I think would be worth considering in a lengthier treatment of the issue, would be to consider hospitality in connection with honour. Many of the societies that are closely associated with rituals of hospitality (ancient Greece, Old Testament Judaism, Arabia, the American South, and so on) are also societies that are closely associated with notions of honour, both personal and familial. It stands to reason that acts of hospitality could be interpreted as either attempts to avoid dishonour (by treating someone poorly who should not have been so treated) or to gain honour (perhaps in the sense of conspicuous consumption). Moreover, many of these same societies were or are characterized by violence in the name of honour. The connection between violence and honour is well known, but it might be equally valid to connect all three: hospitality, honour, and violence as a kind of three-legged stool. But since neither Derrida nor Caputo discusses the connection between honour and hospitality at length, I will not get into it here.

Depending on how we interpret the relationship between risk and hospitality, our reading of Genesis changes. On this (Machiavellian) reading, Abram's hospitality is not despite risk but precisely because of risk: he hopes that by welcoming the stranger, supplying his needs and giving him no cause for alarm or offence, he will soon peaceably leave and continue his journey. Abram's hospitality is a kind of strategy for being left in peace. Just as Florence should have calculated that it would be better served by giving Valentino what he wanted rather than forcing him to take it, Abram calculates that he is better served by giving a stranger what he wants rather than forcing him to take it. In both cases, the idea is that, by freely offering some of my goods and services, the need will not arise for the other to forcibly take all of my goods and services. In this context, it is worth noticing that the passages from Genesis that Derrida discusses immediately precede the chapters describing the events leading up to the destruction of Sodom and Gomorrah. While scholarly and religious commentators disagree about the precise nature of the "sin of Sodom," there is general agreement that the people of Sodom were not hospitable to the guests and foreigners in their midst. We need not concern ourselves, therefore, with sorting out the precise nature of that inhospitality; the important point for my argument here is that Sodom was destroyed by strangers because of a lack of hospitality. (Zeus Xenios isn't the only God that protects guests!) It is precisely this context that suggests that hospitality is less risky, not more risky, than inhospitality. The other, the stranger, brings danger with him; he is always a potential enemy and the smallest spark may light the fire of conflict. By welcoming the other the host avoids offending him/her and, thereby, avoids, or hopes to avoid, an outbreak of violence. Hospitality is not incalculable; rather, it is the *result* of a calculation.

IT WAS FORTUNATE THAT PHARAOH KNEW NOT JOSEPH

I conclude this chapter with a brief discussion of the relationship between virtue and truth. For our purposes only a few key points need to be highlighted. Insofar as (a) truth is an effect of the prince's actions (either by influencing empirical situations or by imposing interpretations of them) and (b) the success of the prince depends on his virtue, it follows that truth is dependent upon virtue. The opening chapter of *The Prince* makes it clear that Machiavelli does not understand virtue in terms of *ratio* (as in "an activity of the soul in accordance with reason") but, rather, in terms of *stato*. Virtue is defined as one of the two ways (the other being fortune) by which one can achieve stato. This suggests that there is a relationship or similarity between truth (understood as the effectual truth) and stato. But what exactly does "stato" mean?

This word, often translated as "state," has been commented upon at length by Richard Black:

> In Florentine usage of the fifteenth and early sixteenth centuries, stato never carried the modern sense of a public embodiment of power, The State, or the commonwealth. Rather, it normally meant "regime," used in the sense of membership of the ruling group of a city, or of power over a territory, city or people. It was never a synonym for "republic" or "city" ... Disapproval is clear, for example, in the political writings of fifteenth century Florentines such as Leon Battista Alberti, Agnolo Pandolfini or Giovanni Rucellai, for whom *stato* had a pejorative sense, associated with tyranny.[29]

Machiavelli's stato is not, therefore, the state but power. States may or may not have stato; officials may or may not be able to enforce their will. The contemporary term "failed state" may be taken to indicate a state without stato. To the extent that virtue is a path to stato, one might say that virtue primarily, if not exclusively, is the ability to project effective force on one's surroundings. This further binds together truth and state. Earlier I argue that *the* effectual truth above all others is the sacrificial distinction between good and bad violence and that it is the acceptance of this distinction (learning to be not good) that enables the prince to enforce his will in other matters. We may now go a step further and note that the enforcement of his will is nothing other than the state. The achievement of the state requires that (a) one endorse the sacrificial distinction between good and bad forms of violence and (b) is competent or effective at using the good kind.

In chapter 1 of *The Prince*, as a path to state, virtue is principally juxtaposed not to vice but to *fortuna* (P I). Machiavelli sees an inverse relationship between virtue and dependence upon fortune: the more virtuous one is, the less the outcome of one's action depends upon fortune. But what is fortune? Anthony Parel argues that fortune is primarily astrological: "there is no real difference between the impact of Fortune and that of the heavens or planets on human affairs."[30] Parel goes on to argue that, in the astrology of Machiavelli's day, this planetary influence was impersonal and predictable; one can compare fortune to the tides, whose ebb and flow is influenced (impersonally) by

29 Black, *Machiavelli*, 100–1.
30 Parel, "Farewell to Fortune," 591.

the moon's gravitational pull. Finally, given the complete collapse of Ptolemaic astronomy and astrology, Parel argues, it is impossible to find anything philosophically useful in Machiavelli's writings concerning fortune. But Parel's account is perhaps *more* specific than is needed for our purposes; it has also met a serious rival in Alison Brown's Lucretian reading of fortune. According to Brown, "although Machiavelli accepted the important role of astrology in our lives ... he was novel in allowing unexpected room in this deterministic universe for the swerve of chance that enabled a bold and clever person to exercise his free will."[31] According to Lucretius, atoms fall, or are supposed to fall, in a straight line through the void. However, they occasionally swerve. The swerve disrupts the orderly cascading of atoms, causing them to crash and bash into each other; from these crashes atoms join and separate creating the things of the world around us. On Brown's reading, fortune seems to designate the random joining and splitting of atoms that constitute the things and events of life, but, precisely because these are the result of a swerve, one has space to act freely. Parel is not convinced by the Lucretian reading: the crux of his criticism is that Machiavelli's language in chapter 25 of *The Prince* uses the language of Ptolemaic astrology, not Lucretius and his swerve.[32] Certainly, Parel argues, if Machiavelli adhered to Lucretius's account, it would have shown up in chapter 25.

Although I am broadly sympathetic to the Lucretian reading, for the argument I am advancing to work, we do not have to settle the debate between Parel and Brown; it is enough to recognize that (a) fortune refers to events that one does not control, without concerning ourselves with defining too closely what does control them, and (b) it is the task of virtue to minimize the effect that these events have on our plans and ourselves. This much Parel and Brown both grant, disagreeing only over how virtue minimizes the effects of fortune; either by waiting for more propitious times (Parel) or stepping into the space provided by the swerve (Brown). In his *Discourses,* Machiavelli challenges Plutarch's claim that Rome's empire was dependent upon fortune: according to Machiavelli, what Plutarch attributes to fortune is actually the effects of Roman virtue. While fortune is not entirely eliminated, Rome – because of her virtue – had less need to rely on it than did other regimes (D II.1). In *The Art of War* Machiavelli makes a similar point, noting that the reliance on fortune on the part of the princes of Italy is accompanied by a lack of virtue (AW II.313). Whether or not fortune is dependent upon

31 Brown, *Return of Lucretius,* 85.

32 Parel, "Farewell to Fortune," 599–601. For Brown's response to Parel, see her "Lucretian Naturalism," 108–10.

the fall of atoms or the movement of planets, the important point for Machiavelli is that a virtuous person will not allow his or her fate to be decided solely by fortune but will, by whatever means possible, attempt to manage and influence the outcome. This requires the sacrificial distinction.

For Machiavelli, after one has had insights into what the fortunes of one's times require, one can manage them, adapt to them, and turn events to one's purposes. In chapter 25 of *The Prince* he notes that fortune is only able to "demonstrate her power where virtue has not been put in order to resist her" (P XXV). There are two famous images used to describe the relationship between fortune and virtue in chapter 25, and both images are violent. The first compares fortune to a raging flood, and virtue to the dams, dikes, and canals that control the floodwater and prevent the flood from doing any serious damage. The point of this comparison seems to be twofold. First, fortune – like a raging flood – is not something that can be controlled. The twists and turns of fortune are precisely those things that, for whatever reason, one cannot control. However, the impossibility of controlling fortune does not entail an inability to manage its effects. While a prince cannot keep the river from rising, he can order things such that the flood neither wash away crops nor flood towns. Virtue, in this analogy, is found in the preparations that precede the flood: the building of dikes and dams. The great earthmoving and water-managing project that Machiavelli describes should call to mind our earlier discussion of truth. Here we find the virtuous prince changing the facts on the ground, creating embankments, canals, and the like where previously there was nothing. The virtuous prince is seen in his effects. We should add that this construction project would not have been accomplished without sweat and hard labour; there are no diesel-powered earthmovers in Machiavelli's example. We can assume that, in constructing the earthworks, the prince forces people to work harder and longer – perhaps at little or no pay – than they would ordinarily work. No doubt many of the labourers will question the need for the system of flood control the prince is forcing them to construct: they may grumble, "Why prepare for a flood that may never come?" Livy notes that Tarquin angered the Roman people by forcing them to dig sewers and flood controls.[33] But these disgruntled labourers return us to discussion of the armed prophets earlier in *The Prince*: the armed prophet – the one who relies on virtue – forces people to obey even when they do not wish to or do not believe him (P VI). In this sense, the first metaphor for

33 Livy, *Ab Urbe Condita*, I.56.

the virtue-fortune relationship implicitly relies on the sacrificial distinction between good and bad violence: the prince limits the power of fortune via the good violence of the armed prophet.

If the first metaphor suggests that virtue is found in the ordering of things such that fortune can be resisted, it also indicates that this resistance to fortune cannot be taken to entail a complete elimination of it. A similar point is made in his discussion of totally new princes in chapter 6 of *The Prince*: here he lists four – Moses, Cyrus, Romulus, and Theseus. According to Machiavelli, these men came to power through their own virtue, relying on fortune only for the opportunity (P VI). Moses was fortunate to find the Hebrews enslaved, Theseus fortunate to find the Athenians scattered, and so on. So, even our most virtuous princes had some (minimal) relationship with fortune. Fortune is never eliminated, only managed. Indeed, it is in the management of fortune that the prince demonstrates his virtue – Moses by liberating the Hebrews and introducing his new modes and orders (the Mosaic Law), Theseus by uniting the Athenians, and so forth. The prince in chapter 25 likewise needs fortune to threaten floods so that he can display his virtue in managing the risk. If he lived in a place that was not prone to floods, he would be forced to find another way to exercise virtue. The dikes and dams of chapter 25 play a role similar to the modes and orders of chapter 6: both are (a) introduced by the prince in response to fortune, (b) forced on a presumably unwilling population, and (c) if they function well over the long term, will be evidence of the prince's virtue.

Machiavelli's second famous analogy in chapter 25 is a more disturbing one. Here fortune is likened to a woman who enjoys (so it seems) being beaten by an impetuous man: "I judge this indeed, that it is better to be impetuous than cautious, because fortune is a woman; and it is necessary, if one wants to hold her down, to beat her and strike her down. And one sees that she lets herself be won more by the impetuous than by those who proceed coldly. And so always, like a woman, she is the friend of the young, because they are less cautious, more ferocious, and command her with more audacity" (P XXV). This passage concludes Machiavelli's discussion of the importance of adapting oneself to the changing circumstances fortune presents. Sometimes it is better to move slowly and cautiously, with planning and foresight, sometimes one should simply run in and hope for the best. It is easy enough to reconcile that much with the metaphor of dams and floods: if it is not currently raining, then one should carefully plan how one will proceed to build the drainage system; once the flood is upon you, it is time to start stacking sandbags right away. Even Machiavelli's praise for audacity could be fit into this reading by arguing that, if one is going to build dams, dikes, and canals, one should try for something on the scale of the Hoover Dam or the Panama Canal rather than a simple beaver dam. If Machiavelli is recommending projects on an audacious scale, then the antagonistic relationship with fortune telegraphed in this passage makes more sense. The opening metaphor of dikes and dams can be taken to suggest only a kind of passive rerouting of water. To prevent this misinterpretation Machiavelli concludes with something more violent. Our relationship with fortune should not be one that peacefully harmonizes with it, but one that strives to beat it down and minimizes the effect it can have on our lives. To be virtuous, it seems, means (among other things) to beat down fortune. Here again, we have a good kind of violence that subdues fortune and, by doing so, benefits the people and the prince.

This returns us to the first chapter of *The Prince*, where fortune and virtue are identified as the two ways in which one can obtain the state: the virtuous person does it with her own arms, while the fortunate one must rely on the arms of another. It becomes clearer, as the text moves on to compare armed and unarmed prophets, that virtue is the more reliable way of obtaining and preserving one's state. Nevertheless, I do not think that virtue and fortune are, as some commentators suggest, antitheses separating like water and oil:[34] instead, I suspect that Machiavelli imagines the pair working in tandem in each individual's life with the caveat that, the more virtuous one is, the less influence fortune has on one's life. Indeed, chapter 25 of *The Prince* suggests that "fortune is the arbiter of half of our actions" but that, with the proper planning and care – virtue – one can decrease or limit the influence of fortune. Likewise, in the *Discourses,* Machiavelli tells us that it is when "men have little virtue [that] fortune shows its power very much" (D II.30). One can imagine something of a pie chart, such that, as the size of the virtue portion increases, the size of the fortune portion correspondingly decreases. Of course, this image is merely a heuristic device. Even the greatest princes – Romulus, Theseus, Moses, Cyrus – needed fortune to give them the opportunity to exercise virtue, although, unlike Savonarola, they didn't rely on fortune for anything more than that.

The contrast between the four armed prophets and Savonarola points us to the close connection between virtue and the ability to force obedience; this connection is deepened by Machiavelli's reference to the virtuous cruelty of Agathocles and Hannibal (P VIII and XVII; D III.21–2). It is here, in his discussion of cruelty well and poorly used, perhaps more

34 This, it seems to me, is the guiding intuition of Benner's *Machiavelli's Prince* (see xxxvii); however, her restatement in "Questa Inconstante Dea" comes closer to the view outlined here.

than anywhere else in *The Prince*, that the sacrificial distinction rises to the surface and appears naked to the world. Virtuous cruelty, or "cruelty well used," is sudden, devastating, and quickly over, accomplishing its goals in a minimum amount of time for the benefit of the people. Hannibal was able to control his polyglot army in difficult circumstances because of inhuman cruelty and infinite other virtues; Agathocles was able to rise to power and provide for the security of Syracuse through his cruel execution of the leading citizens. The cruelty well used of Agathocles and Hannibal is easily read as the good kind of violence and the cruelty poorly used as the bad kind. One could object that Machiavelli never praises the cruelty of Agathocles and that, to the extent that he distances himself from Agathocles, he is resisting, rather than employing, the sacrificial distinction. However, while Machiavelli initially hesitates to describe Agathocles as virtuous, a careful reading of the chapter suggests that he does in fact believe he exercised virtue. There are two passages that are typically used to show Machiavelli's rejection of Agathocles's methods. First: "One cannot call it virtue to kill one's citizens, betray one's friends, to be without faith, without mercy, without religion; these modes can enable one to acquire empire but not glory." Second: "His savage cruelty and inhumanity, together with his infinite crimes, do not permit him to be celebrated among the most excellent men" (both from P VIII). It seems to me that many astute commentators are misled by these passages.[35] Machiavelli says that one cannot *call* Agathocles virtuous (*Non si può ancora chiamare virtù*) and that his crimes do not *permit* him (*non consentono*) to be celebrated, which is not the same thing as denying that he was virtuous or worthy of celebration. It is entirely possible that one may believe both (a) that Agathocles is virtuous and (b) that such an opinion is controversial and it would be unwise to publicize it. The situation here is the mirror image of the one alluded to in the *Discourses*, where one might believe (a) that Caesar is a usurper and tyrant but (b) that one can't go around saying such things (D I.10). Moreover, one may consider that the current state of education prohibits precisely the kind of distinction that enables one to call Agathocles virtuous: the sacrificial distinction. There are two points that confirm this reading. First, Machiavelli later announces that Agathocles's well-used cruelty allowed him to redeem himself in the eyes of God and man. Second, Machiavelli seems to want us to closely associate Agathocles and Hannibal – he uses the words "infinite" and "inhuman" to describe them both, referring to Agathocles's "infinite crimes" (*infinite scelleratezze*) and

35 For a recent example, see Benner, *Machiavelli's Prince*, 113–14.

Hannibal's "infinite virtue" (*infinite sua virtù*) on the one hand, and Agathocles's cruelty and inhumanity (*crudeltà e inumanità*) and Hannibal's "inhuman cruelty" (*inumana crudeltà*), on the other (P VIII and XVII). To the extent that he has a high opinion of Hannibal – something suggested by his comments in *The Prince* and his comparison with Scipio in the *Discourses* (D III.21) – we have reason to conclude that he has a high opinion of Agathocles.[36]

The inhuman cruelty of Hannibal and Agathocles is not used for its own sake – they are neither sadists nor sociopaths – but for the sake of imposing or retaining one's modes and orders. We should keep in mind here our previous discussion of the role good violence plays in forming and preserving traditions; recall that Moses was forced to kill "infinite" people to impose his modes and orders. The example of Cesare Borgia is particularly apt here: having found the Romagna disordered, lawless, and chaotic, he ordered his governor to use whatever means necessary to subdue the Romagna and to establish law courts (P VII).[37] While cruel, Machiavelli argues that this is less cruel than the mercy of the Florentines, which allowed disorder to fester and metastasize (P XVII). The mercy of the Florentines may also be taken as an example of the kind incompetence that Machiavelli suggests accompanies the refusal to make the sacrificial distinction. Machiavellian virtue does not exclude the judicious use of cruelty and force.[38] Indeed, Hannibal and Torquatus both appear as illustrations of virtue in book III of the *Discourses* precisely on account of their cruelty. And elsewhere in book III, Machiavelli contrasts the virtue of the Roman army with the "fury and impetuosity" of the Gauls late in his *Discourses* (D III.36). Machiavelli's sacrificial logic distinguishes between good and bad forms of violence, and the distinction between cruelties well and poorly used is an instance of that more general distinction.

36 A longer and more developed argument for the virtue of Agathocles can be found in McCormick, "Enduring Ambiguity."

37 Viroli, *Machiavelli*, 53–60.

38 Viroli puts the matter this way: "As soon as a dominion is consolidated, cruelties and absolute powers have to be replaced by ordinary civil justice and reason, as the tradition of civil wisdom prescribes; but before the rule of law is in place, politics in the conventional sense of the art of ruling according to reason and justice need the help of the ambivalent but powerful art of the state" (*Machiavelli*, 55–6). While I think Benner is correct in her judgment that Machiavelli disapproves of capricious cruelty and thinks that even well-used cruelty is not sufficient to found a lasting state (Benner, *Machiavelli's Prince*, 115–18), it is important to recognize that, while it is not sufficient, it may at times be necessary. This seems to be Viroli's point and I think Machiavelli's as well.

However, my emphasis on cruelty and good violence in Machiavelli's account of virtue should not lead the reader to conclude that virtue excludes mercy and humanity; recent work on Machiavelli has gone a long way towards correcting the view that Machiavelli is all blood and death and it should be acknowledged. In any case, good violence is good, in sacrificial systems, precisely because it is more productive of peace and stability in a community than are other forms of violence. We should not take these harsh edges to be the entirety of Machiavelli's thought: Viroli is surely right to remind us that, while Machiavelli offers a radical critique of the tradition, the aim of the critique is "to restrict the range of its validity rather than dismiss it altogether."[39] Nevertheless, there is also a certain sense in which, precisely by restricting it, he rejects it: if we take it that the (Augustinian) tradition had a blanket prohibition on sacrificial violence, the Machiavellian restriction of the prohibition to simply one that restricts the bad forms of violence and the concomitant endorsement of the good kind can be readily interpreted as a rejection of the tradition.

39 Viroli, *Machiavelli*, 54.

4

Sacrifice and the City

AS WE SAW, Heidegger points to a close connection between how one thinks about truth and how one thinks about nature. Likewise, there is a close connection between Machiavelli's understanding of truth and his understanding of nature. I begin with Machiavelli's claim in his *Discourses* that "it is truer than any other truth that if where there are men there are no soldiers, it arises through a defect of the prince and not through any other defect, either of the site or of nature" (D I.21). In approaching this passage, we have to keep in mind that, for Machiavelli, soldiering is, or should be, a profoundly moral enterprise (AW I.199–204). As in chapter 15 of *The Prince*, here truth is discussed in a moral context; but this passage is a bit clearer in divorcing morality and truth from nature. Moreover, Machiavelli links both soldiering and truth, as we have seen earlier, to the acceptance of sacrifice. One effect of this passage is to solidify and strengthen the link between truth and sacrifice. The passage occurs in the course of a discussion of the third king of Rome, Tullus, who came to power after forty years of Numa's peaceful reign. Tullus found that he lacked men experienced in military matters. Rather than turning to foreign troops, he introduced modes and orders that encouraged military virtue. Machiavelli's reflection on the career of Tullus culminates in the above passage. Machiavelli's point is that nature does not influence the morals of the people in a decisive way but that, instead, the prince does. What is truer than any other truth is that the manner in which one lives – ethics, morals, and politics – is not determined by anything other than the modes and orders of the prince. The discussion of truth in *The Prince* is taken one step further: not only is there nothing super-sensible or transcendent that functions as a source of moral truth, but there is nothing in this world either. Moral truth and nature are decisively separated. To see this more clearly, we have to unpack Machiavelli's understanding of nature.

THREE TENSIONS

Machiavelli's understanding of nature, like so many other things, is difficult to pin down. There are at least three sets of tensions in his understanding of nature: the first regards nature and morality; the second regards changeability and stability; and the third concerns the difference between nature and convention. The first tension is already at work in the first paragraph of this section – that is, in my claim that Machiavelli does not see nature as the source of morals. As I note in the discussion of truth, Mansfield has remarked that Machiavelli understands truth such that nature cannot be a guide to moral action. However, one can object that this presentation of things can be contrasted with certain claims he makes about nature, human nature in particular, that suggest that his moral and political teachings are in fact based on nature. On this side of the tension, one can point to the many passages in Machiavelli's writings in which he refers to the "envious" nature of men, or in which he says that men "naturally desire to acquire," and so forth (as in chapter 3 of *The Prince*, but the list could go on indefinitely). One could argue that the peculiarities of his moral theory are derived from nature, just a different view of nature – nature red in tooth and claw – than that of natural law theorists. But in these passages nature is not so much a guide as it is an obstacle. To this extent, nature does influence political life in Machiavelli, but as a source of problems rather than as a guide. One should think of the relationship between politics and nature as that between two opposing football teams: the two teams influence each other's actions and reactions, but only in an agonistic sense.[1] For Machiavelli, our natural predispositions are not to be perfected in civic life; rather, they are to be overcome: the wise prince creates modes and orders that channel and tame human nature, transforming it into something productive and good. However, this means that nature as a whole lacks any sort of telic orientation and that so, too, does human nature in particular: we are not oriented towards the good; instead, "men never work any good unless through necessity" and "laws make them [men] good" (D I.3, see too AW VII.160). So the constant atelic movement of nature

1 Benner's *Machiavelli's Ethics* focuses attention on the extent to which Machiavellian virtue requires the acknowledgment of limitations. The virtuous prince, in her analysis, does not try to do everything but, instead, sets about doing what is possible for him, in his situation, moderating his course and moving slowly to build firm foundations for his state. I think that she is largely correct in this, and I would suggest that this involves recognizing the obstacles presented by nature and discerning which can be overcome, which can be avoided, and which must be simply accepted.

demands that the prince figure out how to adapt his modes and orders to withstand those movements. Nature, it might not be too much of an overstatement to say, is the first enemy that must be overcome; in fact, one could read major portions of *The Art of War* as dealing with exactly these issues – that is, how the prince should respond to nature (AW IV.19–25 and V.145–160). While Machiavelli recognizes certain natural regularities or necessities, these do not serve as the basis for a natural law we should follow but, rather, as problems we endeavour to overcome. Indeed, as Erica Benner observes, "the concept of natural law, whether attributed to divine authorship or not, makes little sense in Machiavelli's vocabulary."[2]

This takes us to second tension, that between change and stability. We find that Machiavelli endorses both: he maintains not only that nature has not changed since the time of the Romans but also that it is constantly changing (D I.pr and I.6). The solution to these clashing visions, according to Althusser's reading, is a cyclical theory of history: by moving in permanent cycles, the world can both change and not change.[3] This is suggestive, but not entirely helpful insofar as the cycle Machiavelli has in mind in the passages of the *Discourses* Althusser cites is a political one rather than a natural one. A simpler way of resolving the tension might be to argue that, while nature is constantly changing, the natural principles that govern those changes have not altered since the time of Rome. A true knowledge of history will enable one to see how Rome reacted to those changes and better prepare one to react to contemporaneous changes. So far these considerations operate at the level of Machiavelli's political theory; however, a deeper analysis of Machiavelli can be acquired through a brief comparison with Heidegger's reading of Aristotle's *Physics*. According to Heidegger, although Aristotle conceived of *phusis* in terms of movement, movement was ultimately understood in terms of rest, in the kind of standing still associated with the achievement of an end, a telos. So for Heidegger's Greeks, nature's movements were directed towards a kind of telic rest (ECPA 216–17); for Machiavelli, as noted, there is no telic rest. That is to say, change or movement is taken as a fundamental principle of nature; there is no telic vector to this change, it merely changes. Here the work of Alison Brown and Ada Palmer is instructive. Both Brown and Palmer argue persuasively for (a) Machiavelli's interest in Lucretius and (b) that his primary concern in reading Lucretius is with the account of the atomism and the swerve in

2 Benner, *Machiavelli's Ethics*, 201.
3 Althusser, *Machiavelli and Us*, 34–6.

book II. The metaphysics of Lucretian atomism harmonize readily with the account of Machiavelli I have just offered. For Lucretius, the falling and swerving of atoms produce constant change without telic rest, but the principles underlying the falling and swerving – atomism – remain constant. Brown writes: "they [Machiavelli's notes on book II of Lucretius] all contribute key ideas to his philosophy that have hitherto seemed difficult to reconcile."[4] She points in particular to the reconciliation of precisely the tension under discussion here: the tension between Machiavelli's assertions that the world is constantly changing and that it is not changing. If one accepts that falling, swerving atoms are the basic unit of the world around us, then one can account for both the constant atelic change Machiavelli endorses (because it is all just falling atoms) and the claim that the world hasn't changed (because whatever it is, it is still constituted by swerving falling atoms). This strategy enables us to reconcile Machiavelli's purported atomism with his endorsement of an eternal world: if by "the world" we mean earth, then it is not eternal insofar as it did not and will not always exist; but if we mean the falling and swerving of atoms that give rise to the earth, then it is eternal. And this reconciliation becomes easier if we keep in mind that Machiavelli's endorsement was less a matter of metaphysics than it was of politics. In asserting the eternity of the world, one removes an obstacle to the imitation of ancient education: the belief in an imagined kingdom that surpasses this world

In any case, for Aristotle, and by extension Aristotelian scholasticism, nature is changeable to the extent that natural things are understood as possessing an internal principle of motion, and these motions or changes can be understood in terms of certain telic orientations and forms that remain fundamentally unchangeable.[5] There is logic beneath the changeability of particular natural things; since nature does not proceed randomly Aristotle understands fortune (*tyche*) as, strictly speaking, only in the mind.[6] The Christian tradition saw fortune in a similar way, such that it was only the human misinterpretation of divine providence. The atelic changeability of nature in Machiavellian metaphysics entails the reality of fortune as a force in the eternal world. I return to this point later.

The third tension is in what counts as nature. At times (as in our first two tensions) Machiavelli seems to oppose nature to something like convention, in the manner of the classical philosophers. At other times,

4 Brown, *Return of Lucretius*, 76

5 See Aristotle, *Physics*, 192b10–30 and 193b5–20. For a scholastic version of the same, see Aquinas, *In libros Physicorum*, liber 2, lectio 1, n.5.

6 Aristotle, *Physics*, 198a5–10.

however, he suggests that ossified traditions and conventions become natural. So, he refers to the hereditary prince as a "natural prince" (P II) and refers to the "natural affection" that the people bear towards their hereditary barons (P IV). The list could go on. This tension is particularly vexing insofar as, if taken literally, it borders on the paradoxical. I suspect, however, that, in the later context, he is referring to what *appears* natural to people and in the former to what is really natural. The resolution of this tension returns us to the modes and orders instituted by the new prince. When modes and orders have been in place for many years, for many generations, they begin to seem natural to the people living with them: it seems natural for the hereditary prince to rule or for the people to love their barons. But since there must have been a first prince, or new prince, what appears natural to the people was at one time imposed, with some degree of offence (P III and VI).

GOD AND FORTUNE, MACHIAVELLI AND BOETHIUS

Roughly a thousand years before Machiavelli was implicated in some kind of revolutionary conspiracy, imprisoned, and tortured, Anicius Manlius Severinus Boethius found himself in a similar situation. Like Machiavelli, he responded to his situation by writing; unlike Machiavelli, he died in prison. Boethius's *Consolation of Philosophy* begins with the author in a jail cell lamenting his unjust imprisonment and wishing for death. He is soon interrupted by the appearance of Lady Philosophy. While the figure of Lady Philosophy is somewhat mysterious and susceptible to numerous interpretations, it does not serve our limited purposes here to delve into the precise nature of his guest. It is enough to note that she presents herself as his doctor and offers him a kind of therapy. This consoling proceeds, as she makes clear, in two stages: the first stage will use softer remedies to clear away Boethius's errors, while the second stage will use harsher cures to lead him to the truth.[7] It is worth noting that, among his errors, the principle one – indeed, the one that book II focuses upon entirely – involves fortune. Without wanting to claim that Machiavelli was familiar with Boethius's texts, I do think that it provides a useful contrast to the thought of Machiavelli and that, by juxtaposing the two, we will be able to highlight certain themes in Machiavelli that might otherwise go unnoticed. So what is Boethius's error regarding fortune? Essentially, it is a belief in the reality and efficacy of fortune: Boethius complains that God – who controls everything else in the

7 Boethius, *Consolation of Philosophy*, I.6.

universe – does not care for humankind and, in his negligence, leaves us at the mercy of fortune. Boethius sings:

There is nothing discharged from the old orders
Deserting its posts and proper position
Controlling all things toward their set object
Only human deeds you [God] disdain to reign in
In the way they deserve – you, their helmsman
So it is; why can slippery Fortune
Cause such change and such sport.[8]

In Boethius's complaint, we are at the mercy of fortune because God does not control human deeds. Unlike the rest of nature, which Boethius perceives to be following set orders dictated by God, we are ignored by God. This has a twofold result: on the one hand, we are free, but on the other hand, we are at the mercy of fortune.

Lady Philosophy's goal, throughout the rest of the text, is to persuade Boethius that he – and humankind in general – is not scorned by God but, rather, that all things are ordered by his providence without thereby denying human freedom and responsibility. The details of this explanation are, for our purposes, not important. The important thing for us is the claim that fortune is illusory: according to Lady Philosophy, what mortals refer to as fortune is not really fortune at all but simply a misinterpretation of divine providence. This is to say, the existence of fortune and the existence of providence are taken to be mutually exclusive: if God exists and God's power embraces all things, then there is no such "thing" as fortune. This conclusion, it is worth noting, is already hinted at in the closing argument of book II, in which Lady Philosophy argues that every fortune is good fortune.[9] As she develops her argument, she revises her claim to mean that, in the strict sense, there no such thing as fortune and especially no such thing as misfortune. No matter what happens, the wise will not complain as they will understand every event as a good.[10] According to Lady Philosophy, the apparent ups and down of fortune, all the vicissitudes of life, are incorporated into a single divine plan, a single still point that interprets, governs, and unifies the multiplicity and changeability of the visible world. As Lady Philosophy puts it: "This sequence moves heaven and the stars, balances the elements among themselves one with the other, and transforms these elements in

8 Ibid., I.m.5.
9 Ibid., II.p.8.
10 Ibid., IV.p.3.

the interchange of each with each; the same sequence renews all the things that are born and die, through the development of their offspring and seed, resembling each other from generation to generation. This sequence also ties together the actions and the fortune of mortal men, in an indecomposable interweaving of causes, and since this sequence sets out from *the loom of motionless Providence,* it is necessarily the case that these motions be unalterably well."[11] The more one cultivates virtue and wisdom, the closer one approximates the stillness of the divine; and it is in this approximation and proximity that one can be said to be free.

The crucial difference between Machiavelli and Boethius is not found in the question of freedom. Both admit, in one way or another, that human beings are free and responsible for their actions. No, the crucial difference is that Boethius – and with him the mainstream of the Christian tradition – sees fortune as illusory, as a foolish misinterpretation of providence, while Machiavelli sees it as a real force in the world. This difference, in turn, points us towards a deeper one: according to Lady Philosophy, we can conclude from the omnipotence and omnibenevolence of God that fortune – as typically understood and as described in book I or the early parts of book II of the *Consolation* – does not exist. Ultimately, the denial of the reality of fortune by Lady Philosophy is predicated upon God's transcending of the world: we know that fortune is illusory because we know that God exists outside the world and governs it. For Lady Philosophy, the world is perpetual but *not* eternal.[12] Eternity, in her usage, means not merely "always existing" but a kind of changeless stillness of a permanent *now* with no past or future.[13] The perpetuity of the world (as Lady Philosophy makes clear) is defined – for reasons we don't need to get into here – by the surpassablity of the world. Indeed, for Lady Philosophy the perpetuity of the world is experienced in swiftly passing moments, whatever stability it has derives from and point towards the eternity of God. The non-eternity of the world, in Boethius, means that the world points beyond itself towards the transcendent eternity of God, and this, in turn, means that fortune is illusory. One is free, according to Lady Philosophy, only to the extent that one transcends the world and dwells under the shadow of providence; this theme is present in Lacoste as well, and his words can be taken as a summary of Lady Philosophy's view: "the man who finds complete repose in God escapes the world's rule over him" (EA 26).

11 Ibid., IV.p.6 (emphasis mine).

12 Ibid., V.p.6.

13 For a fuller exposition of this point, see Stump and Kretzmann's classic "Eternity."

Machiavelli, on the other hand, reverses the Boethian position: the eternity of the world means that it points towards nothing but itself: change, not stillness, is the only constant. This being the case, fortune is not illusory, or at least not in the same way as it is in *The Consolation of Philosophy*. But if Boethius offers us a kind of *modus ponens* (if there is an omnipotent God, then fortune is an illusion; there is an omnipotent God, therefore fortune is an illusion), does Machiavelli's position function as a kind of *modus tollens*? In other words, does Machiavelli's admittance of fortune into his ontology entail the rejection of God? Not necessarily. In fact, at times it seems that Machiavelli blurs God and fortune:

> And although one ought not to reason of Moses, he having been a mere executor of the things that were ordained by God ... But let us consider Cyrus and the others [Romulus and Theseus] who have acquired or founded kingdoms: you will find them all wonderful [*mirabilis*], and if their particular actions and orders are considered, they seem not discrepant from those of Moses, who had so great a preceptor. And in examining their actions and life, one sees that fortune provided them with nothing other than the occasion which gave them the matter into which they could introduce whatever form they pleased. (P VI)

Machiavelli begins by separating Moses from the other three on the basis of Moses's discourse with God; however, by the end of the passage he has united them in terms of their debt to fortune. The opportunity to exercise virtue was given by fortune (not God) to both Moses and the pagan founders. Moreover, fortune merely provides the unformed matter that the *virtuoso* informs with "new orders" (P VI). This reverses the Boethian Christian argument: rather than fortune being merely a human misunderstanding of divine providence, Machiavelli presents divine providence as a misunderstanding of fortune. It was not God's will that enabled Moses to act, but good luck. In the same way, he begins chapter 25 with a mention of God and fortune as both governing the things of this world. However, here, too, Machiavelli quickly forgets God to focus on fortune.[14] Nevertheless, there is reason to believe that Machiavelli is

14 In this, I am in agreement with Parel, when he writes: "Instead of being a *ministra* of God, she [fortune] is the mistress of human destiny ... Briefly, in the Machiavellian cosmos, there is no room for God's providence" (*Machiavellian Cosmos*, 65). Against this, in "Amazing Grace, " Nederman argues that readers like Parel over-simplify medieval and late medieval approaches to fortune. According to Nederman, one can find various medieval figures – running from Augustine of Hippo ("What we call random occurrence [*casam*] is nothing but that of which the reason and cause is hidden from view") through John of

not blurring them so much as it seems: God and fortune often appear as two distinct forces operating at times in tandem and at time competitively; the blurring occurs because we don't always know whether events are due to God or to Fortune.[15] Whatever the case, the reality of fortune is a symptom of the deeper gulf between Boethius and Machiavelli and, by extension, traditional Christian theology and Machiavelli. As Viroli puts it, "a God that allows the presence of an occult force in heaven with such great power over the events on earth, and who allows a capricious and furious Fortuna to torment mortals is a very different God from the Christian God that governs nature and the human world through divine providence."[16] In sum, the Boethian denial of the reality of Fortune is predicated on the claim that God transcends the world; on the other hand, Machiavelli's understanding of Fortune is inseparable from a vision of an imminent God as one agent among others acting in the eternal world.

Salisbury – affirming the reality of fortune (626–7). But this isn't exactly the case: as the quoted passage from Augustine reveals, they affirm it only in the same epistemic sense that Lady Philosophy did – that is, that things appear as fortune only because we lack a complete understanding of providence. Fortune is unexpected to us, but not unplanned by God. But, Nederman continues, Machiavelli also attributes plans to Fortune (628). I'm not sure how literally we should take those passages that personify fortune and attribute agency to her though. It is quite possible that those are the same figures of speech that give us the spirit of Music or power of Love and that, by chasing them down, we lose the forest for these trees. In any case, there is no need to decide the issue on that basis alone since Nederman has a more substantive argument as well: Machiavelli's counsel that we should not rely only on fortune but should work hard to take advantage of the opportunities fortune offers mirrors Thomistic teaching on grace and free will whereby fortune is a kind of grace that still needs to be put to work by the will (634–5). There is certainly something to that parallel, but it needs further development. The discussion of grace and free will in Christian theology is inseparable from debates about divine knowledge (or foreknowledge, as the case may be) and power. The few references to scholastic thought that Nederman finds in *The Prince* and elsewhere do not allow us to reconstruct Machiavelli's position on these disputed topics, and we can't say too much for sure regarding grace and free will. As the parallel stands now, I suspect it goes in the opposite direction than intended: fortune is a replacement for grace in an eternal world. Grace, as Nederman points out, is ultimately oriented towards heavenly beatitude, while in Machiavelli's case we are dealing with "secular political aspirations rather than eternal beatitude" (635). In sum, whatever parallels there are between Machiavelli and traditional Christian teachings on this score, they are far outweighed, to my mind, by the gulf between the quest for heaven and the quest for *stato*, between the temporary world and the eternal world.

15 For more on this point, see Viroli, *Machiavelli's God*, 30–2.

16 Ibid., 33.

MACHIAVELLI'S *OZIO* AND LACOSTE'S *OPUS DEI*

There is a sense that the Machiavellian man is haunted by his exposure to fortune. The principle task in life, it seems, is to limit as much as possible the role that fortune can play in one's life, minimizing fortune's strength through the judicious use of virtue. As chapter 25 puts it, she can only demonstrate her power when virtue is not ordered to resist her (P XXV). The exposure to fortune replaces or covers over other sorts of exposure, including especially exposure to God. In his phenomenological study of liturgy, Jean-Yves Lacoste argues that an opening move in liturgical experience is the choice to subordinate one's openness to the world to one's exposure to a world-transcending God (EA 51). By this, Lacoste wants to say that liturgical experience comes *after* other forms of experience; that one arrives at the liturgical after passing through the limits of the world and history. The exposure to God, in Lacoste, is not limited by the world but instead marks one's transcending of the world as a kind of "symbolic exodus" (EA 50). The liturgy, he goes on to argue, symbolizes and realizes a kind of peace and fraternity not given in the world of history and politics. For Lacoste, in being exposed before God one is exposed to something transcending the world of history, ethics, and politics. It is this kind of exposure that Machiavelli denies or prevents: insofar as fortune displaces God and insofar as fortune is understood in a political or moral register – that is, as the counterpart to virtue – there is nothing outside of the world for the Machiavellian person to be exposed to. The importance of fortune derives from the eternity of the world.

One can wonder if Lacoste's description of liturgy in terms of a vigil, something that comes after the work of ethics and history, does not give too much to the Machiavellian view of history. Jean-Yves Lacoste writes in his phenomenology of the liturgy, *Experience and the Absolute*, that "there is an essential link between violence and history" (EA, 55). He correctly notes that, if this is granted, one either embraces a cynical view of history in which there is no real peace or one takes an eschatological view that locates peace somewhere beyond history: "the philosophy of history and moral philosophy, however, come up against violence (or 'ill will') as against an inalienable secret of existence in history: although non-violence can take place in history, it will never be its principle determinant" (EA, 56). In all this, Lacoste agrees with Machiavelli. But for Lacoste, this determination of history by violence means that liturgy can only be something done later, as vigil, after one has exhausted oneself performing ethical and historical obligations. Here we can only ask the question, but we will return to it later: Does Lacoste give up too much to

Machiavelli when he grants violence such a central role? Does this not reproduce Machiavellianism? Despite his insistence on surpassing the world, does Lacoste's surpassing appear as a mere vacation from history rather than as a true surpassing of the world? Is liturgy then not an instance of what Machiavelli called *ozio,* a break from the violent work of seeking peace? Lacoste justifies this break by claiming that liturgy takes time from our sleeping hours rather than from our working hours. But why should *opus Dei* take place only after hours? Isn't this an admission that it is a dispensable *ozio* after all? And cannot this be absorbed into Machiavellianism with the assertion that sleep is made possible by security, and that security is made possible by the armed prophet's virtue? The liturgical surpassing of the world would then be a luxurious illusion, a leisurely dream of an imagined republic, rather than a true surpassing. Without speculating on Lacoste's intentions, we can say that his text admits of this Machiavellian reading but does not require it. Lacoste accepts a Machiavellian world minus the claim that the world is eternal. In other words, he adopts the Machiavellian view of history and politics precisely so as to place God outside of it, protecting and emphasizing the surpassable (non-eternal) nature of the world. In terms of this chapter thus far, it could be described as a quasi-Boethian and quasi-Machiavellian move, mixing the two in equal parts. It agrees with Boethius in allowing for the surpassing of the world and in putting God outside the world, but by interpreting history in the way he does – Machiavellianly – he seems to deny the role Boethius gives to providence. The question for Lacoste, then, is as follows: Is the Boethian God outside the world reconcilable with the Machiavellian view of history, with fortune, rather than with providence?

HOW TO BUILD A CITY

As a preparation for answering the above questions, let us turn to the first book of the *Discourses* for Machiavelli's most sustained treatment of nature. Here he is concerned first of all with the choice of locations for cities. He analyzes the advantages and disadvantages of fertile and infertile lands insofar as the development of civic virtue is concerned. One should note that this is not a worry found in Livy: when Livy considers the geography of Rome, he is only concerned to identify which were the first hills to be settled.[17] Machiavelli argues that building cities in fertile areas will liberate people from the onerous necessity of hard work, thus

17 Livy, *Ab Urbe Condita,* I.6.4.

allowing them to cultivate a life of leisure (*ozio*) rather than virtue. The fertility of the area will remove the need for political structures and institutions to the extent that people will be able to satisfy their basic needs without much effort or risk. However, settling in an infertile and inhospitable area will force people to cultivate civic structures while, at the same time, rendering them incapable (due to poor quality of the land) of raising the crops needed for a flourishing population (thus leaving the city weak and insecure). Neither horn of this dilemma is particularly suited to political life. In fact, in both cases nature opposes the formation of successful communities: in the first, the fertile land provides little incentive to enter into political life; in the second, the inhospitable land threatens the lives of the inhabitants. Machiavelli's solution to this problem is that one should choose the fertile grounds but introduce modes and orders that create an artificial necessity to work in order to make up for the lack of natural necessity. That is to say, since the people are not led by nature to cooperate and work hard, it falls to the leader or founder to compel them to do so: "those [founders] should be imitated who have inhabited very agreeable and fertile countries, apt to produce men who are idle and unfit for any virtuous exercise, and who have had the wisdom to prevent the harms that the agreeableness of the country would have caused through idleness by imposing the necessity to exercise on those who had to be soldiers" (D I.1). The creation of artificial necessity overcomes the fertility of the land by constructing a situation in which the people live *as if* cooperation and hard work were needed to sustain their lives when, in fact, they are not. The founder imposes an artificial necessity that overcomes the limitations of the natural environment and human selfishness to create the ideal political environment. The task of *virtù* is to overcome the inhospitality of nature by introducing the modes and orders conducive to life. A similar point is made in *The Art of War*. There, Fabrizio explains that people are more or less virtuous not because of nature but because of princes; when the princes are not good, virtue does not show itself (AW II.284–91). This is why it is truer than any other truth that, if the people are not soldiers, the prince is to blame.

For Machiavelli, the world is eternal, but it is not a place of dwelling in Heidegger's sense. We have to force the world to accept us. This is done, as we saw, through virtue. In Machiavelli's thought, the pairing of the eternity of the world with the inhospitality of the world means that human beings are never at rest but always struggling against a hostile world. For Machiavelli, as much as for Heidegger, the human being is essentially *unheimlich*. The homelessness of humankind in Machiavelli takes the form of a striving for home. It is precisely because they have no natural habitat that human beings must, under the direction of the founder, come to dwell in cities. There is no guidance or natural law that orients one towards this or that way of life; instead, as we saw earlier, the founder imposes community upon people. In *Being and Time* (1927), the homelessness of Dasein consists mainly in the fact that Dasein is existentially and ontologically a being-in-the-world but not a part of the world, a thing among other things. One is an individualized (*vereinzelt*) Dasein (BT 233). This homelessness is more fundamental, Heidegger continues, than absorption in *das Man*; it is – admittedly— covered over and hidden by Dasein's fallenness into "the they" but revealed in its depths by Angst. A few years later, in *Introduction to Metaphysics* (1935), Heidegger uses *unheimlich* to translate the Greek *deinon*, tying the concept much closer to violence than is apparent in *Being and Time.* The human being is uncanny (*unhiemlich*) and, as such, must forge a home in the world with violence, wresting stability and order from the overwhelming sway of nature (IM 167). Is this far from Machiavelli or are they two sides of the same coin?

One can push this even further, with a reference to the work of Lacoste. In his discussion of precisely this topic in Heidegger, he (Lacoste) notes that Heideggerian homelessness is conditioned on the fact that we are being-in-the-world – that is, that the world precedes us and envelops us: "If we belong to the world … then the world is not something that fundamentally belongs to us or that we have established. It precedes us as something for which we have not wished, as that which pre-exists and outlives us, and where the mode of our presence in it must be understood as that of house arrest" (EA 12). Much the same can be said of Machiavelli's world. We find ourselves in a world neither hospitable nor adapted for our purposes, and we have no escape. In both cases – Heidegger and Machiavelli – the task becomes to make one's way in this world not of one's choosing. In the case of *Being and Time,* we do this by falling into the everydayness of *das Man,* anaesthetizing ourselves in idle chatter so as to ignore or hide from this predicament. In the case of Machiavelli, one embraces the modes and orders of the founder. According to Machiavelli, all cities are built either by those native to the area or by foreigners (D I.1), but in a certain sense everybody is a foreigner. Indeed, those Machiavelli classifies as natives are merely those who do not have to go far to find a defensible place. In no way does he understand "native" as indicating any special connection to the land – moral, spiritual, political, or otherwise. In that sense, as our previous discussion should have made clear, no such relation obtains with the world as such. It is only after one has, under the direction of a founder, carved out a space that one can speak of these kinds of connections. But even then, in Machiavelli, the connection is primarily to the institutions, modes, and orders under which one lives rather than to the land as such. To the extent that one feels a special connection to the land, Machiavelli would argue that one does not feel it with the land per se but, rather, with the land as worked over by the modes and orders of one's city.

According to Heidegger's account in his 1951 essay entitled "Building, Dwelling, Thinking," the "essence of building is dwelling" (BDT 361). Building, in the sense Heidegger has in mind, is not mere construction but, rather, a kind of disclosure of being or articulation of the place. Heidegger writes of a footbridge that it doesn't merely connect the banks, but "the banks emerge as banks only as the bridge crosses the stream." As he goes on, he suggests that the bridge "gathers" the fourfold into a single place, enabling one to dwell within that fourfold. The tone of the Heidegger of the 1950s is less dramatic than that of the Heidegger of earlier essays; as John Caputo puts it, mythopoetry replaced the bombast and struggle of the 1930s.[18] While building Heidegger's footbridge or peasant hut certainly requires hard labour, the tone and imagery of the essays suggest that buildings blossom forth from the earth rather than being imposed upon it. And certainly nobody gets killed. Building the bridge doesn't require sacrifice or violence in Heidegger's telling, despite the fact that there is a strong tradition connecting bridge-building with human sacrifice (via immurement) in the peasant folkways of Germany: to make the bridge secure, one must bury a child in its foundations.[19] But even as Heidegger represses sacrificial violence, the peaceful, bucolic nature of the essay is haunted by death. Early in the essay, Heidegger notes that the essential being of the mortal is "being capable of death as death," and the essay's final pages describe a coffin (BDT 352 and 362). Dwelling, it turns out, is inseparable from death.[20] The closing paragraph of the essay references a housing shortage and offers another iteration of homelessness, this time being not as a translation of "deinon" but as indicating a lack of dwelling. Heidegger's immediate concern is to remind his audience that constructing housing is not the same as building dwellings, but the old buildings that were destroyed and that need to be replaced were destroyed in the Second World War. Heidegger is concerned that the new construction projects will provide

18 Caputo, *Demythologizing Heidegger*, 179.

19 To be clear, this tradition is not peculiar to the Germans – there is a persistent legend about London Bridge being built the same way – but we would expect Heidegger to have some knowledge of the German tradition.

20 This point is made admirably by Young, *Heidegger's Later Philosophy*, 64ff.

homes but not dwellings: dwelling is not an organic outgrowth of earth but, rather, something created and achieved. In this instance, it has to be achieved by those with the power to organize responses to crises: the princes of postwar West Germany. And with this paragraph, Heidegger finds himself, despite himself, returning to the paths blazed by Machiavelli. If gods dwell in the vineyards of Rome, well, the terraced vineyards of the Roman hills were made possible by the modes and orders of Romulus (or, if Heidegger prefers a Greek example, the olive groves of Athens were made possible by the modes and orders of Theseus). This is why Machiavelli will sacrifice most other goods at the altar of stability: for without a stable city, one is thrust back into the inhospitable world. The housing crisis is natural and normal: the *patria*, the *heimat*, dwelling rests on the modes and orders of the prince. The combination of these two realizations entails that the city must be protected at all costs, against all threats, both foreign and domestic.

CALUMNY, ACCUSATION, AND SCAPEGOATS

We have already noted the connection between violence and tradition, on the one hand, and violence and founding, on the other. The armed prophet comes to power through the use of violence, and the modes and orders introduced by the prophet require periodic repetitions of that founding violence to stay vibrant and effective. In both cases, we could characterize these as instances of the fertile, good violence distinguished, in sacrificial logic, from the destructive, bad violence. Both history (what happens) and tradition (our interpretation of what happens) are soaked in violence. The connection between history and violence forged by Machiavelli – that is, a connection in which violence is taken as normal and, indeed, the motor of history – has been widely accepted, even by philosophers who would not consider themselves Machiavellian (as we saw in our discussion of Lacoste). In Machiavelli's work as a whole, violence never recedes from view; nevertheless, the goal of this violence is peace, "the establishment of a new principality adorned and strengthened with good arms and good laws," in which the citizens feel free and secure enough to attend to the joys and sorrows of ordinary life.[21] There is a calming passage in *The Prince*, in which Machiavelli describes the successful ruler in terms that seem far from the violence found on other pages:

21 Viroli, *Machiavelli*, 55.

A prince should also show himself a lover of the virtues, giving recognition to virtuous men and he should honor those who are excellent in an art. Next, he should inspire his citizens to follow their pursuits quietly, in trade and in agriculture and in every other pursuit of men … But he should prepare rewards for whoever wants to do these things, and for anyone who thinks up any way of expanding his city or his state. Besides this, he should at suitable times of the year keep the people occupied with festivals and spectacles. And because every city is divided into guilds or into clans, he should take some account of those communities, meet with them sometimes, and make himself an example of humanity and munificence. (P XXI) 22

It is hard to reconcile this view of city life with the claims made earlier in my paragraph. After all, this situation seems both peaceful and inside of history. But it isn't so clear: the situation described here needs to be read in connection with Machiavelli's earlier discussion of Cesare Borgia's conquest of the Romagna. Borgia did bring peace and stability to a previously corrupt and uncivil place, but he did this by inflicting all sorts of pain and suffering on the countryside, culminating in the murder of his own officer, Remirro de Orco (P VII). Machiavellian peace is the product of (good, sacrificial) violence rather than the antithesis of violence. One might with some plausibility describe it as the peace of Cacus. Describing this peace, Augustine writes:

Let us, however, consider a creature depicted in poetry and fable: a creature so unsociable and wild that people have preferred to call him a semi-man rather than a man. His kingdom was the solitude of an awful cavern, and he was so singular in his wickedness that a name was found for him reflecting that fact – for he was called Cacus, and *kakos* is the Greek word for "wicked." He had no wife with whom to give and receive caresses; no children to play with when little or instruct when a little bigger, and no friends with whom to enjoy converse, not even with his father Vulcan. He gave nothing to anyone; rather, he took what he wanted from anyone he could and whenever he could. Despite all this, however, in the solitude of his own cave, the floor of which, as Virgil describes it, ever reeked with the blood of recent butchery, he wished for nothing other than a peace in which no one should molest him, and a rest which no man's violence,

22 John McCormack points out that the word translated as "spectacles" is *spettacoli*, "the plural form of the same word he uses to describe the Remirro incident." This point can lend a fairly different tone to the passage. And though I won't develop the point here, I suspect that a thoughtful comparison of these *spettacoli* with Machiavelli's discussion of the bloody and violent sacrifices of antiquity in the *Discourses* would reinforce the analyses offered in this book. See McCormick, "Prophetic Statebuilding," 7.

or the fear of it, should disturb ... Thus for all his monstrous nature and wild savagery, his aim was peace: for he sought, by these monstrous means, only to preserve the peace of his own life.23

If Cacus's violent peace is rooted in his monstrous nature, the close connection between the desire for peace and Machiavellian violence is rooted in the doctrine of the eternity of the world. Note that Machiavelli complained, as we saw in chapter 1, that the Christian rejection of the doctrine has, in his sense, made people insufficiently violent and less peaceful. If one is to achieve Machiavellian peace one must injure people so gravely that they cannot respond (P III).

Machiavelli's presentation of peace as the product of sacrificial violence, of cruelty well used, is sometimes taken as one of the novelties of his teaching. And while I don't object to that reading, I think that there is a deeper sense in which we can say that Machiavelli's teaching is not new at all but, in fact, returns to something old. That is to say, it returns to archaic sacrificial religion wherein peace is the product of violence. I've gestured in this direction more than a few times in the preceding chapters, but now it is time to make the point more substantively.

We have to depart a bit more from the text of Machiavelli and turn to those of René Girard and his understanding of the relationship between sacrifice and archaic religion. In *Violence and the Sacred*, he argues that archaic religion develops as a ritualization of what was, at first, a spontaneous act of violence (VS 92). This spontaneous violence develops out of and completes what Girard calls a sacrificial crisis. As already noted, in Girard's terminology, sacrifice is used to distinguish legitimate (good) from illegitimate (bad) forms of violence (VS 37–8). When, for a variety of possible reasons, the sacrificial rites are no longer able to serve that purpose, the community enters into a sacrificial crisis. In such a crisis, the difference between legitimate and illegitimate violence breaks down, and the various rules, taboos, rites, and customs that previously structured and ordered the community are rendered impotent. The violence spreads throughout, respecting neither person, nor rank, nor station. Due to the breakdown of modes and orders, difference is abolished: the combatants become more alike the more they fight – just as two boxers assume the same stance in the ring. This brings us to a surprising paradox: the more we fight, the more similar we become, and as we become more similar, the more we fight. At the apex of this cycle, the rivals become nearly indistinguishable (VS 143–9). The sacrificial crisis

23 Augustine, *City of God*, XIX.12.

culminates in undifferentiated violence, exemplified in the violence of the Bacchanalia in Euripides, where all differences, boundaries, and restrictions are broken down and overturned in the fury of desire (VS 126–30). The temperature continues to rise, until either the burning violence consumes the people or a scapegoat is found. In the latter case, the swirling violence eventually begins to orbit around a specific person as the combatants gang up on this unfortunate individual or group. First one person blames a specific person or group for causing this trouble, then another imitates this desire to punish said person or group, and another, and so on, until the entirety of violence and rage is (re)directed exclusively on this person or group. This unfortunate soul is the scapegoat. The choice of the scapegoat is not motivated by forensic concerns – he is not blamed because he is actually guiltier than the others but, rather, because he is the easiest target: maybe he has a physical or mental impairment that makes self-defence harder; or maybe he is a stranger with few or no allies to defend him; and so on. As with predatory animals, the weakest of the pack is targeted for the hunt. The killing, torture, expulsions of the scapegoat function to redirect the intra-communal violence away from the community. By receiving all the violence of the others, the scapegoat unites the community and restores calm (VS 78–9). In restoring calm, the violence suffered by the scapegoat can appear as beneficial. The death of the scapegoat transforms the villain into a saviour and is the birth of that notoriously ambiguous thing, the *mysterium tremendens et fascinans*, known as the Sacred. The sacred leads to ritualized violence. When facing similar crises, the people remember what has worked in the past and return to it, not this time as a spontaneous murder but, rather, as a ritual sacrifice. If we look for the presence of this archaic sacred, this strange power that causes the rise and fall of the community in Machiavelli, we could do worse than to focus our attention on fortune. According to Girard, the sacred can be easily applied, mutandis mutandi, to fortune: "The sacred embraces all those forces that threaten to harm man or trouble his peace. Natural forces and sickness are not distinguished from the threat of a violent disintegration of the community. Although man-made violence plays a dominant role in the dialectics of the sacred and is never completely omitted … it tends to be relegated to the background and treated as if it emanated from outside man" (VS 58). If Dame Fortuna is a goddess, then she is certainly an archaic one.

One of the defining features of archaic religion, according to Girard, is a belief in the fertility of violence, that legitimate violence – violence properly channelled and directed rather than random and chaotic – can be used not to destroy but to build and preserve the community. We have seen this kind of dynamic at work over and over again in Machiavelli.

The judicious use of cruelty builds up the community (for example, it establishes law and order in the Romagna and prevents riots in Pistoia) by directing violence towards a few individuals rather than allowing it to spread and destroy the entire community. Cruelty well used is nothing other than a revival of the scapegoating violence of archaic religion. Machiavelli's novelty, then, is the novelty of a return to something old, older than ancient philosophy, to the archaic pre-Socratic sacrifices depicted by the tragedians.

One obvious objection to this reading presents itself: Machiavelli tells us, in *The Prince*, that one should only proceed against someone with "manifest cause" (P XVII). That is to say, Machiavelli demands that those to whom the prince is cruel be guilty; he must have a reason for his cruelty. It cannot be, as in the case of archaic religion, merely a temper tantrum. Indeed, one could go further and argue that archaic scapegoating, insofar as it proceeds against someone without cause, is precisely what Machiavelli recommends against. Nevertheless, this objection can be parried: a key element of archaic scapegoating is that the persecuting community *believes* that it has cause; it believes the scapegoat is guilty. Despite what Girard's vocabulary can suggest to the casual reader, the archaic communities do not *know* that they are scapegoating – that is, they do not know that they are killing the innocent (VS 83; THSFW 116–18; SG 1–11). In their eyes, the scapegoat really does have it coming. This is why Girard thinks that there is always an important degree of misunderstanding present in myth. Machiavelli's emphasis on the need for manifest cause is readily interpretable in terms of the ancient rite's demand for unanimity: the victim's guilt must be publicly attested to so that the people can consent to the victim's death. The demand that the prince have manifest cause for proceeding against his victim supports, rather than opposes, the reading offered here.

The punishment with manifest cause that Machiavelli mentions in *The Prince* can be profitably compared with the account, in the *Discourses*, of accusations and calumny. Machiavelli writes: "Between one side and the other there is the difference that calumnies have need of neither witnesses nor of any other specific corroborations to prove them, so that *everyone can be calumniated by everyone*; but everyone cannot, of course, be accused, since accusations have need of true corroborations and of circumstances that show the truth of the accusations. Men are accused to magistrates, to peoples, to councils; they are calumniated in piazzas and loggias" (D I.8, emphasis mine). The problem with calumny is not primarily the lack of evidence but that "everyone can be calumniated by everyone." To be sure, the lack of evidence is one of the reasons this is possible, but the more fundamental problem is that anyone can do it.

Calumny threatens to spread throughout the city, with each person accusing the other, reproaches and recriminations flying through the streets with no respect for proper authority. Instead of appealing through the proper channels established by the orders of the city, the calumniator sidesteps them and ultimately eliminates them. The difference between magistrate and private citizen is neither acknowledged nor respected; in this way the calumniator blurs the distinction between the legitimate (sacrificial) violence of the magistrates and the illegitimate violence of the mob. Calumny is a threat not merely to the one calumniated but also to the modes and orders of the city. It is, in a nutshell, the bad kind of violence that threatens communities. When calumny is allowed to spread its contagion, as it was at Florence, the result is inevitable: "on every side hatred surged; whence they went to division, from division to sects; from sects to ruin" (D I.8). Calumny produces a kind of sacrificial crisis wherein the modes and orders of the city are destroyed. Indeed, one of Girard's descriptions of the sacrificial crisis – "The institutions lose their vitality, the protective façade of the society gives way, social values are rapidly eroded, and the whole cultural structure seems on the verge of collapse" (VS 49) – could be read as a gloss on Machiavelli's account of calumny.

In contrast to the crisis of calumny, the alternative path – accusation – relies on and reinforces the modes and orders of the city. The accusation enables the humours of the people to be vented in an ordered way (D I.7) without hurt to the city. Indeed, it seems that accusations serve to benefit the city by allowing for the *public* punishment of citizens. As Machiavelli explains, when a citizen is crushed by the public, there is little or no disorder in a republic, even if the citizen was wrongly punished (D I.7). Why? Because to the extent that it was done with public consent there is no single individual or group that can be blamed for the crushing, thus avoiding a cycle of vengeance between partisans and sects. In this way, problems in the city can be resolved without endangering the modes and orders of the city. Accusation is not non-violent in contrast to the violence of calumny – both seek the death of another citizen. Nor should we contrast them in terms of adherence to rules of evidence; it is not impossible that the calumniator have evidence for what he whispers in piazzas and loggias or that the public accuser mishandle evidence. Instead, the only thing distinguishing calumny from accusation is that calumny undermines the modes and orders of the city while accusation respects them, in particular the difference between legitimate and illegitimate violence. In short, the distinction Machiavelli draws between accusation and calumny is only an instance of the broader sacrificial distinction between good and bad violence: accusation is a case the good kind of violence, and calumny is a case of the bad kind of violence.

A well-ordered city will provide the means for citizens to accuse one another; a city without good orders will suffer the destructive effects of calumny. Accusation and calumny are therefore not distinct species but two different manifestations of the same reality, the reality of conflict and violence within cities and between citizens. Violence is at the heart of the city. Machiavelli repeatedly affirms the fertility of (good) violence: the city at peace is the product of the prince's (mostly legitimate) violence and, as such, is subordinated to violence. This thought is, as we have already noted, not only not new but also downright archaic. I'm not sure to what extent modern philosophy is determined by Machiavelli – the scholarship on the *wirkungsgeschichte* of Machiavelli varies from Strauss's view that he is highly determinative of the trajectory of modern thought to the opposite extreme, that he is utterly inconsequential (this seems to be Heidegger's view) – but to whatever extent it is, it is to that extent a return to the archaic. I don't hope to add anything to this debate, as interesting as it is, but only want to point out that we can discern the fingerprints of archaic thinking in Machiavelli's work, which is not surprising, considering his fascination with antiquity. When a great mind is motivated to think deeply about ancient modes and orders we should not be surprised to find that the same mind is influenced by them.

5

New Princes, New Philosophies, and Old Gods

I WOULD LIKE TO BEGIN THIS CHAPTER with a discussion of Machiavelli's minor work from 1520, *The Life of Castruccio Castracani.* It is a short and strange work; beginning with a short discourse on fortune and virtue, it turns to a biography of Castruccio and culminates with a series of aphorisms attributed to him. This biography, needless to say, is the stylized biography of Renaissance humanism rather than a biography informed by modern historical scruples; it is designed to depict a moral *exemplum,* a model his readers should follow.[1] J. Macfarland argues for two points that are relevant here. First, Macfarland notes that "Castruccio's life is designed to illustrate several of the political and military principles found in *The Prince,* the *Discourses* and *The Art of War.*" Second, given this, Machiavelli seems to have wanted to hold up Castruccio as a modern example of one who, as it were, successfully put Machiavelli's ideas into practice.[2] The text culminates with a list of aphorisms attributed to reworkings of passage taken from Diogenes Laertius's *Lives of the Philosophers.* Their presence indicates that Castruccio provides us with clues to the understanding of philosophy Machiavelli proposes as an alternative to the philosophy of imagined republics.

Machiavelli begins the biography of Castruccio by reflecting on the fact that very often the greatest men arise from low origins or overcome great torments. Sometimes, Machiavelli remarks, they overcome

1 On this point, and its relevance for reading CC, see Bondanella, "Machiavelli's Archetypical Prince." This paper is particularly important for one of the claims that I advance in this book: that Machiavelli immanentizes religion. Bondanella shows that the biography of Castruccio follows the structure of medieval hero-tales but eliminates every transcendental element, every reference to angels, demons, saints, and so on; instead, politics is all.

2 Macfarland, "Machiavelli's Imagination of Excellent Men," 133–46.

this shame by purporting to be descended from the gods. This, he claims, is appropriate for it shows that fortune, rather than prudence (*prudenza*), is responsible for greatness. His point is unclear – especially since it seems to run contrary to a central teaching in both *The Prince* and the *Discourses* – but it seems to be that when one starts out so low only good fortune can account for a rise to greatness. Castruccio, it turns out, is one of these men. However, as he goes on, we find that Castruccio's success is not based merely on fortune but, instead, involves both fortune and virtue. In this, we are not far from the opening chapter of *The Prince*, in which virtue and fortune are identified as two ways of gaining power. However, if Castruccio's ascent to power is based primarily or predominantly on fortune, he hardly seems a good candidate for imitation or of interest to Machiavelli's friends since they are men who enjoy virtuous deeds (*azioni virtuose vi dilettate*). And in any case, one cannot reasonably expect to imitate another's fortune. So despite the reference to fortune in the opening pages, one could reasonably conclude that Machiavelli is more interested in Castruccio's virtue than in his fortune. If Castruccio owes his success to fortune it is only because she has given him certain opportunities to exercise virtue rather than success per se. In the case of Castruccio, fortune ensured that, as a foundling, he was taken in and raised by an old priest and his sister. Later, fortune would ensure that he has the opportunity to leave the priest and become a soldier. However, from this point onward, Castruccio's rise to power is founded on his virtue. In this, he is no different from the armed prophets of *The Prince*, who, while attaining power through their own efforts and strength, were dependent upon fortune insofar as she created the conditions (e.g., the enslavement of the Hebrews, the dispersal of the Athenians) that the armed prophet exploits. Indeed, commentators have repeatedly drawn our attention to the similarities between Castruccio and the four armed prophets of *The Prince*.[3] Castruccio, however, does not rise to the level of the four armed prophets discussed in the latter insofar as he does not introduce new modes and orders on the same scale. Each of the four armed prophets in *The Prince* founded important civilizations or empires. Castruccio is not nearly as important as those four. He comes closer to Agathocles the Sicilian, a man who also rose from low birth to a position of great power through crime and cruelty. Nevertheless, it has been argued that Castruccio's biography is meant to retell the story of the four

3 See Bondanella, "Machiavelli's Archetypical Prince"; and Schnapp, "Machiavellian Foundlings."

armed prophets in more modern guise; here the failures of Castruccio function to warn us of the difficulty of obtaining such heights.[4]

Castruccio's aforementioned rejection of the life of a priest for the life of a soldier and captain dramatizes Machiavelli's endorsement of ancient education and all that it contains over and against that of the Christian religion. Machiavelli tells us that, as a youth, Castruccio rejects his "ecclesiastical books" for weapons; upon doing so, he begins to display his great virtue of both body and mind (*virtù di animo e di corpo grandissima*). This is the first time that Machiavelli uses the word *virtù* in the narrative of Castruccio's life proper as opposed to in his introductory remarks. So, it is with the abandonment of ecclesiastical things that virtue first appears in the narrative. In chapter 1, we noted Machiavelli's complaint that Christian education, in contrast to that of the Romans, does not teach a distinction between good and bad violence and, thereby, makes one less capable of using violence effectively. In the *Discourses,* his complaint associates the belief in the eternity of the world with Roman virtue; here, he associates virtue with the rejection of ecclesiastical things. This is the flipside of the same coin: the ecclesiastic things that Castruccio rejects presuppose a belief in something transcending the world. It appears both here and in the *Discourses* that virtue requires sacrifice. Later, upon being introduced to Messer Francesco, Castruccio declares that nothing would make him happier than abandoning his studies for the priesthood (or, more precisely, *studii del prete,* the studies of a priest) to become a soldier:

> One day he [Messer Francisco] desired to find out more about the boy, and when he was told the story of his background he resolved to take him under his wing. One day he called Castruccio into his presence and asked him where he would prefer to be, in the house of a gentleman who would teach him to ride and use weapons, or in the house of a priest, where he would be taught nothing but offices and Masses [*uffizii e messe*]. It did not escape Messer Francesco that Castruccio brightened at the mention of horses and arms. The boy stood before

4 Schnapp, "Machiavellian Foundlings," 653–76. See, too, the insightful discussion of this question by Erica Benner in *Machiavelli's Prince,* 72–87. I think Benner is largely correct that Machiavelli suggests Heiro is a more obtainable model than are the four major princes of the chapter; but, despite this, I cannot share her conclusion that the discussion of the four is entirely ironic. I take it that the metaphor of the archer that opens the chapter suggests that, by aiming at the higher target, one may hit the lower one – that is, by modelling Romulus one may become Heiro. The deeper point, however, may be less about how or who to imitate than about the activities of founders. In other words, Benner's suggestion that *The Prince* is a republican book revealing the nature of princely power is, I think, largely correct; chapter 6 reveals the discourse-forming power of founding princes.

him in humble silence, but when Messer Francesco encouraged him to speak, Castruccio replied that if Messer Antonio [the priest] did not mind, nothing would make him happier than abandoning his priestly studies [*studii del prete*] and taking up those of a soldier. (CC 406, translation slightly modified)

This is the key point in Castruccio's life as Machiavelli presents it; after entering into the service of Francesco, Castruccio's rise to pre-eminence continues unabated. It is the decision to abandon the house of the priest that launches him on his career. To understand Castruccio's decision more fully, it is worthwhile to pause and consider the life of a priest and that of a soldier.

THE TRANSFIGURATION OF SOLDIERING

Machiavelli's longest consideration of soldiering is found in *The Art of War*. In the preface to the text, Machiavelli points out that there is a long-standing opposition or disjunction between military and civilian life, such that the two are seen as having little or nothing to do with each other. Indeed, says Machiavelli, when a man enters into the military, he feels the need to change his character entirely, leaving civilian ways behind. Nevertheless, he continues, if the orders of antiquity were still followed, this opposition would not be so drastic. In fact, in antiquity the military life presupposed and perfected that of the civilian, not the opposite: "And if in every other order of cities or kingdoms the utmost diligence was used to keep men faithful, peaceful and full of the fear of God, in the military it was redoubled" (AW Pr.5). Machiavelli suggests that, if the ancient orders were followed, one would again find the most faithful, peaceful, and devout men in the military. But why are the ancient orders not followed, if they are so clearly superior? In the preface itself, Machiavelli avoids making any kind of explicit explanation. Later the main speaker in the dialogue, Fabrizio, when asked why ancient orders are not followed, answers with a lament for the effect of Christian mercy on soldiering. Although I have already quoted this passage, it is worth doing so again:

The other reason [for the lack of military virtue] is that today's mode of living, on account of the Christian religion, does not impose the necessity to defend oneself that there was in antiquity. For then, men conquered in war were either killed or remained in perpetual slavery, where they lived their lives miserably. Their conquered towns were either dissolved or, their goods taken, the inhabitants were driven out and sent dispersed throughout the world. So those overcome in war suffered every last misery. Frightened by this fear, men kept military training alive and honored whoever was excellent in it. But today this fear is for the most part lost. Of the conquered, few of them are killed; no one is kept in prison for long, because they are freed with ease. (AW II.305–08)

It seems to Fabrizio that the relatively lenient punishment for losing a battle or war has made princes neglect the ancient orders. As I argue earlier, the martial incompetence Fabrizio laments is an effect of Christianity's discomfort with violence, which is, in turn, due to the rejection of the sacrificial distinction. These reflections can lead to the conclusion that it is Christianity, as much as or more than anything else, that keeps Fabrizio's contemporaries from embracing ancient orders. In both *The Art of War* and *The Life of Castruccio Castracani* there is an opposition between two ways of life: the life of the priest and the life of the soldier.

The priest spends his life seeking to conform himself to a supersensible and transcendent standard of behaviour. The life of the priest is one committed to sanctification wherein the priest, to paraphrase the name of a famous book, imitates Christ (rather than Romulus). The priesthood, therefore, presupposes a super-mundane standard to which the individual priest is called to conform himself; likewise, the priest exists within a community – the church – that proposes to the world a set of norms to which his behaviour and beliefs must conform. These norms, according to the church's understanding, are derived from a world-transcending God known on the basis of reason and revelation, including here both the Scriptures and sacred tradition. However, both natural law and revelation are, in the end, rooted in a world-transcending God. This God is invisible. As Thomas Aquinas puts it in his great Eucharistic hymn: *praestet fides supplementum, sensuum defectui.* Taken together, Machiavelli's eternal world and new doctrine of truth undermines the priesthood by attacking the claim that the priest conforms himself to a super-mundane truth: the kingdom of God is an imaginary principality. *The Prince*'s rejection of invisible republics and principalities entails the rejection of the clerical life; this entailment is dramatized in the life of Castruccio. The life of the priest presupposes an invisible order and the pursuit of the transcendent peace of heaven. The priest performs precisely those bloodless rites that Machiavelli criticizes in comparison with the blood and gore of Roman religions (D II.2). The life of the priest points towards the heavenly Jerusalem that Augustine appealed to in his rejection of the sacrificial distinction. Castruccio's choice for a life of soldiering rather than holy orders is a good choice, from Machiavelli's point of view, because it is a choice for the Roman model of education over the Christian one (c.f. D II.2). Recall that Machiavelli presents the story of

Castruccio as a story of virtue: the sine qua non of all the virtuous actions performed by Castruccio is his initial rejection of the clerical state. The transfiguration of the soldier and captain in Machiavelli's thought is inseparable from the displacement of holy orders.

CASTRUCCIO'S MARGINAL PHILOSOPHY

The particular details of Castruccio's rise to power largely mirror the activities of Agathocles and Cesar Borgia – that is, the kind of good violence that judiciously mixes cruelty and audacity, force and deception, for the benefit of the community. Let us look closer at the sayings attributed to him that make up the final portion of the text, most of which are adapted from Diogenes Laertius's *Lives of the Philosophers* – the biographies of Bion, Aristippus, and Diogenes the Cynic, among others. They are, by and large, marginal figures; in the words of one commentator, they are "not the canonical fathers of ancient philosophy, but rather atheists philosopher-rascals."[5] Aristippus is the founder of the Cyrenaic school, which held that the chief good is physical pleasure. Unlike the Epicureans, who held a similar account of the highest good but maintained that the truest form of pleasure is freedom from pain and tranquility of mind, the Cyrenaics focused on the moment to moment enjoyment of more straightforward physical pleasures: eating, drinking, sex. This distinction is subtle but important: while both agree on the primacy of pleasure, Epicurean pleasure is a far cry from Cyrenaic pleasure in that Epicurean philosophy suggests that one should postpone or avoid short-term physical pleasures for the sake of long-term tranquility and freedom from desire (as Torquatus argues in Cicero's *de Finibus*).[6] In contrast, Aristippus's sect argued both that we should embrace whatever pleasure is available to us and that physical pleasures were superior to intellectual ones.[7] Bion garnered a reputation for himself as a great atheist and scoffer at the gods and religion – until he fell sick, whereupon he gave himself over to superstitions and charms.[8] Castruccio's death-bed discourse seems to suggest that we should focus on the earlier parts of Bion's life since he – Castruccio – did not fall back onto superstitions when facing death. Diogenes the Cynic is a different sort of philosopher; he is taken

5 Schnapp, "Machiavellian Foundlings," 666. Schnapp's paper is particularly useful on this point in that he shows the importance of the aphorism to the integrity of the text as a whole.

6 See Cicero, *On Moral Ends*, I.55–63.

7 Diogenes Laertius, "Life of Aristippus," VIII, in *Lives of the Philosophers* I.

8 Diogenes Laertius, "Life of Bion," X, in *Lives of the Philosophers.*

not only as a representative of moral seriousness but also as a critic of other philosophers, in particular Plato.[9] Diogenes Laertius also tells us that he responded to a syllogism "proving" that he had horns by announcing that he does not see them; by arguing against the possibility of motion by getting up to walk; and, of course, to the definition of a man as a featherless biped by throwing a plucked chicken at Plato.[10] Diogenes the Cynic, at least in part, elevates the visible or empirical over theoretical philosophical argumentation, whereby a performance or action serves as the best refutation of philosophical theory. Machiavelli's Diogenes is a philosopher of the visible, rejecting imaginary republics. The aphorisms adapted from these three philosophers by Machiavelli defend the pleasures of food and sex, mock marriage and the afterlife, and elevate the political life over all others. Needless to say, each of these quotes is updated when appropriate to seem less anachronistic; however, the adaptation also merges each of these philosophers into Castruccio. Castruccio offers a blend of all three: a hedonistic atheism focused on success in the visible world. Moreover, as Leo Strauss points out, a few of the sayings taken from the life of Aristippus are heard by Castruccio rather than said by him; in these aphorisms he takes the place of Aristippus's auditors, in each case, the tyrant Dionysius.[11] If Machiavelli intends to combine Aristippus, Bion, and Diogenes in his presentation of Castruccio's philosophy, we must conclude that he also intends to include Dionysius the tyrant. This combination of philosopher-tyrant is further cemented by another saying of Castruccio – instead of claiming, as Aristippus did, that he wished to die like Socrates, Castruccio wants to die like Caesar (CC 428).

Although Caesar was more concerned with comparing himself to Alexander than to Socrates, Machiavelli's replacement of Socrates with Caesar in Castruccio's statement shows that Machiavelli *was* interested in such a comparison. Socrates was killed by the people of Athens for introducing new gods and corrupting the youth; Caesar was killed by the Senate of Rome because it suspected his ambition. If Socrates was killed for being too philosophical, then Caesar was killed for being too political. Another way to put it is to say that Socrates dies for an invisible republic or principality, while Caesar dies for the visible one. It is well known that part of the Athenian complaint against Socrates was that he corrupted the youth; if we take his teaching in *The Republic* as representative, one can see that Socratic corruption is intimately connected to the

9 Diogenes Laertius, "Life of Diogenes," IV, in *Lives of the Philosophers.*

10 Ibid., VI, in *Lives of the Philosophers.*

11 Strauss, *Thoughts on Machiavelli,* 223–4.

denial of the eternity of the world. Here we should remind ourselves that Platonism, as we saw in *The Timaeus*, explicitly denies the eternity of the world; but, even before we get there, we can find that same denial in the analogy of the cave. The escape from the cave to the world of ideas is a surpassing of the world. It is not surprising that Heidegger's criticisms of Platonism focus on the analogy of the cave for it is there that the two major themes of (a) Plato's understanding of truth and (b) the surpassability or non-eternity of the world are united. On the other hand, we have seen that Machiavelli connects the life of the ancient Romans, especially ancient Roman soldiers, with the affirmation of the eternity of the world. Here Julius Caesar can be taken, despite Machiavelli's criticisms in other texts, as representing that tradition. If Socrates is the exemplar of the belief that the world is not eternal, the life of Caesar can be said to exemplify the life of one who believes the world is eternal and who, embracing the ancient sacrificial education, uses violence quite effectively. In seeking a death like that of Caesar, Castruccio indicates that success in this world, rather than in the next world, is the highest good. The association of this view with the sayings of other philosophers elevates this above a crass materialism or striving: Castruccio's embrace of sacrifice is not an indifference to, or ignorance of, the highest good but, rather, an alternate account of the highest good. The Socratic life presuppose a vision of the truth as *orthotes* (if we wish to continue with Heidegger's terminology), and its dignity and status are in large part based on that vision of super-sensible and transcendent truth: the philosopher knows about higher and better things than the non-philosopher, and because of a radical commitment to these things, the philosopher rejects sacrifice, harming no one.[12] Machiavelli's doctrine of truth and the affirmation of the eternity of the world elevate the life of Caesar above that of Socrates. Castruccio's and Caesar's devotion to *imperium* is a devotion to truth. Political engagement, rather than contemplation, becomes the highest philosophical activity.

SWEAT AND LABOUR IN THE SUNLIGHT

Surprisingly, it is in the *Florentine Histories* that we find Machiavelli's most developed reflections on the relationship between philosophy and virtue. Since I discuss the passage at some length, for the reader's convenience I quote it in full:

12 Plato, *The Republic*, 586a–d.

> Usually provinces go most of the time, in the changes they make, from order to disorder and then pass again from disorder to order, for worldly things are not allowed by nature to stand still. As soon as they reach their ultimate perfection, having no further to rise, they must descend; and similarly, once they have descended and through their disorders arrived at the ultimate depths, since they cannot descend further, of necessity they must rise. Thus they are always descending from good to bad and rising from bad to good. For virtue gives birth to quiet, quiet to leisure, leisure to disorder, disorder to ruin; and similarly, from ruin, order is born; from order, virtue; and from virtue, glory and good fortune. Whence it has been observed by the prudent that letters come after arms and that, in provinces and cities, captains arise before philosophers. For as good and ordered armies give birth to victories, and victories to quiet, the strength of well-armed spirits [*la fortezza degli armati animi*] cannot be corrupted by a more honorable leisure [*ozio*] than that of letters, nor can leisure enter into well-instituted cities with a greater and more dangerous deceit than this one. This was best understood by Cato when the philosophers Diogenes and Carneades, sent by Athens as a spokesman to the Senate, came to Rome. When he saw how the Roman youth was beginning to follow them about with admiration, and since he recognized the evil that could result to his fatherland from this honorable leisure, he saw to it that no philosophers could be accepted in Rome. Thus, provinces come by these means to ruin; when they have arrived there and men have become wise from their afflictions, they return, as was said, to order unless they remain suffocated by an extraordinary force. (FH V.1)

In endorsing Cato's expulsion of philosophers from Rome, Machiavelli again returns to the sacrificial distinction between good and bad violence. Cato's expulsion was good violence, because – if successful – it would ward off the bad violence courted by philosophy, "honourable leisure." When a city fails to keep philosophy at bay – when it fails to practise the good violence of Cato – it inevitably suffers bad violence. One recent commentator, Mark Jurdjevic, astutely points out that the passage we are discussing precedes Machiavelli's long discussion of the decline of Florence and rise of the Medici.[13] According to Jurdjevic, Machiavelli's preface provides an interpretation of the events narrated in book V: philosophy had corrupted the city and allowed the Medici to dominate it. While philosophy as practised in Florence is the proximate target, it would be a mistake to limit the passage to Florence; Machiavelli seems to have broader vistas in mind in this passage. He presents philosophy as the product of the leisure time provided by the security and

13 See Jurdjevic, *Great and Wretched City*, 60.

stability of good arms. The captain, the warrior, comes before the philosopher; in Lacoste's terms, philosophy is a vigil that occurs after one's duties have been discharged (EA 78). If one finds out what something is by looking to what it is *first,* then Machiavelli's anthropology is simple: the human being is *first* a captain and only second, if at all, a philosopher. Philosophy is something we do in our leisure (*ozio*). Now, at this point, one might suggest that the view of philosophy as leisure activity is not altogether novel: after all, in Plato's *Republic* philosophy is introduced with the guardians, entering only into the "feverish city" awash with luxuries, not into the city of simple necessity. Likewise, in the *Metaphysics,* Aristotle is quite clear that philosophy is only practised after certain physical needs have been met.[14] While Plato and Aristotle admitted that philosophy as a practice has a number of prerequisites, they saw philosophical leisure as the crowning jewel of civic life, not the beginnings of its decline. Philosophy was a good, and it was good because of the nature of the human being; in fact, it was the essential task of the human being: "Man by nature desires to know." For Machiavelli this is *not* the case: philosophy or metaphysics, the search for super-mundane and transcendent truths, is a deleterious luxury not an essential task.

Machiavelli argues that the spoils of peace and good captainship will ruin the city itself because the philosophical search for truth distracts men from the virtuous manufacture of la verità effetuale. Classical philosophy is corruptive for at least three reasons. First, it teaches error insofar as it focuses on invisible "imagined republics" rather than on the visible and attempts to draw normative standards and evaluate politics on the basis of a fantasy. Second, it suggests that philosophical inactivity, leisure (*ozio*), is more noble and worthy than the activity of the captain or founder. These two points lead to a third: philosophical inquiry can be destabilizing by undermining the modes and orders of the city; when the philosopher discovers that there is no transcendent basis for the organization of the city, that it is largely dependent upon the arms of the founder, these beliefs are undermined. This point parallels the "corruption of the youth" argument against Socrates, at least as Aristophanes understood it when he depicted Socratic teaching as undermining the old-fashioned virtue of Marathon via his focus on intellectual endeavours. To the extent that the philosopher teaches others, he or she embraces the role of unarmed prophet. Since the unarmed prophet always comes to ruin, a city populated by philosophers too will suffer. In fact, as the discussions in book I of *The Art of War* suggests, to be a good citizen

14 See Plato, *The Republic,* 372a–375b; Aristotle, *Metaphysics,* 981b10–30.

is to be a good soldier: solid citizenship requires training and discipline, which comes from a good captain.[15] This mirrors the discussion, in his *Discourses on Livy*, of the role of the prince when founding a city (i.e., that he should force the people to be virtuous). We should keep all this in mind when evaluating Machiavelli's praise for the foresight of Cato. It is not the pursuit of wisdom that Machiavelli objects to, but the vision of wisdom offered by philosophers: wisdom as contemplative *ozio*. The honourable leisure represented by philosophy is a kind of naiveté: it supposes that one can speculate peaceably without taking concern for defence against threats. The leisurely philosophers Machiavelli criticizes do not necessarily reject the sacrificial distinction (as Augustine does), but they seem to forget it with equally bad consequences. By forgetting that good violence can be used to chase out bad violence, they let down their guard and become victims of bad violence. In the same passages Machiavelli argues that philosophers only truly become wise "from their afflictions." Wisdom comes not from speculation but from experience: they are wise when they have been ruined and forced to acknowledge the importance of the security and stability provided by captains. When the importance of the captain's work is acknowledged, the sacrificial distinction is acknowledged: the violence of the captain is a good violence that wards off bad violence. For Machiavelli, this is true wisdom.

As noted above, Machiavelli's endorsement of Cato's expulsion of the philosophers cannot be interpreted as a rejection of the pursuit of wisdom or philosophy, per se, but only of a certain model of philosophy. That this is the case can be seen in the image of Castruccio and the collection of philosophical sayings Machiavelli attributes to him. Instead, the kind of philosophy that he rejects is one that is focused on invisible truths, it is contemplative and inactive. It is through this kind of philosophy, he argues, that leisure, *ozio*, enters even into well-ordered cities and seduces its best citizens. This alternative philosophy is a philosophy without *ozio*, without the invisible truths of imagined republics. It is a kind of anti-philosophy that rejects the contemplative leisure of the philosophers that brought so much grief to the city and pursues, instead, the life of the captain, remembering and endorsing the sacrificial distinction between good and bad violence. It is through the visible agonistics of the field, rather than the debates of philosophers, that one finally arrives at truth – la verità effetuale. This agrees with the advice offered by Fabrizio in *The Art of War*: according to him, modern princes err in imitating the ancients in indoor pursuits of delicate and soft things rather

15 See C. Lynch's interpretive essay accompanying his translation of AW, 200–1.

than in rough things done in the sun – the life of the soldier. These pursuits are true and perfect (*vera e perfetta*), while those other ancient pursuits brought decay to Rome and are false and corrupt (*falsa e corrotta*) (AW I.17).

When Machiavelli refers to philosophy as an "honourable leisure" (*onesto ozio*) he admits that classical philosophy does have an undeniable seductive force: even Cato could not keep it from entering Rome. Imagined republics and invisible truths seduce by presenting themselves as the highest and best things. If the threat that philosophy represents to virtue is to be defused, then a mere rejection will not work nearly as well as a counter-seduction. The honour of philosophy – especially Platonism – rests in its claim to surpass the world and offer access to eternal and divine truths. Machiavelli's new doctrine of truth and doctrine of the eternity of the world serves as an inoculation against classical philosophy by denying both. Returning to Castruccio, he represents not a thoughtless absence of philosophy but, rather, a new philosophy that marries Caesar to Socrates, Diogenes to Dionysius. This new philosophy focuses not on the contemplation and discussion of the transcendent and invisible – as did the honourable leisure of the ancient world – but rather on the control and modification of the visible and temporal by means of a distinction between good and bad violence

MACHIAVELLI'S OLD GOD

We are now in a position to discuss more directly the bush we have been beating around: the relationship between Machiavelli and religion. In any discussion of Machiavelli and religion, one should separate two distinct kinds of questions that are often intertwined:

a) What were Machiavelli's personal religious beliefs, practices, and so forth, and how did they influence his thinking about political life?
b) What are the theological or religious implications of his texts?

No less a thinker than Maurizio Viroli has judged that answering (a) is "perhaps an impossible undertaking."[16] Nevertheless, he continues, it is possible to entertain the hypothesis that Machiavelli was a Christian of some sort, the emphasis falling on "some sort." In any case, (b) is the philosophically more consequential question; indeed, as Viroli has shown in *Machiavelli's God*, one can quite seriously point to a Machiavellian

16 Viroli, *Machiavelli's God*, 2.

theology, a vision of God guided by the Republicanism of Florence and the writings of the humanists.[17] Machiavelli's God, Viroli (following de Grazia) argues persuasively, loves good government, patriotic service, devotion to *la patria*, glory, justice, and peace. But this love of peace and justice does not exclude friendship with those who use cruelty well. Machiavelli's God understands that, to save the fatherland and create good governance, one sometimes has to do evil.[18] I return to this point later, but attentive readers will probably already guess where I will go with it.

The passages and topics under discussion in (b) are some of the most debated in Machiavelli. Cary Nederman is certainly correct to describe this as the most contentious area of Machiavelli scholarship, and, in a moment of frustration, Ada Palmer refers to it as a "tired debate."[19] For some scholars (e.g., Leo Strauss or Gennarro Sasso), Machiavelli was a full-blown apostate who, anticipating the Nietzschean critique of Christianity by a few centuries, saw Christianity as both false and weakening. At the other extreme, one finds scholars (e.g., Sebastian de Grazie or Cary Nederman) arguing that Machiavelli is much closer to traditional Christianity and only a bit anti-clerical. And, of course, there are various gradations in between these two views. I should confess that, if forced to choose between the two extremes, Machiavelli's defence of the eternity of the world and the influence of Lucretius pushes me towards the Strauss/Sasso reading; nevertheless, there are numerous passages that support the other reading. What does one who reads Machiavelli this way do with those passages? There are two options. First, one could take them as feints, illusions, or tricks. This is what Harvey Mansfield, representing the Straussian faction, suggests in his review of de Grazie's *Machiavelli in Hell*.[20] While sympathetic with this approach – if I may paraphrase the Spanish scholastic Domingo Soto, while not a Straussian I was raised among them – it, too, quickly opens up the door to highly

17 Ibid., 43–61. The remarks of Jurdjevic, in the first chapter of *Great and Wretched City*, on the importance of Savonarola for the development of Machiavelli's thoughts on religion and politics are certainly relevant here as well. According to Jurdjevic, Machiavelli saw in Savonarola, despite his failures, evidence that political projects can be invigorated by appeal theological themes.

18 Viroli, *Machiavelli's God*, 64–5.

19 Nederman, "Amazing Grace," 617; Palmer, *Reading Lucretius*, 86.

20 Mansfield, "Review of *Machiavelli in Hell*," 764–5. See also the remarks on de Grazia in Sullivan, *Three Romes*, 4–5.

speculative readings inoculated against all possible counter-examples.[21] Second, one could take these passages as evidence of a conflict within Machiavelli, as showing that he struggled to digest and express his own deepest insights. Machiavelli, on this reading, was a man of his time and made use of the religious language and imagery of his day in his writings, at times even though the fundamental orientation of his thought is towards a more radical critique of that same religion. On this view, the contentious history of interpreting Machiavelli's philosophy of religion only reflects Machiavelli's own ambivalence. If one takes this tack, then it seems that the most profitable strategy is to focus on his substantive claims and arguments when directly speaking about religious matters rather than on asides, ejaculations, and turns of phrases that show up in other contexts. If Viroli's account of Machiavelli's writing method is correct – "the products of pain distilled into pages of pure power and vitality ... [infused] with all the intensity of a life he feels slipping from his grasp"[22] – then we should expect this ambivalence. Our Florentine secretary is brilliant, but it is not the brilliance of the systematic word-counting professors. In fact, I think that Viroli's account of Machiavelli's religious view is convincing precisely because it allows us to recognize the ambivalence in Machiavelli's texts. On Viroli's reading, Machiavelli thought Christianity could have a valuable role to play in civic life, but he also thought that it wasn't quite up to the task he had in mind. Viroli summarizes his position as follows: "Machiavelli not only asserted that republican liberty needs a religion that instils and supports devotion to the common good but also that the Christian religion properly interpreted is apt to serve such a task."[23] Strangely enough, I think that this view can be harmonized with my aforementioned sympathy for the more radical readings of Strauss or Sasso: Machiavelli thought that Christianity as commonly practised and understood was false and bad for politics but

21 While I find many "Straussian" readings insightful, I also tend to think that they over-argue the case, spending too much time reading between the lines for hints of Machiavelli's apostasy when – in fact – it is right there on the surface. There is no need to draw strained analogies between the "Marius" and "Maria" (as Mansfield does at NMO 46n.39), between Rome's militarism and Paul's epistles (as Sullivan does in *Three Romes*, 54–5), and so on to show that Machiavelli is not a traditional Christian.

22 Viroli, *Niccolò's Smile*, 153.

23 Viroli, *Machiavelli's God*, xi. Viroli's position seems to find its contrary in that of Vicki Sullivan. According to Sullivan's reading of Machiavelli, "the religious is not only pernicious, it is wholly superfluous" (*Three Romes*, 7). But Sullivan comes closer to Viroli's position a bit later, when she introduces the idea of a "temporal Christianity that can fortify political life" (*Three Romes*, 10 and 147–71).

that some adjustments it could be good for politics. Viroli suggests something like this in his biography of Machiavelli: "He [Machiavelli] recognized that fear of God had beneficial effects on the way people lived and could be a powerful tool to support the law and authority of a prince or republic ... But his god was a political god [*sic*], a friend to princes who achieved great things (such as Castracani), or perhaps one should say a rhetorical god that he used to exhort princes to achieve great things. His god had very little in common with the Christian God, being neither a principle of faith nor a source of hope."[24]

Machiavelli's reading of Lucretius might offer more clues to his views on religion. Lucretius is notoriously unfriendly to religion: it is based on fear and ignorance, and the sooner the bulk of humanity can be freed from its spell, the better. In fact, it is precisely this freeing that he hopes his poem will accomplish (DRN I 60–135). Machiavelli does not follow Lucretius on these points. Instead, he argues that religion – properly understood or used – is a great boon for societies and cultures. The claim that religion can be put to good uses is not incompatible with the claim that it is false, or even that it is rooted in fear and ignorance. While we can be confident that Lucretius's critique of religious belief was understood and digested by Machiavelli, it seems clear that he did not adopt it entirely; perhaps he saw in the example of Savonarola – despite his failures – that false beliefs can make good politics.[25]

The view that Christianity is false, and as currently practised weakening, is not incompatible with the view that, reinterpreted, it could be good for political life. In the same way, I might believe that my guitar is out of tune and bad for playing music, but retuned it could be good for music. One need not believe a creed to believe that it is useful for other people to believe it. While on Viroli's reading, Machiavelli really and truly believed in his version of Christianity, it is not clear to me whether Machiavelli thought this God was real or whether he thought it was simply good for people to believe these things about God. We should not, however, distract ourselves with the attempt to peer into Machiavelli's

24 Viroli, *Niccolò's Smile*, 207. See, too, the similar remarks in his *Machiavelli*, 23–4. There Viroli notes that the Machiavellian vision of God as a friend to founders and statesmen has its roots in Cicero's *Dream of Scipio*. But even then, there is an important difference: "[Machiavelli's] political God is more 'understanding' than the God of Cicero and the humanists. For them, God is ready to help and reward founders, rulers and redeemers of republics who have practiced the political virtues: justice, fortitude, prudence and temperance. For Machiavelli, God is willing to excuse also princes who perpetrated 'well-committed' cruelties, if that were necessary to establish their power, or to redeem kingdoms or republics."

25 See Brown, *Return of Lucretius*, 80; and Jurdjevic, *Great and Wretched City*, 15–60.

soul. Whatever the case may be, the more important point is that the God described in Machiavelli's major works is an interventionist one that acts to help the friends of liberty and punish her enemies; rather than making the rain fall on both the just and the unjust, this God pushes the tower of Siloam down so as to smite enemies of liberty. God rewards and befriends those who fight for the fatherland and allows them to commit any number of evil deeds when prosecuting war on behalf of it. Perhaps the essential moment of Machiavelli's theology is the admission that the murderous Agathocles was able to restore his relationship with God not despite but precisely because of his murders, his well-used cruelty (P VIII). It is a God that accepts, promotes, and rewards the sacrificial distinction between good and bad violence. This kind of God could be properly described – following Girard's taxonomy – as an archaic God, a God of fertile violence, a God that delights in sacrifices ("cruelty well used") rather than a contrite heart. Machiavelli's God is not so much a new God as it is a very old one. In Machiavelli's political theology, the old gods, the oldest of the old gods, the gods of sacrifice and scapegoating, reappear. I do not mean here that Machiavelli reverts to a conscious belief in pagan divinities, but that he reproduces the sacrificial structure of archaic religion: to the extent that he wants to reform Christianity to make it better suited for political purposes, his reforms seek to make it more, not less, sacrificial.

As we have already noted, although there are passages in the *Discourses* in which Machiavelli describes Christianity as the true religion, he also describes the practices associated with the followers of the false religion (i.e., Roman paganism) as more desirable because of their political and military effects: "Neither pomp nor magnificence of ceremony was lacking there, but the action of the sacrifice, full of blood and ferocity, was added, with a multitude of animals being killed there. This sight, being terrible, rendered men similar to itself. Besides this, the ancient religion did not beatify men if they were not full of worldly glory, as were captains of armies and princes of republics" (D II.2). The message seems to be that the superiority of pagan rites lay in their violence. To be sure, this was a good violence that served to benefit the public by warding off bad violence, but it is precisely this sacrificial distinction that Christianity rejects. If Christianity teaches men to submit to beatings rather than to avenge them (D II.2), then this is arguably because Christianity refuses to distinguish between good violence and bad violence. But it is this distinction that the Roman sacrifices, "full of blood and ferocity," taught with aplomb.

In book I of his *Discourses*, Machiavelli suggests that the important part of religion is not the beliefs as much as it is the rites and ceremonies:

"Those princes or those republics that wish to maintain themselves uncorrupt have above everything else to maintain the ceremonies of their religion uncorrupt and hold them always in veneration; for one can have no greater indication of the ruin of a province than to see the divine cult disdained. This is easy to understand once it is known what the religion where a man is born is founded upon, for every religion has the foundation of its life on some principle order of its own" (D I.12). Now while Machiavelli is well known for his indifference to matters liturgical – he seemed to disdain the divine cult, rarely, if ever, attending church services – a concern for the proper celebration of rites is hardly the calling card of one antagonistic to religion. In fact, there is a long-standing tradition in liturgical Christianity that views the proper celebration of rites as the sine qua non for proper belief: *lex orandi, lex credendi.* The first part of the passage quoted above can be easily squared with that tradition. However, the departure from that tradition comes in the final sentence, in which Machiavelli claims that every religion founds itself on a principle of its own. I take this to mean that the religion is itself the origin of its rites, that the creation of rites and ceremonies of the religion is equivalent to the creation of the religion. This claim is not biblical. In biblical religions – Judaism and Christianity – liturgy comes not from the religion but from God: witness the long passages in Deuteronomy and Leviticus describing the proper sacrifices and form of worship, including vestments and prayers. Moreover, the religion pre-existed the rites: the Jews are Jews *before* passage out of Egypt and before the introduction of rites in Deuteronomy and Leviticus. According to the Old Testament, the Jewish religion was born when God introduced the rite of circumcision to Abraham to seal the covenant. The rites do not give birth to the religion but, instead, God is the source of both the religion and the rites. We might say that, while Machiavelli endorses the view encapsulated by lex orandi, lex credendi, he does so only after decisively sealing prayer and belief off from the invisible God. Later in the same section he writes: "Thus princes of a republic or of a kingdom should maintain the foundations of the religion they hold; and if this is done, it will be an easy thing for them to maintain their republic religious and, in consequence, good and united. All things that arise in favor of that religion they should favor and magnify, *even though they judge them false*; and they should do it so much the more as they are prudent and more knowing of natural things" (D.12, emphasis mine). The upshot of these two passages is that the rites of a religion are more important than is the theological explanation of those rites.[26]

26 An informative and persuasive discussion of Machiavelli along these lines can be found in Hochner, "Ritualist Approach to Machiavelli." For Hochner, the importance of religion for Machiavelli turns on the effects of its ceremonies and rites rather than on the

These rites do not refer to something apart from themselves, but, instead, there is a self-contained circle or feedback loop whereby the rites serve the foundation and the foundation serves the rites. Finally, (c) it does not matter whether the prince believes the religion or not, he should do his best to preserve it so as to reap the political benefits it bestows. Taken together, (a), (b), and (c) paint a picture of religion reduced to its immanent or worldly aspects: the point of religion is to support the virtues of the good citizen, in particular by instilling a distinction between good and bad violence.

MACHIAVELLI'S MYSTERIOUS GERMANS

Machiavelli's criticisms of Christian practice, as Viroli points out, are balanced by praise of the German states, which were also Christian.[27] Machiavelli's persistent and enthusiastic praise of German and, to a lesser extent, Swiss modes and orders are a nagging problem for readings of Machiavelli that wish to present him as mainly an enemy of Christian orders. It is not surprising that Vicki Sullivan's *Three Romes* mentions the Germans only in passing. Noting that Machiavelli admits that Germany is uncorrupt in contrast to Spain, Italy, and France because it prevents the kind of inequality found in the three others, she emphasizes that the clergy could be considered a source of this problematic inequality.[28] But were there no clergy in Germany? It is also hard to reconcile his praise of German states with his claim that the harmful effects of Christianity are due, at least in part, to the Christian repression of ancient orders and ceremonies (D II.5). Surely they were just as repressed in German as in Italy. How then could it be that the Germans, equally lacking ancient pagan rites, maintained the civic virtue that Italy lacked? Maybe there was an important difference between the German and Italian rites? Prior to the promulgation of the Missal of Pius V in 1570 (which suppressed rites and uses less than two hundred years old) there was a great deal of local variation in Catholic liturgy – differing episcopal sees (e.g., Braga, Milan) and religious orders (e.g., the Dominicans, the Carmelites) each had their own rites, and these could vary quite a bit one from the other.

beliefs or theology behind the rites (595). Hochner reads Machiavelli's preference for ancient Roman rites over Christian rites in these terms: the bloody violence of the ancient rites worked more effectively than modern Christian rites at binding the people together and forming a love of freedom. This can easily be rephrased in Girardian terms – that is, that the rites bind the people together by uniting them against a sacrificial victim that carries the problems and discords of the community on its back (i.e., a scapegoat).

27 Viroli, *Machiavelli's God*, 179–81.

28 Sullivan, *Three Romes*, 125.

Nevertheless, despite the variety, the basic structure of the Mass was more or less constant; liturgical historians remind us that, despite the variations, all the rites are recognizably Western and based largely on the Roman rite. The rituals of German Catholics in 1513 would not be *that* different from those of Italian Catholics.

So, if the Christian rituals tend towards pomp and *ozio*, why were the Germans states so much better than the Italian states? The German puzzle suggests that Christian rites are in themselves insufficient for producing the problems Machiavelli associates with Christianity. But this is hardly what Machiavelli explicitly states. One possible solution (Viroli's) to this riddle is to argue that it is not so much Christianity that is corruptive as it is the profoundly bad example of the prelates and princes associated with the Church of Rome, which taught the Italians not to esteem religion. The Germans are better off because they are further from the papacy's bad example. This suggests that Christian theology is less important for Machiavelli than are the scandalous lives of Christian churchmen. But this solution seems to cut against Machiavelli's general emphasis on the importance of rite: Why contrast ancient and modern rites at all if the real deciding factor is how close one is to the bad example of the papacy? A neater solution is to say that (a) Germany is superior to Italy but (b) both are inferior to ancient Rome. I take it that the truth of (a) is fairly well established. We can find evidence for (b) in book I of the *Discourses.* Towards the end of the first book, Machiavelli is discussing the importance of an uncorrupted citizenry, and he points out that Rome, when uncorrupt, was religious, and that one still sees this goodness and religion in the Germans (I.55). But he is careful to note that only a "good part of that ancient goodness" is present in the Germans, not the totality of it. To explain which part remains, Machiavelli's attention then turns to the German tax-gathering practice. According to Machiavelli, taxes are paid on an honour system, whereby each person pays what he thinks he owes, with no witness or tax-collectors supervising. Despite the opportunity, there is no fraud or cheating. This strikes him as a great and impressive example of civic virtue. And surely it is. Machiavelli then turns to possible explanations for this great virtue. It turns out that the virtue of the Germans rests on a foundation of murder: "Those republics in which a political and uncorrupt way of life is maintained do not endure that any citizen of theirs either be or live in the usage of a gentleman; indeed they maintain among themselves an even quality and to the lords and gentlemen who are in that province they are very hostile. If by chance some fall into their hands, they kill them as the beginning of corruption and cause of every scandal" (D I.55).

The killing of gentlemen to ward off corruption is presented as a good kind of violence; whence the success and virtue of the Germans rests on an implicit acceptance of the sacrificial distinction between good and bad violence. This explains their success *despite* being Christian because, even if they practise the rites of Christianity, they have absorbed the lessons of Roman rituals: the sacrificial distinction between good and bad violence. The example of the Germans gives us clues, therefore, to how Machiavelli understands the good kind of Christianity: it will be a Christianity that embraces the sacrificial distinction.

THE RECLUSE AND THE WANDERER

Place plays a paradoxical role in the work of Lacoste. On the one hand, place is a central category. To be human is precisely to be in a place. But on the other hand, liturgy is defined by the non-place. This is not to say that liturgy takes place in some nowhere but, rather, that liturgical actions reorder our relationship towards place such that the place itself is subordinated to what transcends it. Liturgy surpasses the world and, in so doing, creates a non-place. The church building is enclosed on all sides (unlike the proverbial Greek temple) precisely because in the liturgical actions one is supposed to take leave of the world rather than harmonize with it (EA 36). The transcending action of liturgy can only be understood, Lacoste thinks, on the basis of a prior confrontation with (Heidegger's understanding of) world and earth. The world and the earth occur as two distinct, but related, ways of thinking the reality of place. The world is articulated in *Being and Time*; the earth in the later works as part of the fourfold. Dasein in *Being and Time* was in a godless world; with the works of the 1950s the world becomes absorbed into the fourfold of earth, sky, gods, and mortals. The gods here are not transcendent but, as we noted in chapter 1, a sacred that is entirely immanent (EA 17–18). Now, Lacoste continues, we are well served to consider world and earth not as two mutually exclusive options, but as two points in a constantly oscillating dialectic rooted in the more fundamental "double secret of place" (EA 19). But what is this secret?

The secret of place is one of possibility: both being at home and not being at home are equally possible. There is no reason, Lacoste continues, to treat Unzuhause as more fundamental than Zuhaus. Both are equally possible and legitimate ways of relating to place. At times one will feel un-at-home in the world, at times one will dwell with the earth. This possibility is what "Heidegger failed to think" (EA 19). This understanding of place as the possibility of both world and earth leads Lacoste to the further point that neither is able to account for the dynamics of liturgy.

This also enables us to explain why liturgy is impossible for Machiavelli. The impossibility of thinking liturgically in Machiavelli is rooted in the impossibility of thinking of place. It is impossible to think place in Machiavelli because his account of nature entails that there is no earth, only world. That is to say, in Lacoste's understanding of the earth, it is a place of shelter and protection (EA 14); for Machiavelli, it is not the earth that shelters and protects but the city or, more accurately, the virtue of the prince. We do not dwell on the earth but, if we dwell at all, we do so in the city. In fact, the Machiavellian person – whether citizen or prince – never dwells; he always struggles and worries. There is the constant struggle against nature, against rivals, against internal factions and disorders. When these are overcome, he must plan for future problems (P XXIII). This vision entails that there can only be the world, a world we are thrown into and struggle against.

This denial of earth entails the impossibility of liturgy insofar as the possibility of liturgy is established on the basis of the discovery of the dialectic between earth and world made possible by the deeper reality of place. In denying the earth, this argumentative strategy is cut off: for Machiavelli, Unzuhaus is more fundamental. We can see this a bit more clearly if we look at the relationship of liturgy and the city or community. Lacoste points to two figures that he finds exemplify the non-placed nature of liturgical experience: the recluse and the wanderer. The recluse, in the manner of the desert fathers, hermits, and stylites, leaves the world behind as much as possible, retreating to his cell so as to subordinate everything to God (EA 27). The recluse, of course, is in a place, but it is a place that is a non-place; he wants to be nowhere. He strips his connection to specific places to the minimum – although Lacoste doesn't mention it, it is worth noting that many ceremonies concerned with one's final entry into cloistered monastic life involve a mock burial – so as to focus on the absolute. In a similar manner, the wanderer leaves behind his particular city to wander the world not so as to find other places, but so as to be in no particular place. In so doing the wanderer challenges the right of place to determine one's identity (EA 30). In both cases, the wanderer and the recluse refuse to be determined by one's place and, without ever overcoming it entirely, resist the rights of place. In so doing, they short circuit the dialectic of world and earth. Neither dwells in the earth, but nor does either live in a godless world; instead, they point towards a third way, neither world nor earth – non-place.

The development of the concept of non-place plays a central role in Lacoste's argument, and it, in turn, works by diving through the opening made in his analysis of world and earth. And, as we saw, it is precisely this analysis that Machiavelli would challenge by denying the existence of the earth of the fourfold. For Machiavelli there can be neither place nor non-place as Lacoste understands it; instead, one might write of worlds and cities, cities in world, created through the struggle against the world and preserved through the judicious use of good violence. One cannot dwell in the Machiavellian world or, rather, "dwelling" is a leisure (*ozio*) made possible by the virtues of a prince. This entails that for Machiavelli there can be no liturgy in Lacoste's sense. That is to say, there can be no relation with or experience of a world-transcending absolute because liturgy as vigil relies upon and presupposes the protection afforded by the prince and his modes and orders. Liturgical actions, as far as Machiavelli is concerned, are actions in a world and are exhausted by their worldly elements. In sum, because for Machiavelli we have only a world but not the earth, liturgy must be interpreted entirely in terms of its worldly elements, its visible elements, its rites.

MACHIAVELLI'S PROPHETS

This reduction of religion to its worldly aspects can be seen clearly in *The Prince*'s account of prophecy and the discussion of the relationship between religion and obedience in *The Art of War*. As we saw in *The Prince*, Machiavelli divides prophets into two types, the armed and the unarmed. The armed prophet, according to Machiavelli, is characterized by the ability to make people who no longer believe in you obey you (i.e., the ability to force obedience). Machiavelli includes only one canonical prophet, Moses, in his list of armed prophets, indicating that his understanding of prophecy departs from the traditional one (P VI). Interpreting this difference is difficult. Nathan Tarcov outlines what I take to be the two main possibilities. After noting the make-up of Machiavelli's list, Tarcov writes: "This finding could suggest that Moses was no different from the others and that he can be understood in purely secular terms, but it could also suggest that the others were prophets too, that God was 'no more friendly' to Moses than to them. According to the Bible, Cyrus was ordered by God to let the Jews return to Judea and rebuild the temple in Jerusalem."[29] Additionally, in a footnote accompanying the quoted passage, Tarcov points out ancient writers (Livy, Plutarch) who associate the other two founders with gods. However, nobody who accepts the biblical account as true could also accept the pagan accounts as true, except perhaps as some kind of metaphor or allegory. The only way all four figures can be taken as prophets without equivocation is to

29 Tarcov, "Belief and Opinion in Machiavelli," 575.

secularize prophecy, eliminating both biblical and pagan pieties. If we follow the biblical standard, then only Moses (and maybe Cyrus) counts as a prophet; if we follow the pagans, then only Romulus and Theseus are prophets (and maybe Cyrus) but certainly not Moses.

Biblically, the prophet reveals the truth to the people in the form of a message from God or the gods; the prophet announces a world-transcending truth; he represents the rupture of worldly immanence by announcing something that surpasses the world. Moreover, the biblical prophet typically announces that the favour of God has fallen on the weak, the victimized, the "stranger, widow and orphan." However, Machiavelli's prophets do not announce these things; they are creators, founders, of new modes and orders in the world. If God is no friendlier to Moses than to, for example, Theseus, it may be because they both use violence well in the founding of new modes and orders. Machiavelli comes close to identifying new modes and orders with new beliefs when he writes that the principle problem princes proposing them will face is "the incredulity of men, who do not truly believe new things" (P VI). The new modes and orders include new beliefs; a prince's regime cannot survive on force alone, but neither can it rely on beliefs alone. While force is prior, both are necessary in the long run.[30] This is why the new prince is a prophet. But these prophets do not reveal what God wants people to believe; instead, they persuade and force the people to believe what they – the princes – wants them to believe. According to Machiavelli: "From this arises that all the armed prophets conquered and the unarmed ones were ruined. For, besides the things that have been said, the natures of peoples is [*sic*] variable; and it is easy to persuade them of something but difficult to keep them in that persuasion. And thus, things must be ordered in such a mode that when they no longer believe, one can make them believe by force. Moses, Cyrus, Theseus and Romulus would not have been able to make their peoples observe their constitutions for long if they had been unarmed, as happened in our times to Brother Girolamo Savonarola" (P VI). A glance at one of his prophets, Romulus, will clarify Machiavelli's point. Romulus, the founder of Rome, is a prophet insofar as his founding activity included the ordering of Rome such that the martial virtues were encouraged. The encouragement of martial virtue included not merely laws but also beliefs about

30 There is an insightful discussion of this point in ibid., 577–8. There Tarcov argues quite strongly and persuasively for the mutual interdependence of force and belief in chapter 6 of *The Prince*. While the founders may begin with force, they nevertheless also rely on persuasion. The trick, so to speak, is to be in a position to use force to keep people persuaded when necessary.

what is fine and noble and that encourage those virtues. Moreover, these beliefs were, in turn, supported by the ability of Romulus to force obedience. In another context, Machiavelli points out that it is not enough to simply have good orders: one must make them be "observed with greatest severity" (AW VI.111). This severity, he continues, includes both harsh punishment and generous rewards for departing from or fulfilling the orders, respectively. Taken together, the mix of punishment and reward creates a situation in which the citizen both hopes and fears. This is part of the lesson Machiavelli would have us learn from his murder of Remus: Romulus had to have sole authority in ordering the city and could not countenance any rival (D I.9).

The armed prophet is characterized by the ability to force obedience when the people no longer believe in you. There is a very insightful discussion of this passage in *Machiavelli's Prince.* According to Benner's reading, the idea that one could force belief is simply ludicrous, and Machiavelli is only playing with the idea to explain the attitude of impatient and impetuous princes. The centerpiece of her argument is that belief can't be compelled – "the idea that physical arms can force belief sounds unrealistic as well as draconian" – although she later admits that one can control behaviour.[31] This is probably correct, and I suspect this is what Machiavelli was trying to get at with the caveat that by controlling behaviour one can, in the long term, control belief. What did Moses's modes and orders do if not first control behaviour and, by doing so, belief? One need not, however, appeal to Mosaic heights to see how compelling certain behaviour can, in turn, compel certain beliefs. I strongly disapprove of men wearing hats indoors. Why is this? The source of my disapproval, it seems to me, is the fact that during my formative school years, male students were forbidden from wearing headgear inside the school. This rule was enforced by the teachers and administrative staff with great rigour as they assigned detentions and Saturday-school for violations of the policy. From this I learned (a) to take my hat off upon entering the building and (b) to look with annoyance and disapproval at classmates who could not or would not manage such a simple task. Now, nearly twenty years later, the belief stays with me and I still take my hat off indoors, even though I no longer fear hearing from the vice-principal. If one takes the long view, the modes and orders of a Romulus or a Moses may be seen to have been able to control not only the behaviour of his contemporaries but also the beliefs of his descendants. It seems to me that something like this dynamic is at work both in Machiavelli's claim in

31 Benner, *Machiavelli's Prince*, 82.

book III of the *Discourses* that the education one receives as a child – including what is rewarded and punished, praised and blamed – is internalized and will regulate one's behaviour as an adult (D III.46) and in *The Prince*'s description of ecclesiastical principalities (P XI). One could plausibly argue, after all, that Israel is as much an ecclesiastical principality as any other. The unarmed prophet, such as Savonarola, on the other hand, lacks this ability to compel belief by controlling behaviour – instead, he or she is at the mercy of the members of the crowd, who only obey for as long as they believe the words and promises of the prophet. Because of this dependency on the goodwill of the populace, unarmed prophets always come to ruin (P VI). The unarmed prophet relies on fortune for his or her success, while the armed prophet relies mainly on virtue (P VI, compare with P I). In either case, if the prophet succeeds in introducing his new modes and orders, over time he or she will be held in veneration, and he or she may even seem natural, in the sense that the hereditary prince in chapter 2 of *The Prince* seems to be a natural prince.

ROMULUS AND FOUNDING VIOLENCE

Romulus's greatness, in Machiavelli's *Discourses*, is inseparable from his ability to compel obedience. The killing of Remus stands out, for Machiavelli, as the greatest example of this *virtù* and the lengths to which one must go to in order to obtain or exercise virtue. Curiously, it is this act more than any other Romulean act that he focuses upon as constituting the founding of Rome. In his discussion of the killing of Remus, the auguries mentioned by Livy are ignored; instead, Machiavelli uses it as an opportunity to discuss the importance of being alone, *un solo*, when founding or reorganizing a regime (D I.28). While Livy describes Romulus as attending to the rites of the gods prior to giving law to the Romans, Machiavelli focuses on Remus's death as *the* founding act. Killing Remus is a kind of sacrifice, an instance of good violence that produces order and stability in the community. While not a religious event per se, one also notes that the Romulean asylum – that is, Romulus's offer of protection to miscreants, criminals, and runaways if they would move to his city and live under his laws – does not figure much into Machiavelli's discussion. In contrast to this, the classical tradition saw the Romulean asylum as a fundamental event.[32] If sacrificial logic distinguishes good violence from bad violence by identifying victims towards

32 Livy, *Ab Urbe Condita*, I.8.4–7. For more on this, see the fascinating discussion in Bruggisser, "City of Outcasts." Bruggisser shows that early Christian writers, Augustine among them, read the Romulean Asylum as a shadowy prefiguring of the church's

whom bad violence can be safely directed, the Romulean asylum can be interpreted as anti-sacrificial: rather than expelling strangers and weirdoes from the community, it founds the city by welcoming them. Founding, according to Machiavelli, is a necessarily sacrificial act, and something like the Romulean Asylum has no role in it. Sacrifice is called for because – as we saw in the prior discussion of nature – it is not natural for human beings to live peacefully together. The religious elements of the founding of Rome by Romulus are systematically stripped from Machiavelli's retelling of it. They only reappear as something secondary, added by Numa, not at all essential to the virtue of the Romans, which is derived mainly from Romulus's good arms.

Machiavelli's discussion of the murder of Remus can be fruitfully contrasted with the work of René Girard. Like Machiavelli, Girard argues that founding always requires a murder. There is a Machiavellian tint to much of Girard's writings on foundations, but this tint – like all tinting – is superficial. It is worth taking some time to explain the difference between the Machiavellian and the Girardian conceptions of the founding murder. The most obvious difference has to do with the number of killers and their motivations. Girard's founding murder is always a collective murder. People, according to Girard, are naturally imitative, and, as we saw, this imitation gives rise to various crises the resolution of which takes the form of the violent lynching of a scapegoat, uniting the people in the mimetic desire to punish. Girard believes that the above dynamic, in its most general form, is found in all human situations. However, archaic communities differ from modern ones by the lack of something like a judicial system, the lack of a system of laws and restraints on both imitation and the violence to which can give rise (THSFW 12–13). The imitative struggle in archaic communities is therefore a much wider and potentially more destructive force. The contagion of desire is both the cause and the cure for this violent struggle: unlike the desire, for example, to possess something, the desire to hurt or punish someone can be shared collectively. We can all get a hit or kick in on the victim. When someone – typically an outsider or "weirdo" of some sort – is blamed for the conflict, the desire to punish him or her can also spread like a contagion and, in some cases, replace the initial conflict-causing desire for an object with the unifying desire to hurt this person. This person is the "scapegoat," and this scapegoating functions as a kind of catharsis that enables the remaining people to coalesce into a community. The inside,

gathering of people from all nations. To the extent that they read it this way, one could see why Machiavelli – if he was aware of this tradition – might want to downplay the importance of this moment in Roman history.

the community, is defined by the expulsion or murder of the scapegoat who, from the point of view of the insiders, deserved the punishment. Because of the cathartic and unifying effect of the scapegoating mechanism – now what is imitated is the desire to blame and punish this or that particular individual – the community will desire those effects again and again, imitating the original murder, ritualizing the initial scapegoating into a kind of ritual scapegoating (VS 269; THSFW 25). This ritual scapegoating precedes and makes possible religion and politics.

For Girard, then, the city is the child of religion, and religion is the child of collective violence (THSFW 32). With this formulation we can pin-point two areas where Machiavelli diverges from Girard. First, for Machiavelli, as we noted, religion is the child of the city or the prince. Religious beliefs are counted among those modes and orders that the new prince introduces. Second, while both Girard and Machiavelli point towards founding violence, the nature of this violence is different. Girard's is a mob violence, the collective murder of a scapegoat: "Only a group can found something, an individual never can" (BTTE 23). Machiavelli's founding violence is performed by "un solo," not the collective. It is not the product of rage or panic but of calculation: "This should be taken as a general rule: that it never or rarely happens that any republic or kingdom is ordered well from the beginning or reformed altogether from anew outside its old orders unless it is ordered by one individual. Indeed, it is necessary that one alone give the mode and that any ordering depend on his mind. So a prudent orderer of a republic, who has the intent not to help himself but the common good, not for his own succession but for the common fatherland, should contrive to have authority alone" (D I.9).

Machiavelli provides two examples to illustrate this rule: Romulus's murder of Remus and Cleomenes's murder of the Spartan ephors. In both cases, Machiavelli argues that the killers were acting correctly because they calculated that the bloodshed would enable them to order (or reorder) the fatherland in a better way.

Beyond noting the differences between Machiavelli and Girard on founding murders – differences we return to shortly – we should note that Machiavelli's approval of Romulus was something quite novel. It is probably not surprising that St Augustine disapproved of the murder of Remus and saw the story of Romulus and Remus as replaying the killing of Abel by Cain. Augustine notes that Cain, like Romulus, is the founder of a city.[33] But the ancient Romans themselves had qualms about

33 Augustine, *City of God*, XV.5

Romulus. Livy himself suggests that the killing was not justified, and Cicero is even harsher in his judgment.[34] Both the Augustinian and Ciceronian condemnations of Romulus turned on the idea that there are considerations higher than those of political expediency in play when contemplating such deeds. For Augustine, one must consider the laws of the city of God, for Cicero, the laws of nature, both of which would prohibit fratricide. And neither one believes, as do both Machiavelli and Girard, that murder is necessary for the formation of functioning communities. In the case of Cicero, community naturally flows from human nature; for Augustine, murder may be a prerequisite for the city of man, but not for the city of God. Machiavelli justifies the murder of Remus with many of the same themes used to justify Cesare Borgia's behaviour in the Romagna; Girard, for his part, interprets the tale of Romulus and Remus as an instance of the more general theme of mimetic rivals (VS 61) found throughout archaic history and literature.

Nevertheless, our discussion of Machiavelli's and Girard's respective takes on Romulus and Remus, founding murders in general, points towards a deeper divide between the two authors. For Girard the founding murder is the spontaneous act of a mob, while for Machiavelli it is the calculation of a prince. One could explain this difference by pointing to Girard's greater access to ethnological and anthropological researches, by saying, in short, that Machiavelli was mistaken. But that would be to let Machiavelli off the hook too easily: it suggests that his error (if it is indeed an error) was unavoidable given the information he had at hand. But against this, one can point out, as Girard does, that Livy offers two accounts of Remus's death. In the first account, Livy's Latin can be interpreted as suggesting that a crowd or mob (*ibi in turba ictus Remus cecidit*) killed Remus, not merely one man. The word *turba* suggests not merely a fight or disturbance, but one involving a number of people (SG 91–2). It is only in the second account, an account from which Livy distances himself, calling it a *vulgatior fama*, that Romulus kills Remus in a duel.[35] On the other hand, this sort of approach hides the deeper issues at work here. Machiavelli's focus on the calculation of the prince, as opposed to the violent spasms of the mob, point towards the largely unheralded rationalism of Machiavelli. By rationalism, I mean the belief that the basic structures of our lives are the result of planning or decisions rather than

34 Livy, *Ab Urbe Condita*, I.6.4; and Cicero, *On Duties*, III.41.
35 Livy, *Ab Urbe Condita*, I.7.2–3.

the upshot of unhappy accidents.[36] Even if the founding act is violent, it is a planned violence, a violence that institutes the modes and orders of the founder. These modes and orders, as we saw, include religious beliefs and practices. To provide a variation on a formulation used earlier, for Machiavelli religion is the child of the city, the city is the child of violence, and violence is the child of calculation. This, in turn, means that any and all of these are subject to revision as times and situations change our calculus and that there is, fundamentally, nothing hidden. Girard, on the other hand, offers a different ordering: the city is the child of religion, and religion is the child of a spasm of violence. Here, beyond the subordination of the city to religion, Girard points towards a kind of irrationalism. It is not calculation that founds states but panic and rage – scapegoating. This panic and rage, as we noted earlier, gets formalized into ritual practices that eventually give rise to the city and all that goes with it. The founding mob knows not what it does. There is a mystery, there is something hidden – the scapegoating violence that founded the city – that cannot be seen or understood within the city (THSFW 46–7; SG 11). The hiddenness of the scapegoating mechanism means, for Girard, that one rarely understands the city in which one lives.

NUMA'S NYMPH AND ROMULUS'S CORPSE

According to Roman traditions, a nymph revealed the proper religious rites for the Romans to Numa. However, Livy is incredulous, writing that Numa only pretended (*simulat*) to meet with the goddess while in fact he created the rites of his own accord; a point repeated by Machiavelli.[37] Machiavelli's praise of the politically salutary effects of religion, which has been pointed to by numerous recent commentators, is best read in the context of Machiavelli's view that, although Numa told the Roman people his rites were revealed to him by a goddess, he knew that they were made up. Recall that Machiavelli thinks that princes should maintain

36 Speaking of this kind of rationalism, René Girard writes: "Our rationalist bent … leads to an innocence of outlook that refuses to concede to collective violence anything more than a limited and fleeting influence, a 'cathartic' action, similar, in its most extreme forms, to the catharsis of the sacrificial ritual" (VS, 81). This kind of rationalism works by treating only private or organized acts of violence as productive, while collective acts of violence are treated as destructive (at worst) or temporary catharsis (at best). Against this, Girard's anti-rationalism contends that it is precisely in the unplanned and spasmodic violence of the collective, in particular in its attack on the surrogate victim, that violence is productive. We see later that this "rationalism" is present not merely in the thought of Machiavelli but also in that of Heidegger and Derrida.

37 See Livy, *Ab Urbe Condita*, I.19.5; and Machiavelli's D I.11 for some examples.

rites even when he believes they are false (D.12). Prophecy is understood primarily in terms of *inventio* rather than revelation; the prophet does not believe the modes and orders he persuades or forces his people to believe. There are good reasons for believing that, for Machiavelli, this applies to revealed – Judeo-Christian – religion as much as it does to Roman religion.[38] This is mirrored in Machiavelli's two subcategories of prophet: the armed and the unarmed. Romulus is described by Machiavelli as an armed prophet, and Numa fits his description of an unarmed prophet and is compared with his unarmed prophet par excellence, Savonarola (D. I.11). This point can be expanded upon with a reference to Machiavelli's discussion of the two in his *Discourses on Livy*. There he points out that Numa was forced to depend upon religion because of his lack of *virtù*. Romulus organized Rome without recourse to religion because his strength was enough; Numa, on the other hand, needed religion so that fear of heaven could supplement the lacking fear of Numa. Moreover, Romulus is the condition for the possibility of Numa: his organization of Roman religion presupposed the prior organization of Rome by Romulus in that Numa's "arts of peace" coasted off the momentum given to Roman life by Romulus's arts of war (D I.19). The difference between Romulus and Numa, or the armed and unarmed prophet more generally, lies not in the nature or source of their message, but in their ability to project force and to demand acceptance of the truths they have made. So, prophecy is not what traditional theology thinks it is but, rather, the imposition of new modes and orders. The Machiavellian prophet speaks neither to God nor for God but to human beings. The new prince is a prophet insofar as he is one who creates new modes and orders. The new prince imagines a republic or principality and forces the people to believe in it, even as he refrains from doing so.

The transition from Romulus to Numa is precipitated, in Livy, by the mysterious death of Romulus. It is striking that, in his discussion of that transition in his *Discourses on Livy*, Machiavelli does not address this strange death. Let us turn to Livy to see what Machiavelli leaves out:

> When these deathless deeds had been done, as the king was holding a muster in the Campus Martius, near the swamp of Capra, for the purpose of reviewing the army, suddenly a storm came up with loud claps of thunder, and enveloped him

38 See the discussion in Fontana, "Love of Country and Love of God," 647: "Machiavelli's subversion of pagan religion reveals itself as a veiled attempt to subvert revealed religion, whether Judaic, Islamic or Christian. Indeed, by unveiling the methods used by the founders of pagan religion Machiavelli is simultaneously uncovering the natural and human foundations of revealed religion."

> in a cloud so thick as to hide him from the sight of the assembly; and from that moment Romulus was no more on earth. The Roman soldiers at length recovered from their panic, when this hour of wild confusion had been succeeded by sunny calm; but when they saw the royal seat was empty, although they readily believed the assertion of the senators, who had been standing next to Romulus, that he had been caught up on high in the blast, they nevertheless remained for some time sorrowful and silent, as if filled with fear of orphanhood. Then when a few men had taken the initiative, they all with one accord hailed Romulus as a god and a god's son, the King and Father of the Roman City, and with prayers besought his favor that he would be graciously pleased forever to protect his children. There were some, I believe, even then who secretly asserted that the king had been rent to pieces by the hands of the senators, but in very obscure terms; the other version obtained currency, owing to men's admiration for the hero and the intensity of their panic.[39]

It seems clear, from Livy's telling, that the members of the Senate, for whatever reason, saw the sudden darkness as a chance to kill Romulus, and then, to cover up their crime, they claimed that he was a god ascended to heaven. The bloody senators' appeal to the piety of the soldiers to hide their regicide. Why doesn't Machiavelli talk about this? It seems, after all, a supremely "Machiavellian" moment. Upon closer inspection, this event runs counter to Machiavelli's thought. First, the murder of Romulus by the senators is precisely the kind of thing that is not supposed to happen to good and virtuous founders in the Machiavellian scheme.[40] Indeed, reading Machiavelli one gets the impression that Romulus died in his sleep – the strange cause of his death is never addressed in his major writing. While Machiavelli does discourse at length on how to kill kings, emperors, and tyrants, this is usually in the context of conspiracies or assassinations, not a mob beating someone to death. It is not that Machiavelli is unaware of the violence of mobs – the *Florentine Histories* is replete with tales of riots and lynching – but that he is against them and wants to discourage them as much as possible. One cause of the superiority of ancient Rome to Florence, according to Machiavelli, is that the former was able to solve problems between the estates in the city by introducing new orders rather than rioting and lynching (D I.4 and

39 Livy, *Ab Urbe Condita*, I.16.1–5.

40 This is one reason Benner suggests that Machiavelli isn't as enamoured of Romulus as most readers take him to be (*Machiavelli's Prince*, 78) and, in fact, doesn't actually think it would be a good idea to imitate Romulus. I suspect that the resolution of the issues is that she is quite correct to say that Machiavelli does not want anyone to imitate the historic-Romulus, but he does recommend imitation of Romulus as redacted in his texts.

I.8). The argument for the superiority of Roman orders requires the downplaying of precisely those kinds of events, so the vulgatior fama is preferred in the account of Romulus and Remus, and Romulus's death is never discussed. This takes us to Machiavelli's second reason for ignoring the death of Romulus: the senate covers up its regicide with an appeal to religion. But in Machiavelli's version of ancient Rome this is impossible. This is because, in his telling, Romulean Rome was largely irreligious, religion only being imported by Numa: "One sees that for Romulus to order the Senate and to make other civil and military orders, the authority of God was not necessary" (D I.11). But this does not mean that Machiavelli thinks that religion is unimportant, only that it is not omnipresent. In any case, if Machiavelli was to dwell on the apotheosis of Romulus, it would ruin the chronology of his founding narrative: first Romulean politics and then Numean religion.

Finally, the third reason Machiavelli avoids talking about Romulus's death, in Livy's telling, is that the divinization of Romulus occurs after his murder by the senators. Machiavelli's victims – in contrast to the victims of archaic lynching – never become sacred; they are nearly immediately forgotten. If Girard is correct, the archaic understanding of the sacred is inseparable from the murder victim: the scapegoat is taken as both cause and cure of the communities' problems and, insofar as that is the case, is perceived to be a being of great, although ambiguous, power. One thinks here of Oedipus, who is blamed for bringing a plague to Thebes and is later seen as a god-like source of blessings. According to Girard, Christianity undermines this process by asserting (with reference to the death of Christ) the innocence of the victim and removing that ambiguous power once attributed to him or her. In Christian education, the victim is not the cause of the problems, and therefore killing him or her is not the cure. Recall Augustine's argument that even a victorious prosecution of a just war will not solve our problems. In this much, at least, Machiavelli remains a kind of Christian: his victims never become gods. But he also remains pagan insofar as the victims have it coming: the violence directed against them is good, fertile, and productive violence. Neither raised to the altars as gods nor exonerated as innocents, Machiavelli's victims are simply buried and forgotten.

THE CHICKEN MEN

Machiavelli points out in his *Discourses on Livy* that Numa's ways of peace are inseparable from, indeed founded upon, the work of Romulus. Indeed, although Machiavelli will praise the Romans for their use of religion, this praise is not praise of piety per se, but of the clever political use of the piety of others. When he first broaches the topic, Machiavelli remarks that the religion founded by Numa served to "make easier whatever enterprise the Senate or the great men of Rome might plan to make" (D I.11). So religion may profitably be used to arouse an army or keep order in the city. But one should note here that this is a political religion whose aims and goals are derived not from the will of the gods but from the will of the political leadership:

> Among the other auspices they had in their armies certain orders of augers whom they called chicken-men; and whenever they were ordered to do battle with the enemy, they wished the chicken-men to take their auspices. If the chickens ate, they engaged in combat with a good augury, if they did not eat, they abstained from the fight. Nonetheless, when reason showed them a thing they ought to do – notwithstanding that the auspices had been adverse – they did it in any mode. But they turned it around with means and modes so aptly that it did not appear that they had done it with disdain for religion. (D. I.14)

When discussing the sacred chickens again in book III of the *Discourses*, Machiavelli hastens to add that "virtue must accompany these things [auguries and auspices]; otherwise they have no value" (D III.33). Religion is something created by and for the senate and people of Rome; or, as John Najemy puts it, it is "a human and historical phenomenon."[41] There is neither theological nor philosophical justification for accepting or rejecting religious doctrines; instead, such decisions are based on the utility that they represent, subordinating heaven to the earth, the invisible to the visible. The integrity of the rites is respected but subject to varying interpretations as the situation requires. Religion, one might say, boils down to its rites and the interpretation of those rites.

This returns us to *The Art of War*, the sixth book of which is ostensibly about how to order a military camp. Arguably, however, it is about more than this since the camp is described as a kind of city, a "mobile city" (AW VI.84). In this context, the problem of obedience comes up in a special way: soldiers are, after all, armed. The discussion of the armed prophet and the unarmed prophet in *The Prince* seems to operate on the

41 Najemy, "Papirius and the Chicken-Men," 665. Particularly pertinent for the theme of this book is Najemy' s discussion of the issue as it appears in the context of Machiavelli's discussion of the eternity of the world: "He [Machiavelli] puts change of religion (*le variazioni delle sètte*), along with changes of language in the first category of the causes of obliteration of historical memory that come from mankind ... Here, for Machiavelli, religion is fundamental to culture and civilization: certainly no mere pack of lies but not exactly a unique revelation of divine will either" (666).

assumption that the people at large are unarmed – they are cowed by the arms of the prince, and the downfall of the unarmed prophet comes when the people cease to listen to him, not when they take up arms against him. In short, *The Prince* largely seems to assume that all violence, good or bad, comes from the prince. Of course, in a military context, the people are armed. And, as the rest of *The Art of War* makes clear, Machiavelli thinks that the paradigm of the citizen-soldier is a good one – that is, that that people at large should be armed and, thereby, capable of fairly violent acts. So how then can one get armed people, who outnumber the prince, to obey? In *The Prince*, Machiavelli says that arming the people turns them into the prince's friends (P XX), but he also reminds us that we cannot count on the love of our friends to support us in all difficulties (P XIX). Friendship needs to be supplemented by fear. But what kind of fear can hold the fickle nature of humankind in check? Certainly not fear of the prince whom the armed people outnumber and outgun. We need fear of something else. In *The Art of War* Machiavelli writes: "And because to check armed men neither fear of the laws nor that of men is enough, the ancients added the authority of God. And therefore with very great ceremony they made their soldiers swear to the observance of military discipline, so that if they acted against it, they not only had to fear the laws and men, but God. And they used every industry to rule them with religion." (AW VI.125–6). There are three points to make about this passage. First, religion is an appendix to the authority of the laws and of men. It is not the original authority but, rather, something added as a firewall to stand firm if fear of laws and man decay. Second, we find an emphasis on ceremony, on the rites performed, rather than on the content of the religion. What is important in religion is the ceremony, not the theology. This reinforces the points made earlier in this regard. Finally, we see that religion is used to rule. The point of religious ceremonies is, in the final analysis, to rule men who are armed by instilling them with fear of God – with fear, one might suggest, of a supremely powerful armed prophet – even in the absence of fear of laws or other men. This ruling takes the form of the sacrificial distinction between good and bad violence and the direction of good violence outside the community – towards its victims and enemies – and the prohibition of bad violence within the community. We should keep in mind his discourse on the relationship between fear and love in *The Prince*, where we see that fear creates a more stable bond between subject and prince than does love to the extent that the latter "is held by a chain of obligation, which, because men are wicked, is broken at every opportunity for their own utility, but fear is held by dread of punishment that never forsakes you" (P XVII). Fear of God, presumably, functions in the same way.

This fear enables the commanders to rule their army without ruling them, keep their states without defending them, and govern their subjects without governing them (P XI).

THE PATRIOT GAME

With the foregoing in mind, let us return to Numa so that we can further refine our understanding of religion according to Machiavelli. But to set the stage for Machiavelli's discussion, I first look in more detail at what Titus Livy himself has to say about Numa. As was already mentioned, Livy credits Numa with establishing numerous Roman religious rites and priesthoods; this made him the "second founder of Rome."[42] It is the religion of Numa that, to a certain extent, tamed the warlike spirit of the early Romans with the admixture of *pietas*: "Fearing that without external dangers and cares which fear of enemies and military discipline provide, luxuriant idleness might occupy their souls, he reckoned the thing to lead the multitudes and efficiently civilize the rude was to fill them with fear of the gods."[43] According to Livy, the primary goal of Numa's religion is to preserve the people in their virtue during those times – rare in the history of Rome – when there is nobody to fight.[44] In this case, Numa's religion is invented for purely political or social reasons: as a preservative of virtue. Civic virtue, in Livy's telling of the history of Rome, requires *metus hostillis*, the fear of the enemy, to buttress the modes and orders of the founders. The brilliance of Numa, in Livy's telling, is that he realized that fear of the gods can substitute for the fear of enemies. The people should fear something, either an external enemy or vengeful and powerful gods.[45] Numa's religion was designed to mould the imaginations of the Romans in such a way that, even in the absence of enemies, civic virtues are preserved. Numa gives his Romans imagined republics and princes to keep them in line. In all this, Livy seems perfectly Machiavellian.

However, the above needs to be supplemented since as it stands it is not an entirely accurate description of Livy's account because it suggests that there was no religion in Rome prior to the ascension of Numa to the throne. As noted earlier, this is not the case: although Numa codified, organized, and encouraged Roman religion, Livy *never* suggests that Rome was irreligious prior to Numa. Instead, we find various occasions in

42 See Livy, *Ab Urbe Condita*, I.18.1–I.21.6

43 Ibid., I.19.4–5.

44 Ibid., I.19.3.

45 Ibid., I.19.4–5.

his account of the reign of Romulus and the foundation of Rome where religious beliefs and practices are present. For example, Romulus and Remus consult auguries when initially building the city; the Sabines are invited to Rome as a part of a religious festival; and when Romulus dies the senate claims he had ascended to the gods.[46] Perhaps most important, Livy tells us that it was only *after* attending to the worship of the gods that Romulus gathered the multitude (*multitudine*) to give them his laws: "When Romulus had duly attended to the worship of the gods, he called the people together and gave them rules of law, since nothing else but law could unite them into one body (*unius corpus*)."[47] In fact, this passage comes after a long description of the mythic origins of Romulus's rites. Note the sequence: first Romulus worships, then he gives laws, and then finally these laws unite the people. Livy emphasizes this sequence because it is this law giving – not killing Remus – that truly united this multitude into one body. When Numa is first crowned by the Romans, he hearkens back to Romulus's founding of the city and requires that, just as Romulus wove auguries and rites into the founding of Rome, so they should also be woven into his coronation.[48] Roman religion cannot be said to begin simply with the advent of Numa; rather, Livy tells us that the very foundation of Rome was, at least in part, religious. To be sure, Numa's reign was characterized by a devotion to religious matters that outstripped that of Romulus, but it goes too far to suggest that the founding of Rome was an entirely secular affair in Livy's account.

However, this is precisely what Machiavelli's discussion of Romulus and Numa in the *Discourses* suggests. As we noted, Machiavelli presents the Rome of Romulus as devoted to military affairs entirely and that of Numa as devoted to religion. Rome, prior to Numa, is secular. This opens up an important theme for Machiavelli as he wonders who is more deserving of praise: his Romulus, who ignores religion to focus on the development of martial virtue, or his Numa, who introduces religion to the Romans (D. I.11). While at first seeming to suggest that Numa is more deserving of praise, Machiavelli concludes by arguing that Romulus is superior insofar as his martial virtue can stand without religion, but Numa would not have been able to introduce religion without the foundations laid by the strength of Romulus. In *Discourses* I.11, Machiavelli seems to argue that Numa's religion is more fundamental in that it introduced good orders into the city and that, where there are good orders, one can easily introduce good arms. However, in *Discourses* I.19 he takes

46 Ibid., I.6.4; I.7.2–3; I.9.6-8; I.16.1–8.
47 Ibid., I.8.3.
48 Ibid., I.18.6–10.

this back, saying that Numa's Rome was precarious and under the sway of fortune. Elsewhere he asserts that good arms are the foundation of good laws (P XII). Romulus's Rome, in contrast to Numa's, was more reliant on its own virtue. Numa relied on the virtue of Romulus rather than on his own arms: it was the strength of Romulus's rule that allowed Numa to cultivate religion and peace. If Tullus, the third king, was not closer to Romulus than to Numa, Machiavelli continues, Rome would have been crushed by her neighbours (D I.11 and I.19).

Machiavelli's (a) emphasis on Numa's dependency on the prior accomplishments of Romulus and (b) secularized retelling of the founding of Rome by Romulus confirms my claim that religion, for Machiavelli, is a secondary phenomenon: what is primary is the *virtù* of Romulus, his ability to use good violence. The eternal world is primarily the world of Romulus; the morality and theology espoused by various religions only exists in the space carved out by people like Romulus. They are modes and orders introduced by the prince, not realities discovered by the prince. The importance of Machiavelli's account of Romulus and Numa can be seen by contrasting it with the Augustinian claim that human beings naturally seek God: "inquietum est cor nostrum, donec requiescat in te."[49] Machiavelli's account of the origin of religion denies this: people do not naturally seek God; instead, God is introduced only after the primary political problem of ordering our lives together has been solved. Indeed, religion is a product of the modes and orders introduced by the prince rather than vice versa: he who would act politically must love his city more than his soul. This famous phrase (which Machiavelli uses in his account of the War of the Eight Saints at FH III.7 and adopts for himself in his letter to Francisco Vettori of April 1527 [L #225]) as well as the juxtaposition of Romulus and Numa in the *Discourses* can be elucidated with reference to two important points Machiavelli makes in *The Prince*: first, that all those who rely on belief as a opposed to force (i.e., unarmed prophets) come to ruin and, second, that good laws presuppose good arms (P VI and XII). The two claims summarize the view contained in his account of Numa: the priority of good arms to good laws signifies the priority of force to morality and reason; the weakness of the unarmed prophet is the weakness of Numa.

Although Numa did not come to ruin, as we saw earlier, he would have been ruined if he had not had the reputation of Romulus to protect him; one may recall here Cosimo Medici's assertion in Machiavelli's *Florentine*

49 Augustine, *Confessions*, I.1.1.

Histories that one does not hold power (*stato*) with *pater nosters* (FH VII.6). This reading is compounded by a crucial text from the *Discourses*:

> Lucius Lentulus, the Roman legate, said that it did not appear to him that any policy whatever for saving the fatherland was to be avoided … the fatherland is well defended in whatever mode one defends it, whether with ignominy or with glory … That advice deserves to be noted and observed by any citizen who finds himself counseling his fatherland, for where one deliberates entirely on the safety of his fatherland, there ought not to enter any consideration of either just or unjust, merciful or cruel, praiseworthy or ignominious; indeed every other concern put aside, one ought to follow entirely the policy that saves its life and maintains its liberty. (D III.41)

The fatherland is so important that no other consideration should limit what one is willing to do to save it. The fatherland is the one thing that matters; it is, in a sense, a god deserving of all our labours, work, and care. We do not limit our deliberation by references to norms derived from imagined republics but, instead, focus our attention entirely and completely on what must be done to protect our visible *patria*. We do this, in part, because, for Machiavelli, this *patria* is our only *patria*; the Machiavellian is not a wayfaring stranger or pilgrim in this world, building up his treasures in Heaven and journeying towards the eternal Jerusalem of the City of God. No: the Machiavellian's treasure and heart lie in his visible *patria* in the eternal world. He must defend it, therefore, at all costs for the *patria* is the entirety of his possession, his world, and his life. This is why he must love it more than his soul: the *patria* functions as a kind of highest good. Any violence that defends the *patria* is good violence. The patriotism that Viroli rightly recognizes in Machiavelli is a function of the apotheosis of the *patria*. But while Viroli sees Machiavellian patriotism as a net positive, the Irish writer Dominic Behan reminds us (in his song "The Patriot Game") that "the love one's country is a terrible thing." Why? As the song continues we find that it is precisely this patriotism that sends O'Hanlon (the song's narrator) to kill policemen, deserters, and traitors. O'Hanlon has no mercy for the quislings that sell out the *patria*! He is sure that his violence is a good violence. The apotheosis of the *patria* entails the embrace of sacrifice.

6

The End of the World

IN CHAPTER 56 OF BOOK I OF HIS *Discourses on Livy*, Machiavelli turns to the subject of auguries and similar signs. The tone here is largely sceptical: Machiavelli admits that great signs, such as lightning strikes, voices, and the like, often appear prior to great events but that "whence it arises I do not know" (D I.56). Later in this same section he ventures to speculate a bit more:

> The cause of this I believe to be discoursed of and interpreted by a man who has knowledge of things natural and supernatural, which we do not have. Yet it could be, as some philosophers would have it, that since this air is full of intelligences that foresee future things by their natural virtues, and they have compassion for men, they warn them with like signs so that they can prepare themselves for defense. Yet however this may be, one sees it thus to be the truth, and that always after such accidents extraordinary and new things supervene in provinces. (D I.56)

This passage should be unpacked sentence by sentence. In the first sentence he says that if a man had knowledge of natural and supernatural things – a knowledge that we don't have – then he would know the causes of these events. The events themselves are visible, but the causes of the events are invisible. Machiavelli's scepticism applies only to our knowledge of the invisible causes of these visible events. In the next sentence he refers to the position of "some philosopher." Mansfield finds it noteworthy that Machiavelli refers specifically to a philosopher rather than to a prophet or an ecclesiastic, suggesting that the entire chapter is a critical response to certain aspects of Savonarola's preaching.[1] But it is equally important that Machiavelli refrains from endorsing the

1 Mansfield, *New Modes and Orders*, 165.

philosopher's opinion: he merely admits it as a possibility. After all, in the first sentence, he disclaims having any kind of knowledge of these things; hence he has no grounds for either accepting or excluding that possibility. The entertainment of the philosophical thesis in sentence two is conditioned by the affirmation of the sceptical thesis in sentence one. The philosophical or even theological interpretation of the causes of these events is reduced to mere guesswork. Finally, in the third sentence, Machiavelli tells us that the entire debate about causes is irrelevant because the important point is just that these things *do happen*, not the causes of these events.

Machiavelli does not care where the voices come from. He is aware that people perform auguries and that people believe them, but he knows not what to make of them beyond that. His dismissal of all questions regarding the source of the voices is more important than one might initially suspect. These voices subtly suggest that the visible world might not be eternal, that entities transcending the world may exist and may in fact interact with us to some small degree. If one investigates too closely the causes of these voices one may find oneself speculating about "imagined republics." His agnostic statements regarding the voices no doubt emerge from the same source as does his affirmation of the eternity of the world (i.e., the desire to do away with the transcendent) but it testifies to the possibility that there is something that transcends the world. Machiavelli shuts down this possible interpretation by emphasizing that the only thing that really matters is how the voices operate in *this* world. By a sleight of hand rather than force of argument, he manages to focus our attention less on the possibly world-transcending source of voices than on the management of the voices in this world. For Machiavelli, the important thing is that the prince learns how to manage these auguries correctly; the augury is reduced to the effectual truth. Whatever aspects of the augury there may be beyond the world we cannot and should not speak of. Indeed, we are prohibited from speaking of the augury in itself: we can only speak of the way we relate to it. Similarly, when he discusses Savonarola earlier in the *Discourses*, he remarks that he doesn't know whether or not Savonarola actually spoke with God. But he does know that the people of Florence believed that he did and that this belief enabled him to do a great many things (D I.11). What might normally be taken as the crucial question – did he or did he not converse with God? – is pushed to the side as less important than the political benefits that can be accrued.

The parallels with both Heidegger's argument that theology as a speculative science of God (i.e., of the cause of auguries) is impossible and his argument that the one describing Dasein's being-towards-God (the effect of auguries in this world) is possible and desirable surely announce themselves here, and I won't belabour the point. One might be justified in thinking that these parallels are merely superficial and that focusing on them masks a more general difference of tones, concerns, and whatnot between the two such that these purported parallels are merely accidental and of no real importance. This would be mistaken: while there is a gap between Machiavelli and Heidegger, we can only properly understand it by first understanding the deeper agreements between the two.

THESEUS VERSUS HEIDEGGER

We can get at the deepest point of agreement between Heidegger and Machiavelli by returning to the 1930s and looking at Heidegger's 1935 text, *Introduction to Metaphysics.* After we have understood the deep agreements, we will be able to appreciate their equally important divergences. At a key point in his text, Heidegger turns to Heraclitus and Parmenides for an understanding of the archaic Greek *logos.* We learn, in his analysis, that the logos is intimately related to rank and hierarchy, the strong can gain access to it and the weak cannot: "Because Being is *logos, Harmonia, aletheia, phusis, phainesthai* (*logos,* harmony, unconcealment, *phusis,* self-showing), it shows itself in a way that is anything but arbitrary. The true is not for everyone, but only for the strong" (IM 142). This position is compounded in his discussion of Parmenides and *Antigone,* where Heidegger argues that the logos is intimately connected with the doing of violence:

> Being-human, according to its historical, history-opening essence, is *logos,* the gathering and apprehending of the Being of beings: the happening of what is most uncanny, in which, through doing violence, the overwhelming comes to appearance and is brought to stand. (IM 182)

The connection between logos and violence is the reason that the truth is only for the strong. In the face of an undifferentiated scattering, one must be strong enough to force being to be gathered in this or that way. This point builds on an earlier section of the text, in which Heidegger claims that the world of the Greeks was the product of the struggle (*Kampf*) of statesmen, artists, and writers to wrest being apart from seeming (IM 116). Commenting on these and related passages, Hans Sluga writes: "Violence is, for Heidegger, man's basic trait insofar as he uses force against what is overwhelming."[2] The violence of man, for Heidegger,

2 Sluga, "Conflict Is the Father of All Things," 211.

consists primarily in his struggle against the seeming (IM 161–2), which is to say, in the aforementioned founding struggles of statesmen, artists, and writers. This founding violence, Sluga cautions, is not to be understood as mere brutality but, rather, as creative, giving birth to the *polis,* to culture, to Greece. Paradoxically, Heidegger suggests that these founders are *apolis*: precisely insofar as they violently found the city, they are not limited by the laws of the city. So, Heidegger writes:

> Rising high in the site of history, they also become *apolis,* without city and site, lonesome, un-canny, with no way out amidst beings as a whole, and at the same time without ordinance and limit, without structure and fittingness [*Fug*], because they as creators must first ground all this in each case. (IM 163)

Later, Heidegger tells us that, when decadence has set in and the vibrancy of the founding has faded, other violent men will be needed to return the polis, by force, to the moment of founding.[3] We are only a hop, skip, and a jump from *The Prince* and the *Discourses.* Lest I be misunderstood, let me make clear that I am not claiming that every aspect of Heidegger's *Introduction to Metaphysics* finds an analogue in Machiavelli or vice versa. That would almost certainly be wrong. But I am claiming that both agree in seeing founding as dependent upon the violent acts of a few gifted individuals. Likewise, the forceful revivification of the city in the face of decadence by a few violent men mirrors exactly the recommendation for reform in a corrupt city recommended in the *Discourses* and discussed by us in an earlier chapter.

However, it is precisely at this point, the point at which the German metaphysician and the Italian diplomat seem to agree on fundamentals, that we discover the deeper chasm separating the two from each other. Heidegger's uncanny violence is quite different from the bloodletting of Machiavelli. There will be the temptation to conclude that Heidegger offers us deep ontological structures while Machiavelli stops with a fairly superficial ontic analysis. According to this temptation, Heideggerian violence is reflective of the violence of being, a deeper or more primordial and ultimately more important violence that Machiavelli fails to

3 C. Bambach, commenting on Heidegger's discussion of *Antigone* in IM, writes: "Genuine political order demands a daring violence-initiating act by a founder – either a state founder or an artist or a poet or a thinker who can lead [*führen*] the *Volk,* who might dare to become a leader [*Führer*] through the intro-duction [*Ein-führung*] into the metaphysical truths of the *dike/techne* conflict." See Bambach, *Heidegger's Roots,* 152. With the exception of the last part about metaphysical truths, Heidegger is in agreement with Machiavelli. I address their metaphysical differences shortly.

think. After all, Heidegger tells us clearly that his violence is meant in "an essential sense" and that this is a far cry from brutality and arbitrary cruelty. Heidegger's essential violence, in marked contrast to Machiavelli's founding violence, is primarily directed towards the "overwhelming" rather than towards people (IM 160). Indeed, the violence of poetry, thinking, and building does not kill or destroy but, rather, discloses, allowing human beings to enter into being; the peculiarly human form of violence is *techne*, "the knowing struggle to set Being, which was formerly closed off, into what appears as being" (IM 170–1). All this seems worlds away from the bloody daggers of Machiavelli's founding violence, and his account of violence seems shallow compared to Heidegger's account of essential violence. This conclusion is certainly plausible (it is probably the one that Heidegger would suggest), but it requires that one be a Heideggerian – that is, that one believe that the deeper violence of being is real and that Heidegger gets at those deeper structures. We can find the strength to resist this temptation if we avoid presupposing the correctness of Heidegger's account of being. If we succeed, we will see that Heidegger – despite his reputation to the contrary – is not as deep a thinker as is Machiavelli. Heidegger's interest in deep ontological structures prevents him from noticing what Machiavelli discovers. In fact, Heidegger stops short: his analysis recognizes a few aspects of founding violence but misses the most crucial parts. Heidegger's essential violence is mainly a metaphysical or ontological violence rather than an ontic violence: the techniques of founding, the speeches and fights, the dead bodies and blood-stained weapons are never discussed. Machiavelli is aware of the extent to which essential violence orders and discloses being: this is part of what he means when he says that founders are prophets introducing new modes and orders. But he is also aware that one must force the people to accept these new modes and orders, that good arms precede good laws or, in other words, that the founding of the polis always involves coercion. In Heidegger the struggle to found the city is spiritualized or ontologized into a struggle with being rather than with beings, with other people, and with nature. Indeed, Heidegger's founders are primarily artists and thinkers; even his statesmen seem like theoreticians rather than princes.

What Machiavelli sees and Heidegger misses is that new modes and orders are not introduced in the lecture halls of philosophers and the theatre of poets. The founding of the city precedes and makes possible the theatre in which *Antigone* is performed. As Machiavelli puts it in the *Florentine Histories*, "letters come after arms and … captains arise before philosophers" (FH V.I). Heidegger only thinks the latter half of founding, the introduction of new modes and orders, forgetting the ontic violence that is prior to and necessary for the introduction of new modes and orders: "all the armed prophets conquered and the unarmed ones were ruined" (P VI). He is distracted and dazzled by great art and great books, focusing his attentions on the content of the modes and orders introduced by poets, thinkers, and statesman, and missing the ontic violence that introduces and enforces those modes and orders. So, while Heidegger correctly recognizes the relationship between the Greek *logos* and founding violence he thinks only one part of that founding violence, oblivious to the corpses piled at the founder's feet. His focus on Heraclitus and Parmenides leads him to neglect Lycurgus and Theseus. It is not that Heidegger makes an error in his ontology, it is that his error *is* ontology. From a Machiavellian perspective, Heidegger's account of the origin of the city flounders precisely because he looks for some metaphysical source that the founders manage to harness rather than studying how the act of founding itself manufactures metaphysics. At the last moment, he is distracted by something that has never been seen or touched, an imaginary republic, being.

In short, Heidegger's ontological approach comes very close to the insights of Machiavelli but ultimately fails and obfuscates the actual ontic murders and beatings that made the Greek world possible. He reads the violence required in founding primarily as a kind of metaphysical struggle with the overwhelming rather than as a struggle with, or against, others. Heidegger's account of founding violence only accounts for the founding acts of unarmed prophets (who always come to ruin), forgetting the more fundamental lesson of the armed prophets: to disclose, to introduce new modes and orders, requires virtue, requires that one be able to force others to believe and obey. This applies not only to the account in the 1930s but even more so to "Building, Dwelling, Thinking" and other more bucolic texts from the 1950s. We noted earlier that Heidegger describes a bridge built over the stream. The bridge creates a path from rural farm to city market, leading ultimately to a castle (BDT 354). But he neglects the man in the castle who presumably ordered the bridges and roads to be built in the first place, who employed sheriffs to clear away highwaymen, ensuring that Heidegger's peasants could tarry and linger in safety. This returns us to chapter 21 of *The Prince*: the ability of Heidegger's peasants to follow "their pursuits quietly, in trade and in agriculture and in every other pursuit of men" presupposes the security provided by the prince's sacrificial violence (P XXI).

VIOLENCE AND THE LOGOS

If we criticize Heidegger for not being Machiavellian enough this should not distract us from the equally important point that he is very Machiavellian: his linking of founding with fertile violence walks the path blazed by Machiavelli. Moreover, even as Heidegger's ontological preoccupations prevent him from fully digesting the violence of founding, that same preoccupation enables him to give a richer account of the way the founder's new modes and orders disclose the world. Because of this, his discussion of logos in *Introduction to Metaphysics* can help us better understand what Machiavelli implies but leaves unspoken. In the beginning of his discussion of Heraclitus in *Introduction to Metaphysics*, Heidegger laments that the Greek thinker has been subjected to innumerable "un-Greek" misinterpretations. The root of these errors, it turns out, is the conflation of the Heraclitean logos with that of Christianity (IM 133–4). It becomes incumbent upon Heidegger to disentangle Heraclitus from the Gospel. Heidegger goes on to summarize what, in his view, is the crucial difference between the Christian and the Heraclitean logos:

> But in principle we can say: in the New Testament, from the start, *logos* does not mean, as in Heraclitus, the Being of beings, the gatheredness of that which contends, but *logos* means *one* particular being, namely the Son of God. Furthermore, it means Him in the role of mediator between God and humanity. This New Testament representation of *logos* is that of the Jewish philosophy of religion which was developed by Philo, in whose doctrine of creation *logos* is determined as the *mesites*, the mediator. Why is the mediator *logos*? Because *logos* in the Greek translation of the Old Testament (Septuagint) is the term for word, "word" in the particular meaning of an order, a commandment; *hoi deka logoi* are the ten commandments of God (the Decalogue). Thus *logos* means: the *keryx angelos* the messenger, the emissary who transmits commandments and orders; *logos tou staurou* is the word of the Cross. The announcement of the Cross is Christ Himself; He is the logos of salvation, of eternal life, *logos ziies.* A world separates all this from Heraclitus. (IM 143)

Heidegger is correct in his desire to separate the Greek from the Christian logos, but he misunderstands the difference. Heidegger suggests that the principle difference is that Christianity takes the logos as a being or a thing rather than as a gathering that contends. This amounts to another version of a forgetting (on the part of Christianity) of the ontological difference. But there is a deeper difference between the two accounts of the logos to which Girard points in his discussion of this section of Heidegger's *Introduction to Metaphysics*. Girard begins by noting:

> His [Heidegger's] essential contribution does not lie in an insistence on the notions of "bringing together" and "reassembling," which he shows to be present in the term *logos*. He also states something much more important: the logos brings

together entities that are opposite, and it does not do so without violence. Heidegger recognizes that the Greek logos is inseparably linked with violence. (THSFW 265)

Pointing to the passage quoted above, Girard notes that Heidegger likewise finds violence in the Christian logos, presenting it as the logos of commands and commandments, "whose only function is to transmit orders of a dictatorial master" (THSFW 268). In Heidegger's presentation both versions of the logos are violent. The difference between the Greek and the Christian logos turns only on (a) the source and (b) the nature of the violence. Beginning with (a): in Greece, the violence is found in the creative activity of thinkers, poets, and artists; in Christianity, the violence is located in the commands of a dictatorial God. Turning to (b), in Christianity, insofar as the logos is considered as a being or thing (albeit a very special one), the violence of the Christian logos is only the ontic violence of commands, threats, and punishments rather that the ontological struggle with the overwhelming that characterizes the violence of the Greek logos. It is at both these points that Girard demurs, and I think rightly so. Girard notes that, in the prologue to John, the logos suffers violence at the hands of human beings; the logos is unknown, rejected, expelled by the world (THSFW 271). While the Heraclitean logos violently gathers together opposites, the Johannine logos is expelled: "He was in the world, and the world was made by him, and the world knew him not. He came unto his own, and his own received him not" (John 1:10–11). Girard argues that one must distinguish between the violence *enacted* by the Greco-Heideggerian logos and the violence *suffered* by the Johannine logos. It is not the case that the Johannine logos inflicts violence upon human beings, free or otherwise, but, rather, that human beings inflict violence on the logos. This difference is more fundamental than the difference Heidegger highlights between gathering and a particular being. The proper contrast is not (as Heidegger would have it) the contrast between two kinds of violence, but a more fundamental one between violence and non-violence, between victimizer and victim. The Christian logos is not for the strong but for the weak because the logos itself is weak.

Girard's criticisms of Heidegger has a bearing on Derrida's work as well: Derrida's rejection of logocentrism is predicated on a Heideggerian understanding of the logos; precisely because the logos is violent and exclusionary, logocentrism must be rejected (to the extent possible) in the name of hospitality to the other. Girard suggests that this is too quick: given the fact that there are two modes of the logos, the Heideggerian logos of violence and the Johnanine logos of suffering, the rejection of the first need not entail the rejection of the second. The fact that this is not often appreciated, for Girard, is testimony to the prophetic quality of John's Gospel: the Christian logos is *still* not recognized and it is *still* expelled (THSFW 272). In supposing that the logos of violence is the only logos (even if only in order to reject it), Heidegger and Derrida both represent not the dawning of a new way of post-metaphysical thinking but the return of the oldest way of thinking – that of the old gods of sacrifice. The dynamic we noted earlier in our discussion of Machiavelli's God plays itself out again here: the purported novelty is actually the return of something old and forgotten, a repetition of archaic religion; Heidegger's logos is scrubbed clean of blood and gore but it remains a sacrificial idol.

In the case of Heidegger, we find corroborating evidence in his 1943 postscript to "What Is Metaphysics." There we find him, right before he introduces the idea of "originary thinking (*Das anfängliche Denken*)," appealing to the notion of sacrifice. In a shocking set of sentences – John Sallis calls it one of Heidegger's most astonishing[4] – Heidegger tells us:

> The need is for the truth of being to be preserved, whatever may happen to human beings and to all beings. The sacrifice [*Das Opfer*] is that of the human essence expending [*Verschwendung*] itself – in a manner removed from all compulsion because it arises in the abyss of freedom – for the preservation of the truth of being for beings. (PWM 236)

We couldn't ask for a clearer expression of the sacrificial distinction than this one: human beings are to be sacrificed, or even wasted (one possible sense of *Verschwendung*), to preserve the truth of being. The good violence used to found and preserve communities is called upon here to preserve the truth of being. We may wish to interpret Heidegger's sacrificial language as a kind of philosophical metaphor, as suggesting that the philosopher must give up certain things in the pursuit of truth, as Socrates gave up his life rather than stop philosophizing. Certainly, the above passage suggests that the sacrificial victim is not compelled insofar as the sacrifice arises in the "abyss of freedom." But this does not settle the issue: nothing in sacrifice requires compulsion, as the Roman *devotio* reminds us. Let us read a bit more:

4 Sallis, *Echoes*, 152.

> Sacrifice is the departure from beings on the path to preserving the favor of being. Sacrifice can indeed be prepared and served by working and achievement with respect to being, yet never fulfilled by such activities. Its accomplishments stems from that inherent stance out of which every historical human being through action – and essential thinking is action – preserves the Dasein he has attained for the preservation of the dignity of being. Such a stance is the equanimity that allows nothing to assail to its concealed readiness for the essential departure that belongs to every sacrifice. Sacrifice is at home in the essence of the event [*Ereignis*] whereby being lays claim upon the human being for the truth of being. (PWM 236–7)

At times, it is hard to make heads or tails of Heidegger, and this is one of those times. The passage abounds with abstractions and convoluted phrasings. Nevertheless, it seems clear that this sacrifice is offered in the face of a kind crisis. It occurs when one feels threatened: Thomas Mautner has suggested that the entire discussion of sacrifice in PWM is designed to defend German morale in the face of the defeats mounting as the Second World War drew to a close.[5] Even if one does not agree with Mautner's strategy of reading Heidegger's texts in the light of the social and political context of their composition, one can still agree that, in PMW, there is a close tie between anxiety and the sacrifice of beings in the name of thinking being. In either case, the sacrifice of beings – including human beings – responds to a kind of crisis, the crisis of a lost war or the crisis of anxiety. Sacrifice resolves the crisis with the turn towards being, with the violent founding (per *Introduction to Metaphysics*) of a new polis. The sequence crisis-sacrifice-resolution that Girard finds in archaic thought is reproduced here with a shocking degree of exactitude. This shouldn't be surprising. Heidegger, after all, spent a good part of his philosophical career attempting to return to the thinking of the archaic Greeks; if Heidegger was truly successful in his attempt to rethink his pre-Socratic forbears, then he is only another step away from the archaic world the pre-Socratics inhabited. The pre-Socratic experience of being that Heidegger points us towards is the same world as the executed *pharmakos* and Bacchic frenzy. The great tragedies, among other witnesses, show us that the pre-Socratic world Heidegger loved is inseparable from murder: in *The Bacchae*, Pentheus is torn apart by the Dionysian crowd. Girard claims that Heidegger's thought remains bound by the scapegoating mechanism. To the extent that Heidegger returns to

5 Mautner, "Self-Sacrifice in Heidegger," 393–95.

archaic Greek sources he binds himself even more tightly to that mechanism (THSFW 267).

Precisely because he returns to Greek thought with such rigour and brilliance, Heidegger returns to the archaic belief in the efficacy of sacrifice, the belief that the sacrifice of the pharmakos can resolve the crisis, that Dionysius will be satisfied after the death of Pentheus and order restored or renewed. The structure of sacrificial thought is present in those passages of PWM in which the preservation of the truth of being is tied to, and dependent upon, the *Verschwendung* of human beings. However, the sacrificial moment in Heidegger is probably meant primarily in spiritual (*geistige*) terms rather than in practical ones. Just as Heidegger's essential violence isn't meant to be the same as ontic violence, in the essential sacrifice nobody dies. I do not want readers to suspect me of accusing Heidegger of engaging in human sacrifice during nocturnal rituals deep in the Black Forest! In fact, there is a kind of obliviousness to human things in this section of the post-script: the Thinker could hardly be bothered to kill a man. My point is that, even if this doesn't involve the actual murder of human beings, Heidegger's text repeats the murderous structure of sacrifice whereby the death or expulsion of the victim resolves the crisis. In fact, just as we complained earlier that Heidegger's focus on essential violence led him to miss the more fundamental importance of Machiavellian violence, we might complain here that his naive use of sacrificial logic prevented him from taking his own language seriously enough to think through the implications of his own words.[6] If he had done so, he would have found that the logic of sacrifice presupposes ontic violence, the actual death or expulsion of a victim. From there, he might wonder if it makes sense to adopt the language and structure of sacrifice without also adopting the practice. Is the appeal to sacrificial structures warranted when there is no sacrificial victim? Is the sacrifice without sacrifice we find in PWM a kind of empty cliché or is something more at work? Whatever the case may be, the important point for us, for now, is that in both IM and PWM we find, in antiseptic ontological guise, the same structure of violence and sacrifice we identified in Machiavelli and archaic religion.

6 A similar point is made in Sallis, *Echoes*, 163: "Granted that he [Heidegger] did broach a thinking of the political, it is surprising that he says so little."

DECONSTRUCTING BURIDAN'S ASS

Derrida is well aware of sacrifice and its problems, and he certainly goes far beyond Heidegger's understanding.[7] This is particularly clear in *The Gift of Death.* Although separated by decades, there are good reasons for reading *The Gift of Death* (1992) in close connection with his much earlier essay (1967) entitled "Violence and Metaphysics."[8] Since the latter takes the form of a long debate with Levinas, and presupposes a fairly detailed knowledge of his texts, my discussion focuses on the former. However, it is worth noting some of the general conclusions reached by Derrida in "Violence and Metaphysics." As far as the purposes of this book are concerned, the most important of these conclusions is that violence and non-violence cannot be as clearly separated as Levinas is accused of supposing.[9] The Face of the Other both prohibits violence and makes violence possible because it is only the other whom I can kill: "Only a face can arrest violence, but can do so, in the first place, only because a face can provoke it" (VM 147). The upshot of "Violence and Metaphysics" is that there is not a space outside of, or apart from, violence; rather, it is violence all the way down – peace is mixed with violence. Indeed, Derrida goes even further: when he describes peace as a telos he can be taken as suggesting that peace only arises from violence (VM 116). This is, of course, textbook Derrida: first he finds a philosopher making a binary opposition that privileges one of the binary points, and then he shows that things are not as binary as they seem – the two points are hopelessly entangled and almost indistinguishable ("Like pure violence, pure nonviolence is a contradictory concept"), such that the privileging of one over the other is arbitrary (VM 146). But beyond this textbook manoeuvre, something much more important (for our purposes at least) is going on: Derrida begins to argue that, given the inescapability of violence, the point is to (somehow) use violence to limit violence, "a violence against violence" (VM 117). Derrida's violence

7 In 1993, Derrida published an essay (in French) entitled *Le Sacrifice.* It is surprisingly irrelevant to the discussion that follows: the essay is mainly concerned with the relationship between theatre and philosophy and only briefly mentions sacrifice as a possible source for Greek tragedy, without developing the idea in any meaningful way.

8 These reasons are offered in both de Vries, *Religion and Violence*; and in Hanson, "Returning (to) the Gift of Death."

9 I want to avoid a detailed exegesis of Levinas. For the purposes of this argument, I am only interested in what "Violence and Metaphysics" tells us about Derrida. I am stipulating, for the sake of argument, the general correctness of his reading of Levinas.

against violence calls to mind the sacrificial distinction between a good violence that preserves the community from destruction and a bad violence that destroys. Indeed, one might gloss the just quoted phrase as pointing towards a good violence against a bad violence.

In *The Gift of Death* Derrida returns to some of the themes that occupied him in "Violence and Metaphysics." There he writes (among other things) of "sacrificing ethics" (GD 68). My ethical obligation to *this other person*, according to Derrida, forces us to sacrifice our obligations to help the other others. This sacrificial dilemma (which is to be distinguished from the sacrificial distinction) is such that "I am responsible to anyone (that is to say to any other) only by failing my responsibility to all the others, to the ethical or political generality. And I can never justify this sacrifice; I must always hold my peace about it" (GD 70). This seems like the reverse of Machiavelli: for Machiavelli, I may sacrifice *this other* precisely because of my ethical or political responsibilities. This is good violence in a nutshell. Derrida's sacrificial dilemma is something different: it is the sacrifice of my political obligations for the sake of this other person *hic et nunc.* But beyond the content, there is a formal difference: Derrida's dilemma concerns two (or more) obligations, which is not the case in Machiavelli. In Derrida's sacrificial dilemma, I am given a choice between two disjuncts, each of which entails the negation of the other. When I choose the first disjunct, I inevitably "sacrifice" the second. However, according to the posing of the problem, I owe each disjunct that same (infinite) loyalty. If one allowed the inability to decide to prevent one from deciding, one would betray both – so one must decide even though the decision is undecidable. To say that something is undecidable has a specific meaning for Derrida. It does not mean that one cannot decide, such as when a decision is taken out of one's hands (as when higher authorities set a policy) or when something is unchangeable (as in Aristotle's *Ethics*, when he says we do not deliberate about that which is not in our power).[10] Instead, it means that one must decide, even though there are no firm grounds for deciding. Like the bales of hay set before Buridan's proverbial ass, there is nothing to distinguish the two options; however, unlike Buridan's ass, one must and does choose. In choosing to oblige P, one betrays Q, or vice versa. It is not to Derrida's purpose to cut this Gordian knot but, rather, to linger with it so as to make his readers aware of the treacherous ground of obligation, a ground often concealed by talk of ethics, politics, and social functioning (GD 61–2; 85–6). In a sense, this repeats, in a new register, the claim in "Violence and Metaphysics" that there is neither pure violence nor pure non-violence. In choosing

10 Aristotle, *Nicomachean Ethics*, 1112a20–b.

non-violence with one person, I inevitably treat the second person with violence; at the very least, I fail in my responsibility to her or him. We are meant to be aware of both our obligations to the other, and our constant, inevitable, betrayals. The point of Derrida's discussion of this sacrificial dilemma is to mourn the problem, not to solve it.

The distance between Derrida's sacrificial dilemma and the sacrificial distinction is, however, not as great as one might suppose or wish. Certainly, although he admits that pure non-violence is impossible, Derrida would like to minimize the amount of violence in the world. The problem, as we have already seen, is that the minimization of violence is accomplished by more violence. The violence that minimizes violence is implicitly a good violence that is preferable to the bad violence of "the worst." We already saw an implicit appeal to the sacrificial distinction at work in "Violence and Metaphysics," and it is at work again here. That is to say, Derrida's sacrificial dilemma assumes that the choice for one or the other disjunct is both (a) at the service of the other and (b) to the detriment of other others. When I choose P, P is benefited and Q sacrificed. But this is exactly what happens in good sacrificial violence: in order to benefit some, violence is directed towards others. The sacrificial dilemma in *The Gift of Death* is a homily on the sacrificial distinction, but not a replacement of it. As far as homilies go, it is a good one; one might go so far as to call it Augustinian. However, despite the proximity to Augustine, it is only half-way Augustinian. Derrida's analysis calls to mind Augustine's discussion of the sorrows of the just warrior: unlike Augustine, Derrida does not offer an alternative to it. Derrida's point is precisely that there is no alternative forthcoming. This is our situation. It is inevitable and sad. While Derrida's emphasis on the unhappiness of all of this may seem to prove his distance from the sacrificial distinction, there is nothing in the sacrificial distinction per se that precludes sadness. Augustine was well aware that Brutus cried while the execution of his children was carried out under his orders and supervision (CG III.16) – for the uninitiated, Iunius Brutus, after the expulsion of Tarquin and the founding of the Roman Republic, discovered that his own children were conspiring to return the ousted tyrant to the throne. As consul, Brutus had no choice but to order the execution of his offspring. The duelling obligations of Brutus can be readily interpreted as an instance of the kind of sacrificial dilemma described by Derrida, and the unhappiness of poor Brutus is precisely Derrida's point. Certainly, Brutus had an infinite obligation to his sons, but he also had an infinite obligation to the other others in Rome, and by fulfilling one, he necessarily betrayed the other. In a way, whichever decision he made would have been the wrong one. Describing precisely this same incident, Machiavelli unhesitatingly describes Brutus as unhappy. He, too, is aware of Brutus's competing obligations to his sons and his city. However, Machiavelli nonetheless maintains that, despite this unhappiness, the violence of Brutus was of the good kind: when it comes to communal strife and conflict, "there is no remedy more powerful, nor more valid, more secure, and more necessary, than to kill the sons of Brutus" (D I.16). This is *why* Brutus would have betrayed his obligations to the city had he not punished his traitorous sons so severely.[11]

The sacrificial distinction simply states that there are good and bad forms of violence: the good violence is fertile, it founds and preserves communities, while the bad violence is destructive, threatening, and undermines communities. Derrida's sacrificial dilemma in *The Gift of Death* runs alongside the sacrificial distinction but never challenges it. In fact, in "Force of Law" and "Faith and Knowledge," Derrida's discussion of founding violence replicates the logic of the sacrificial distinction. Let us know turn our attention to those essays.

However, before we can discuss these two essays in any detail, a few words regarding Derrida's vocabulary are in order. It is undeniable that Derrida often exhibits a fairly idiosyncratic vocabulary; not only is he well known for introducing neologisms, but he often uses older words in unique ways. It serves our purposes well, therefore, to note the idiosyncratic meanings he gives to two key terms – "the sacred" and "sacrifice." Derrida's take on the word "sacred" is at variance with most other uses of the term: not just that of Girard but also that of scholars of archaic religion like Benveniste, Otto, and van der Leeuw among others. Derrida's usage of the word emphasizes the association of the sacred with a kind of purity, of being unscathed or undefiled, "saintly, sacred, safe and sound, *heilig*, holy" (FK 84). Derrida's gloss on the sacred emphasizes the *fascinans*, forgetting or downplaying the *tremendens* part, even as a long footnote cites Benveniste to the opposite effect (FK 84n30). The sacred figures of the archaic world are ambiguous and unpredictable; capable of both great blessing and cursing, they are often scarred or deformed. So Zeus is a rapist and protector of guests, Hephaestus is deformed, Odin is missing an eye, Loki both assists and frustrates the gods, and on and on. This is why the archaic sacred is both *tremendens* and *fascinans*,

11 Interestingly, Kierkegaard alludes to this incident early in *Fear and Trembling*, a text Derrida comments on at length in *The Gift of Death*, but Derrida doesn't mention Brutus in his commentary. Kierkegaard's point is to distinguish Abraham's sacrifice from that of Brutus: Brutus's actions can be understood because, in applying Rome's laws, he preserves the republic from the bad violence of a royalist counter-revolution. Kierkegaard's point, in our terms, seems to be that Abraham's sacrifice cannot be understood in terms of the sacrificial distinction: there is no bad violence being avoided by killing Isaac. See Kierkegaard, *Fear and Trembling*, 58.

scary and fascinating. Moreover, Derrida's idiosyncratic understanding of the sacred leads to an equally odd use of the world "sacrifice." Insofar as his usage of "sacred" strips it of its negative connotations, he associates "sacrifice" with a "making safe" or a "purifying" of oneself or another. In Derrida's usage, "sacred" and "sacrifice" both rest on the quest for an illusory purity – illusory because, just as there is no pure non-violence, so there is no pure sacrifice.[12] Nothing, Derrida argues, can be made entirely pure, entirely safe, and entirely sacred; so the so-called pure sacrifice is always already, unbeknownst to the believers in sacrifice, compromised and impure.

Whatever one thinks of Derrida's argument, the fact is that Derrida's "sacrifice" is only half a sacrifice in the usual sense of the term. Sacrifice, in the usual sense, always mixes safety and danger: no one ever thought that the safe "pure" sacrifice Derrida critiques was possible. The near obsessive/compulsive concern with the proper celebration of rites typical of sacrificial acts is not rooted in a prudish desire for purity. Instead, one is concerned that everything be done right, because sacrifice is dangerous and all hell will break loose if things go wrong. Likewise, the sacred must be set off from the masses not merely because it is very good but also because it is very bad, or at least very dangerous. Sacrifice and the sacred are like guns, which are safe when handled correctly but can be deadly when mishandled (and so best kept out of the reach of untrained hands); Derrida presents them as porcelain dolls best kept high on a shelf, lest the children break it. In a sense, Derrida's work on these points is devoted to untying his own knots: the mix of impurity and purity, safety and danger, that Derrida labours to discover in sacrifice was, in fact, there all the time.[13] In any case, the point here is not to dispute Derrida's definition of the sacred but to avoid confusion by emphasizing that, in Derrida's writing, the analogue to the ambiguous archaic sacred is not "the sacred" but "the mystical." Whence, in what follows, my emphasis is on "the mystical" rather than the sacred.

Derrida's approach to the question of religion, in his famous "Faith and Knowledge," bears unmistakable similarities to Machiavelli on at least two points: (a) the subordination of religious belief to ethics and politics and (b) the sacrificial distinction between good and bad

12 For a brief discussion of the association between safety and sacrifice in Derrida, see Caputo, *Prayers and Tears of Jacques Derrida*, 43–4.

13 However, it is arguable that Derrida's forgetfulness of the *tremendens* leads him to a fairly simplistic and one-sided understanding of religion in terms of "the safe and sound, the unscathed, the immune" (FK 42–3) rather than in terms of the dangerous, the scarred, and the diseased.

violence. To (a) we note that, very early in the essay, when Derrida is describing how he and his interlocutors will address the question of religion, he writes of his commitment to the binding of philosophy to the city: "But we also share, it seems to me, something else – let us designate it cautiously – an unreserved taste, if not an unconditional preference, for what, in politics, is called republican democracy as a universalizable model, binding philosophy to the public "cause" to the *res publica*, to "public-ness" (FK 47, emphasis removed). Derrida's philosophy is not to be a philosophy of *ozio* – even if the paper is being delivered in Capri – but a philosophy at the service of city; this understanding of philosophy, in turn, guides his approach to religion. To the extent that philosophy is a public servant, when it approaches religion, it must approach it in terms of the city, of ethics and politics. This paragraph anticipates the key move of Derrida's essay, the introduction of the messianic without a messiah. Rather than awaiting one anointed by God, messianism without a messiah awaits justice (FK 56). Justice is a way of being towards the text one inhabits, a way that deconstructs the violence of the tradition, opening up alternative interpretations that are less oppressive. Derrida takes the messianic as that other which interrupts and surprises us by entering into our moral and ethical traditions and disrupting them. Despite the difference in tone, this is not far from what Machiavelli's prince does when introducing new modes and orders. Of course, one might object that Derrida's messiah is far from Machiavelli's prince, but Derrida knows better, admitting that the arrival of the messianic can bring about the worst just as easily as it can the best (FK 56). There is no guarantee that the interruption of history by the messianic will lead the lion to lay down with the lamb: the lion might just as easily eat the lamb. Cesare Borgia lurks as an implicit possibility within Derridian messianism precisely because it is, as Derrida insists, purely formal, without content. The formality of Derrida's messiah is precisely the source of the danger he calls "the worst"; if there was more content to messianism, we might be able to explain how the coming of the messiah precludes the worst. We might say that Isaiah tells us that the messiah will suffer rather than cause suffering, or that John the Baptist tells us that the messiah is concerned with the forgiveness of sins rather than with extracting vengeance. But the "general structure of experience" that Derrida is interested in tells us nothing of the sort. Derrida is sober enough to know that, shorn of content, we are left with a pure interruption that is, in principle, capable of going either way. Derrida's messianic other can come peacefully or with war, introducing the best or the worst; the messianic can be, we might say, armed or unarmed.

These Machiavellian elements are even more pronounced as Derrida turns to the origins of laws, and it is here that we find him employing the sacrificial distinction between good and bad violence. Echoing Heidegger's discussion of the apolis condition of the founder, Derrida notes that, in a certain sense, the initial promulgation of law is illegal: "The foundation of law ... is a 'performative' event that cannot belong to the set it founds, inaugurates or justifies" (FK 57). With no law to guide the promulgation of law, the promulgation is a decision in the face of what cannot be decided; in some, if not all, cases, the source of undecidability is the sacrificial dilemma. This point is developed at greater length in his essay entitled "The Force of Law," in which he describes the founding act as "violence without ground" (FL 242). Because it founds the law, there is no law to justify it; as in Machiavelli, good arms precede good laws (P XII). Here we have the fertile, good violence of sacrificial systems: the violence that founds and preserves the community. As Derrida continues, we see that the sacrificial system is here in all its glory: not only is the founding a good kind of violence, it is through the violent founding of law that one hits upon "the mystical." Founding violence is mystical not to the extent that it points towards something mystical in the sense given by mystical theology (i.e., something transcending or surpassing the world) but only to the extent that it is un-reasonable, beyond or before reason. It is mystical because there is no reason, natural or supernatural, for laying down this or that set of laws that would justify it. It consists merely of "a *coup de force*, of a performative and therefore interpretive violence" (FL 241). The mystical appears in the apparently arbitrary choice for one set of modes and orders over another that reason cannot justify or negate, and it is – precisely because of this – quickly covered over and imbued with a kind of mystical authority that gives birth to religion.

By now the reader should hear echoes of Machiavelli's discussion of the new prince all through Derrida's discussion: the armed prophet's imposition of new modes and orders is echoed in the founding violence of which Derrida speaks; the use of loaded religious language, like "prophet" and "mystical," as a way of getting at the elusive nature of this founding act echoes Machiavelli's practice; even the focus on founders rather than on mobs echoes Machiavelli. Derrida, arguably, goes beyond Machiavelli insofar as he maintains that the modes and orders of the prince can be and ought to be deconstructed in the name of justice (FL 242–3). However, I'm not entirely convinced that this move does not find analogues in Machiavelli's praise of various statesmen and leaders who thrived precisely by knowing when to subordinate the law to the demands of the singular and, indeed, when to create new laws to respond to new singularities. Something like this is present in his comparisons of Venice, Florence, and ancient Rome (D. I.4 and I.6; FH's preface and section III.1). But we must leave things at the purely suggestive level since to dig too deeply into this would take us too far afield.[14]

It is more pertinent to note that, for Derrida, both the foundation of law and the messianic disruption of law rest on decisions taken in the face of the undecidable. The undecidable approaches when we are tasked with deciding regarding something that is foreign to rules and law but that must be decided with a view to rules and laws (FL 252–3). The undecidable returns to the mystical foundation of authority already discussed, repeating in a new context the initial founding violence. Similarly, Machiavelli notes that it is necessary to return to the founding violence periodically to address needed reforms in the regime (D III.1). In both cases, one acts in a way that cannot be justified with reference to the law – in the case of founding because one is creating the law, in other cases because one is departing from it in the face of that which is radically heterogeneous. Derrida himself points us towards the connection between the undecidable and the mystical, referring to Pascal and mysticism precisely at this point in his essay on law (FL 254). This reference to Pascal and the mystical take us directly to a discussion of a formal messianic structure that precedes the particular messianic beliefs of world religions. We already noted the role of decision in the foundation of law. Returning to the messianic, Derrida writes that the messianic interrupts history by deciding to let the other come, although he comes without grounds, without a "horizon of expectation" (FK 56). So, when the messiah comes nobody will expect it – there will be no Isaiah, no John the Baptist, preparing the way– and, as such, one will have no reason to accept the messiah, so that accepting or rejecting will be undecidable. In fact, one could argue that Derrida's formalization of messianism is inseparable from this undecidability: if there was some determinant content to guide our expectations and reception of the messianic, it would be decidable. As things stand, the messianic introduces possibilities we have no means of adjudicating between while nonetheless forcing us to choose. The decision made in favour of welcoming the messiah is the mirror image of the decision that founds the law. Law is founded by a decision in the face of the undecidable – and religion is the child of this

14 A more detailed discussion of these questions, however, can be found in Saralegui, "Maquiavelo y la Partitocracia."

law. Later this law is interrupted by another decision in the face of another undecidable.

As noted, Derrida insists on interpreting religion formally; he is interested in an "abstract messianicity" that precedes all particular messianic beliefs (FK 56). As such, although he admits that at times it will prove difficult to do so, he will as much as possible avoid immersing himself in the details of a particular religious tradition. He emphasizes the Latinity of his discourse and the dependency on Abraham as problems to be dealt with rather than as a good to be embraced. The interest in formal structures apart from any detailed study of any particular religious texts separates him sharply from Girard's reliance on ethnological and anthropological reports. Nevertheless, in *Violence and the Sacred* (1972) Girard comes close to Derrida's formalism in that he believed himself to have – by means of ethnology and anthropology rather than formal analysis – isolated a structure common to all religions – the scapegoat mechanism (VS 306). Indeed, he is quite enthusiastic about Derrida's work (VS 296–7). However, in *Things Hidden* (1978), we find that Girard's early enthusiasm for Derrida has waned; he now worries that Derrida is not radical enough in his analysis to the extent that he refuses to go beyond Greek philosophy to ask about Greek religion; he adds that the discovery of the scapegoat at the root of Greek religion both justifies and completes deconstruction (THSFW 62–4). We can deconstruct traditional discourses because they are lies designed to obscure the founding murder. Of course, one could defend Derrida on that score by pointing to precisely the texts we have been discussing, texts not yet written at the time when *Things Hidden* was being composed (1974–77).[15] But that will not do enough to bridge the gap since *Things Hidden* is concerned with arguing for the uniqueness of the Judeo-Christian scriptures insofar as in them and them alone, among all ancient texts, the innocence of the scapegoat is constantly asserted. So, Girard notes that the innocence of the victim is asserted again and again in the Bible, from Abel to Jesus, while in the other archaic myths there is always a belief that the scapegoat really is polluted – Oedipus *did* kill his father and marry his mother,

15 For more on the relationship between Derrida and Girard, see the works of McKenna, notably "Ends of Violence," and *Violence and Difference.* Also of interest are Girard's comments in an interview with Thomas Bertonneau (see Bertonneau, "Logic of the Undecidable"). One key point that has to be kept in mind in any discussion of the two is that, while Girard, in THSFW, suggests that Christian revelation offers a way out of sacrifice, this position is revised in subsequent works. He now admits that there is no way out of sacrifice, so to speak, but that, instead, Christian revelation enables one to recognizes oneself as a persecutor. On this point, see BTTE 35 and 82.

even if unintentionally (THSFW 149; OWSC 35). "In biblical texts, victims are innocent and collective violence is to blame. In myth, the victims are to blame and communities are always innocent" (OWSC 35). This point only emerges for him via a careful study of Christian and non-Christian texts (THSFW 176–8). In the case of Girard, an interest in the concrete details of scapegoating eventually led him to argue for the uniqueness of the Judeo-Christian scriptures.

So, Girard's emphasis on particulars leads him, ultimately, to distinguish between religions, while Derrida's formalism prevents him from seeing what makes each religion unique. Derrida's "faith without dogma" (FK 56–7) leads him to a cloudy religion where the important differences are hidden in a fog. If the reader will allow me a bad joke at Derrida's expense, it is passing strange that a man so interested in difference ends up wanting to treat all religions as more or less the same.

Without delving into the complex relationship between Derrida and Girard, we should note that Derrida's "mystical" has precisely the same ambiguous quality that Girard discerned in the archaic sacred: it "engenders, organizes observes or perpetuates it [the social structure], or, on the contrary, mishandles, dissolves, transforms and on a whim destroys it" (VS 242). More fundamentally, just as Girard argues the archaic sacred emerges from violence and is inseparable from it, so, too, does the mystical in Derrida's essays. The mystical is nothing but archaic sacred violence translated to a philosophy conference at a hotel in Capri. As I note earlier, when Derrida is talking about "the mystical" he is talking about the same phenomenon Girard calls "the sacred," but when Derrida is talking about "the sacred" he is talking about something entirely different. However, Girard's interest in the sacred/mystical is nearly the opposite of that of Derrida. For Girard, the point is a critique of the sacred/mystical on the basis of the Gospel; for Derrida, the point is to use the ambiguity of the sacred/mystical to further the deconstructive project. What Girard questions – how and why did the sacrificial distinction develop? – Derrida takes for granted, as a kind of inescapable necessity. Although Derrida relies on the sacrificial distinction, he arguably does so in order to problematize the results of violence. Derrida's treatment of violence accepts that there is a kind of fertile, good, founding violence but also that it is possible for any particular act of violence to be of the bad kind. In fact, more to the point, he suggests that any instance of the good kind could be reinterpreted as an instance of the bad kind; this is, in fact, one way of understanding what deconstruction seeks to do. Likewise, it would seem to follow that any instance of the bad kind could be reinterpreted as an instance of the good kind. Derrida would have us accelerate the dance between these two poles such that one can never say for certain with which kind of violence one is dealing, whence a need for constant vigilance. Despite these revisions and caveats, it is nevertheless the case that Derrida, in principle, recognizes the sacrificial distinction and presents it as both lamentable and unavoidable.

Heidegger and Derrida both point towards the fundamental importance of violence, but each fails to think it through with the clarity of Machiavelli. Machiavelli recognizes that violence, in its most fundamental form, is not the violence of thought but, rather, the actual violence of people killing other people. Violence is murder, or at least attempted murder. Because of the clear-sightedness of Machiavelli's account of violence, because of its emphasis on what Heidegger might call merely ontic violence, he is able to think the meaning of violence more deeply than Heidegger. Indeed, it is his understanding of violence that enables Machiavelli to see the importance of founding as a way of managing violence, as a way of minimizing violence. Recall that the Machiavellian defence of cruelty, as seen in his discussion of Cesare Borgia among other places, requires that cruelty, to be defensible, must be oriented towards securing stability. At the same time, however, the necessity of cruelty and violence for the achievement of stability requires eschatological hopelessness in Machiavelli's thought: violence is justified as the only way to peace. The most hopeful passages he ever wrote – the final chapter of *The Prince* and the call to liberate Italy from the barbarian occupiers – are inseparable from violence. Machiavelli's hope is in war, in more violence. It is the sacrificial hope that the right kind of killing will solve our problems.

The violence of the liberator counters the violence of the occupier. We have a cycle of violence rather than an end to violence. The inevitability and inescapability of violence, in Machiavelli, is linked to his understanding of the world as eternal. Recall that, because the world is eternal, history is more or less cyclical: the only thing that stops the cycle of regimes is that, in their weaker stages, they are conquered by stronger ones (D I.2). Since history is ineluctably violent, we have an eternal cycle of violence. This cycle of violence cannot be stopped, for what would stop it? Everything in the world is in history, in violence. And since the world is eternal, we cannot appeal to an imagined republic or imagined prince who would come from on high to put an end to the violence. The best we can hope for, according to Machiavelli, is the management of violence by carving out spaces where we can live in relative peace under the protection of strong princes. These peaceful situations are made possible by violence, or at least the threat of violence, and are always complicit in that violence. This is why, as Derrida correctly observes, they are unjust and can always be deconstructed. But again, as Derrida correctly observes, this deconstruction will not produce new non-violent structures but only different forms of injustice. This is why deconstruction is a never-ending task; like the world, deconstruction is eternal.

EL CHUPACABRA AND DEMOCRACY-TO-COME

If the world is basically violent – as Machiavelli, Heidegger, and Derrida all agree – is not hoping and working for peace testimony to a yearning for something beyond the world? If so, this hope has to be separated from Derrida's hope for something like a "democracy-to-come." In "Violence and Metaphysics" Derrida adduced "pure peace" as a kind of unachieved and unachievable telos; arguably, the later Derrida's hope for a "democracy-to-come" develops this concept in such a way as to both highlight and obscure the impossibility of peace. First, the highlighting: nothing in history or experience suggests that the *demos* will ever renounce violence. How could it? The *demos* is constituted by violence: to renounce violence would require the renunciation of the *demos.* Indeed, one could go so far as to say that the very idea is contradictory. Second, because of Derrida's association of deconstruction with various left-wing movements there is a tendency to think of his emphasis on democracy-to-come as a kind of promissory note for progressive politics, whereby if we just had the right policies and reforms (if we just deconstructed the right things) the democracy-to-come could someday get here. On my reading, the first of these two poles is the more fundamental one, and this is why the deconstructionist can only hope for a democracy-to-come.

In an important sense, Derrida's democracy-to-come can be compared to *el Chupacabra,* the legendary beast that stalks Texas and Northern Mexico sucking the blood from goats and other small livestock. The interest in el Chupacabra stems from the fact that it does not fit into any zoological taxonomy; we do not know what it is or when it will appear. Whenever we think we have caught el Chupacabra it turns out to be, upon closer inspection, something else, for example, a coyote with mange. Nevertheless, the legend of el Chupacabra lives on. Likewise, the democracy-to-come can never arrive; if it was to arrive it would turn out to be something else, some particular kind of democracy, and as open to deconstruction as any other regime. Just as el Chupacabra can only exist as something absent, as el Chupacabra-to-come, the democracy-to-come can never actually arrive. Nevertheless, Derrida would insist that the comparison with el Chupacabra is misleading: we use the democracy-to-come not to tell stories around campfires but to critique existing regimes. Precisely because it has not yet arrived, it is capable of avoiding the historical and non-universal aspects of particular regimes and of deconstructing them.[16] In this sense, Derrida's "democracy-to-come" functions less like el Chupacabra and more like the Platonic *kallipolis* of *The Republic.* The point of Socrates's description of the city in speech is not, he reminds his interlocutors a number of times, to build the city, but to acquire a standard by which to judge and criticize existing cities.[17] Indeed, there are good reasons to believe that Socrates took the city in speech to be physically or practically impossible. Needless to say, associating Plato and Derrida in this way is a striking claim to make: it suggests that Derrida's later work returns to precisely the kind of metaphysics he was always attempting to avoid. And there are numerous differences between Plato's kallipolis and Derrida's democracy that will be obvious to anyone familiar with the two thinkers; one might begin by pointing to the specificity with which Plato describes his city in contrast to the vagueness of Derrida's democracy. Derrida's vagueness, however, is not accidental, nor is it the result of laziness; rather, it follows directly from his understanding of the democracy-to-come: insofar as it is not to be identified with any particular regimes, it must remain open-ended and vague. Indeed, it cannot even be identified with democracy as we know it except to the extent that it is oriented towards the future and exhibits an openness to change and possibility not found in other forms of government.[18]

The vagueness of democracy-to-come is mirrored in the vagueness of the messianic without a messiah. This is, in part, why John Caputo reacts so forcibly to the suggestion that determinate religious beliefs be taken seriously by deconstruction; he correctly perceives that this would be the end of deconstruction: "Once you have an identifiable Big Being like that, once you know it, you have undermined the experiential structure (the possible/impossible) under analysis." I take Caputo's point to be that (a) insofar as *determinate* religious beliefs (e.g., creedal Christianity) would claim to identify and know the "Big Being" it is (b) incompatible with deconstruction's interest in the possible/impossible.[19] Once we trap el Chupacabra it ceases to be a mysterious beast that troubles our zoology and ontology (because we don't even know if it is real) and becomes just another creature in the books. As long as we are looking for el Chupacabra we will be frustrated at not finding it, but when we do find it (if we do) we will be disappointed. It may be the case that we are

16 See the discussion in Nass, *Miracle and the Machine,* 184–6.

17 For example, see Plato, *The Republic* (369a; 420b–21c; 472b–c; 497b–592a–b). See, too, Glaucon's summary at 543c–44b.

18 See Plato, *The Republic,* 422a.

19 Caputo, "Return of Anti-Religion," 36.

destined to be frustrated and unhappy; a great deal of commentary on Derrida emphasizes the "playful," "ironic," and "irreverent" aspects of this thought – this trend probably reached its nadir in the unfortunate scene in the *Derrida* documentary in which he is asked if deconstruction is like *Seinfeld* – and not nearly enough attention is paid to the sadness that permeates his work. Caputo's reference to the *Prayers and Tears of Jacques Derrida* is an obvious exception to this comment, but Caputo sometimes undermines his own title by emphasizing the *Viens* of deconstruction, the hope for the impossible. Sometimes there is too much emphasis on the "hope" and not enough on the "impossible." The hope will not be fulfilled; el Chupacabra is never caught. That is why it is so sad.

However, there is another way of looking at these same issues. Earlier I note the structural similarities between the Platonic kallipolis and the Derridean democracy-to-come insofar as – despite differences in details – both function as non-existing or non-actual grounds for criticisms of existing or actual regimes. If that is the case, then one can develop a Machiavellian critique of Derrida. Just as we saw that Machiavelli understands founding better than Heidegger does, we might wonder if – despite the numerous affinities between Machiavelli and Derrida to which I have pointed – his criticisms of imagined republics apply to the democracy-to-come. Machiavelli writes: "And many have imagined republics and principalities that have never been seen or known to exist in truth" (P XV). This applies to the democracy-to-come: like el Chupacabra, it has never been seen nor has it been known to exist. Indeed, as we saw, it is in principle not known to exist. Machiavelli might argue that, when dealing with political problems, an appeal to this imagined democracy-to-come would not be any more helpful than would an appeal to the Platonic *kallipolis.* It makes much more sense for ranchers to equip themselves to handle really existing coyotes than imagined chupacabras. But, one might object that there is more at issue in Derrida's democracy-to-come than merely pragmatic concerns – with the caveat that to dismiss entirely the reformist politics it is meant to ground would be to do a disservice to Derrida's moral seriousness – in that the democracy-to-come reflects the quite real (and not imagined) possibility of interruption, of surprise, and so forth.

One of Derrida's most astute commentators, Jack Caputo, repeatedly affirms that deconstruction is on the side of the losers: "Deconstruction is on the watch for exclusion, the victims, the injustice produced by the law, which even the best laid laws inevitably produce. Laws always silence, coerce, squeeze or level someone, somewhere, however small. Deconstruction's justice does not aim at disinterested impartiality but at a preferential option for the disadvantaged, the differends, the losers, the leftovers, the little bits and fragments."[20] This theme is an important one for Caputo; his readers can almost hear the pounding hooves of his high horse at full gallop when he turns from textual exegesis to issues of social justice, of protecting the losers. This is to his credit. But he sometimes forgets, or under-emphasizes, a point emphasized by Machiavelli: while it is true that the strong wish to oppress while the weak simply wish not to be oppressed, when those oppressive structures are deconstructed and replaced with new ones, we will not be free of disadvantage but merely have disadvantaged and advantaged different people. In other words, the deconstruction of social structures always makes new losers. There is no guarantee that the new winners will not be just as morally blameworthy in their treatment of the losers as was the case in the previous dispensation. Indeed, it is highly likely in that the deconstruction of modes and orders entails the introduction of new ones, which requires that one offend partisans of the old orders so severely that they cannot threaten the new ones (P III). Of course, it would then be the task of deconstructive justice to minister to those people, the new losers. The deconstructive quest for justice is an infinite task, but it is always – at exactly the same time, for reasons Caputo adduces above but doesn't dwell upon – a creation of injustice: even the best laid laws inevitably produce it. In a strange paradox, the passion for doing justice that Caputo lauds and identifies with deconstruction is inseparable from acts of injustice. This is why Machiavelli, despite aforementioned similarities, is more clear-sighted and more incisive than deconstruction

One might point to the final chapter of *The Prince*, in which Machiavelli imagines the coming of a liberator for Italy, as his own experiment in imagining a democracy-to-come. Nevertheless, there is a crucial difference: Machiavelli never would have accepted the idea that the liberation of Italy is inevitably deferred. He has a plan he seeks to execute, and this is a far cry from imagined republics that are in principle deferred. Finally, one can wonder if this deferral of democracy-to-come doesn't transpose the lost origin, which Derrida began his career rejecting, into a lost *telos*; instead of a pristine beginning to which we cannot return, Derrida substitutes a pristine end that we cannot attain. To fully explore this point would require a more careful reading of Derrida than I am inclined to give here; instead, I will satisfy myself with the claim that, whatever may be the case regarding the last point, Machiavelli's rejection of imagined republics entails the rejection of the democracy-to-come as much as it does the rejection of the classical imagined republics. The vagueness of

20 Caputo, *Against Ethics*, 87 (emphasis mine).

Derrida's imagined republic doesn't make it any less imagined. In sum, Machiavelli saw the consequences of sacrifice further and deeper than did either Heidegger or Derrida.

LITURGY AND DEFENESTRATING BISHOPS

In his *Experience and the Absolute,* Lacoste attempts to develop an account that begins with Heidegger but goes beyond it, an account that shows how being-towards-the-absolute is a legitimate phenomenological category. This is, as he puts it, a liturgical critique of Heideggerian phenomenology. The liturgical, for Lacoste, signifies this way of being towards the absolute; it is "the resolute deliberate gesture made by those who ordain their being-in-the-world as a being-before-God" (EA 39). We discuss some of his ideas earlier in the text. One of the key points I made about Lacoste earlier is that his admission that the liturgical critique of phenomenology is not verifiable in history gives too much to the Machiavellian account of history; an account that we see can encompass the work of Heidegger and Derrida.

We should take a closer look at Lacoste's understanding of liturgy. Recall Lacoste's argument that the dialectic of world and earth he finds in Heidegger indicates that neither can be originary but that both rest on the deeper principle of place. Liturgy's modification of being-in-the-world reminds us of this – that is, that "being-in-the-world is the initial and not the originary" (EA 92). The distinction between the initial and the originary is important. By means of this distinction, Lacoste is granting the phenomenological primacy of the world, of history, and, therefore, of violence. But, at the same time, he is indicating that, while this is the first thing that we experience, it is not the ultimate or foundational principle. The distinction on the one hand acknowledges the appropriateness of the analysis offered by Heidegger, Derrida, and others, but it also indicates that, despite the appropriateness of these descriptions, they do not get at the deepest truths. Nevertheless, Lacoste is at pains to remind the reader, throughout *Experience and the Absolute,* that liturgy is an interruption supervening upon the atheism of the world. There is nothing in the world, in history, which compels one to enter upon liturgy. The non-eternity of the world cannot be apodictically proven. The dialectic between world and earth can continue uninterrupted for as long as one wishes. The liturgical might point towards something originary, but it is an origin hidden from experience. And while in framing the question this way Lacoste avoids the accusation of holding a Pollyanna view of history, he does this at the price of appealing to a lost origin. The appeal to the lost origin could easily be objected to on deconstructionist grounds – that is, as reintroducing a transcendental signifier that is both beyond our ordinary experience and also the ultimate explanation of it. Lacoste would then be offering metaphysics of the most traditional sort. Whatever one thinks of this critique, I will not dwell on it except to nod in its direction as we pass by. I do this not because I think it is unimportant, but because the modifications of Lacoste's argument that I am going to suggest will remove the threat of this particular objection.

The liturgical experience, Lacoste continues, is not dependent upon history but, rather, upon a vigil or nocturnal event that occurs outside of the daylight business of history. When the sun has set, and the violent work of the day is over, one has the luxury of escaping from the dialectic of world and earth and entering into an experience of the absolute. The liturgical night is not, of course, to be identified with a time of the day. After all, most church goers still go on Sunday morning. The point is that the night is a time of mystery and shadow set apart from the working day. Liturgy is both a kind of *ozio* that, like philosophy in the *Florentine Histories,* comes after the work of captains and princes is accomplished and the peace-as-telos that Derrida alludes to in "Violence and Metaphysics." Moreover, one need not stay up praying at night; liturgy is a decision (EA 22). To enter upon the liturgical vigil requires one to resist one's natural diurnal rhythms. There is nothing in the world or on the earth that compels one towards liturgy but, instead, one enters upon it as a sort of gamble or bet – the bet that one can, within the world, orient oneself towards the absolute. Nevertheless, and this is a crucial point for Lacoste, whatever one thinks of the odds, the fact is that people do make this bet. Making this bet, in turn, dramatically transforms our being in the world. For example, Lacoste argues that, for one who has made the liturgical bet, "death ceases to be the final reality to which we can reconcile ourselves by making it our highest possibility, as Heidegger believes" (EA 60).[21] In transforming our relationship with death, liturgy transforms our relationship with the world as such, "the Absolute's eschatological claims over us are substituted for the world's historical claims" (EA 61). One way of reading Lacoste is as describing the transformation that occurs whenever one makes the liturgical bet and as showing that traditional phenomenology – including especially that of Heidegger – is incapable of describing this transformation. Since, as a

21 E. Falque has made a similar argument to the effect that belief in the resurrection of the body has determinant and important effects on our phenomenal experience of the living body, such that a phenomenology of the resurrection is both possible and desirable. See Falque, *Metamorphosis of Finitude.*

matter of fact, people do make this bet, this entails that traditional phenomenology is inadequate as a description of how the world is experienced by these people.

Nevertheless, as Lacoste admits, the liturgical experience that he seeks to describe is always describable in other forms; a critique of liturgy is just as possible as a liturgical critique. Derrida or Heidegger can always claim that the liturgical gambler is betting on a losing horse, deluding himself. Indeed, one way of reading Machiavelli is as saying precisely this: the liturgical experience that Lacoste describes does indeed get at something of how many people experience the world, but these people are deluded followers of imagined republics. It is interesting to note that, so far as I know, the only time Machiavelli describes liturgical action in any detail is in his description of an assassination attempt:

> And thus they decided to kill the Medici in the cathedral church of Santa Reparata; since the cardinal would be there, the two brothers would attend in accordance with custom. They wanted Giovan Battista to assume the task of killing Lorenzo, and Francesco de' Pazzi and Bernardo Bandini to kill Giuliano. Giovan Battista refused to consider doing it, either because the familiarity he had with Lorenzo had softened his spirit or because some other cause moved him; he said he would never have enough spirit to commit such an excess in church and accompany betrayal with sacrilege. This was the beginning of the ruin of their enterprise, because, since time was pressing, of necessity they had to give the task to Messer Antonio da Volterra and to the priest Stefano, two men who by practice and nature were very inept for so great an undertaking. For if ever any deed requires a great and firm spirit made resolute in both life and death through much experience, it is necessary to have it in this, where it has been seen many times that men skilled in arms and soaked in blood have lacked spirit. The decision thus made, they determined that the signal for action should be the taking of communion by the priest who celebrated High Mass in the church. (FH VIII.5)

For those not familiar with the order of a High Mass, the priest's communion takes place immediately prior to the distribution of communion to the faithful. If Italian practice, then, is anything like contemporary practices, there is a disorganized movement towards the altar rail. Attendees do not, in contrast to contemporary American practice, wait quietly for the usher to come to their pew. The moments following the priest's communion is the best time to kill someone at mass insofar as it is then when one can move about without calling much attention to oneself. In any case, Machiavelli's discussion of the entire conspiracy can be taken as a historical critique of liturgy. The sacred moments of the liturgy are transformed into signals and opportunities for violence. Battista's respect for the absolute is the beginning of failure for the Pazzi conspiracy. The description of the conspiracy has two effects. First, through the person of Battista it reminds us that the rites of a religion can be useful for keeping people in line. Battista's hesitancy recalls the discussion of religion in *The Art of War,* which we analyzed earlier (i.e., that religion can be used to rule those who are armed). Second, it shows how an undue respect for the absolute leads to failure. The conspirators failed because they had more respect for religion than did the Medici. The violence that followed upon the assassination attempt led to more bloodshed than would have happened if it had succeeded. And even worse for liturgy, the failure of the conspiracy made possible the Medici's further consolidation of power. If Battista had understood that the assassination was a kind of good violence – even good enough to perpetrate at mass – then the plot would not have been ruined. The source of the plot's failure was, ultimately, Battista's formation by Christian education. It was his inability to distinguish between good and bad violence that led to the deaths of his allies and co-conspirators, and the tightening of the Medici's grip on the city. In the aftermath of the failed conspiracy, Archbishop de Salviati, who collaborated with the failed assassins, was thrown out the palace windows and his naked corpse hung for all to see (FH VIII.8). Here, in de Salviati's defenestration, is the Machiavellian critique of liturgy. Liturgy is good for timing assassinations and keeping people in line; but to take liturgy as an opening towards the absolute is delusional – in so doing one is only opening oneself to imagined republics and principalities and, thereby, inviting failure and misery. The partisans of the Medici, in throwing Archbishop de Salviati out a window, showed exactly how much history respects liturgical experience.

LITURGY IS FOR LOSERS

So, we seem to have fought to a draw: the liturgical critique of history is countered by a historical critique of liturgy, just as Lacoste said it would be. The old gods and God find themselves equally unable to vanquish each other. This, however, would not be a draw. If the choice between the old gods of violence and the new God of peace, between Machiavelli and the Absolute is undecidable, then Derrida wins. The choice for one or the other will be undecidable in his sense, and, therefore, whatever one chooses, the resulting structures could be deconstructed. Heads he wins, tails you lose. If this is the case, then the loss will be doubled. If the choice for the Absolute could be deconstructed it would have been shown to be a mere illusion or delusion, wishful thinking, on the part of those who bet on liturgy. Lacoste's claim that the decision to live liturgically fundamentally alters one's being-in-the-world would turn out to be merely the mapping of ontic illusions with no importance for deeper ontological questions. These questions would still be answered via the traditional atheism Lacoste locates in Heidegger. Heidegger's analysis, in turn, leads us back to the bloodiness of Machiavelli's analysis of founding. It is not simply to say that if the liturgical critique fails, we can still hope, within history, for a democracy-to-come, but, rather, that if the liturgical critique fails, then there is no democracy-to-come.

On the other hand, if the historical critique of liturgy can itself be subjected to a historical critique, a historical critique that points towards liturgy, then the choice for the absolute can be justified. The standard of justification here has to be specified, however. To say that it is justified is not to say that is admits of apodictic proof, but only that there are enough reasons for choosing the absolute that it is decidable rather than undecidable. I note at the outset that Machiavelli offers something like a moral argument for sacrifice, asserting that there are certain goods that can only be achieved if one accepts the sacrificial distinction between good and bad violence. I now propose the reverse of that: there are certain goods that can only be achieved by resisting sacrifice.

If we return to the fifteenth chapter of *The Prince*, in which Machiavelli expounds on the effectual truth, we will notice that the rejection of imagined republics and principalities is concomitant with the recommendation that "a man who wants to make a profession of good in all regards must come to ruin among so many who are not good. Hence it is necessary to a prince, if he wants to maintain himself, to learn to be able not to be good, and to use this and not use it according to necessity" (P XV). To succeed among those who are not good, it is necessary to learn to be like them, to learn how to imitate the non-good. This recommendation of imitation of the non-good builds upon his prior recommendation, earlier in *The Prince*, that one imitate the founders of new regimes, the four armed prophets Romulus, Theseus, Cyrus, and Moses: "For since men almost always walk on the paths beaten by others and proceed in their actions by imitation … a prudent man should always enter upon the paths beaten by great men and imitate those who have been most excellent, so that if his own virtue does not reach that far, it is at least in the odor of it" (P VI). The connection between imitation and the rejection of imagined republics is not accidental. Machiavelli places a high premium on imitation – imitation of the ancient Romans, of the non-good, of the founders, and so on. We imitate those things we see in *this* world rather than orienting our lives towards a supersensible and transcendent good. This imitation, however, inevitably leads to conflict.

If more than one person takes his advice to imitate Romulus, one of them will end up suffering the fate of Remus. Romulus and Remus came into conflict not despite their similarities but precisely because of them: because they both desired the same thing, rule over the new city they were founding.[22] The imitation of those who are not good leads directly into competition with others who are not good. Christian education resists competitive imitation by turning towards a world-transcending "imaginary republic." Since the Machiavellian does not accept the reality of imaginary republics, he thinks this move is guaranteed to fail: they will never get what they want because what they want does not exist. To believe in an imagined republic is to condemn oneself as a loser. It is a delusion, an illusion, a hallucination, an ideology or false consciousness; it is anything but what the one so oriented thinks it is. In other words, within the eternal world, to orient oneself towards something transcending the world can only be to swallow the illusions of imagined republics and the inevitable failure that comes with chasing illusions.

Perhaps the best illustration of this point is found in the sign that Pontius Pilate – surely a product of the Roman education lauded by Machiavelli – affixed to the Cross of Christ. It reads in Latin, Greek, and Hebrew: "Jesus of Nazareth, King of the Jews" or in its common Latin abbreviation INRI (*Iesus Nazarenus, Rex Iudaeorum*).[23] There is good reason to interpret this signage as a continuation of the mockery to which Jesus had been subjected since the beginning of the Passion, part and parcel with the crown of thorns (John 19:1–3). There is no indication that Pilate took the sign seriously: it was probably one last joke at the expense of another crucified loser. However, from a different perspective, it takes on a radically different meaning: for the believer, the crucified man *really* is the King of the Jews, the Davidic King who fulfills the Old Testament prophecies, the Messiah, the Son of God. The Roman centurion at Golgotha is the flip side of Pilate: while Pilate mocks the loser on the cross, the soldier recognizes this same loser as the Son of God (Matthew 27:54). The crucial point here is that what appears as a typical sacrifice – the good violence that executes one trouble maker to avoid the bad violence of riots or revolution – motivates others to become suspicious of sacrifice. Returning to Pilate's sign and the jokes of the soldiers during the scourging at the pillar, we should recognize these as references to Pilate's prior conversation with Jesus at the Praetorium:

22 Livy, *Ab Urbe Condita*, I.6.
23 John 19:19 (cf. Luke 23:38).

Pilate therefore went into the hall again and called Jesus and said to him: Art thou the king of the Jews? Jesus answered: Sayest thou this thing of thyself, or have others told it thee of me? Pilate answered: Am I a Jew? Thy own nation and the chief priests have delivered thee up to me. What hast thou done? Jesus answered: My kingdom is not of this world. If my kingdom were of this world, my servants would certainly strive that I should not be delivered to the Jews: but now my kingdom is not from hence. Pilate therefore said to him: Art thou a king then? Jesus answered: Thou sayest that I am a king. For this was I born, and for this came I into the world; that I should give testimony to the truth. Every one that is of the truth heareth my voice. Pilate saith to him: What is truth? (John 18:33–8)

So, in the biblical account the kingship of Jesus is irreducible to the sacrificial violence of kingship as understood in the world. Whatever kind of kingship Jesus possesses, it is one without the power to defend him; it is a kingdom that refused to use violence to resist violence, rejecting the sacrificial distinction. But the non-violence of this kingdom seems inseparable from its not being of this world – if it were, Jesus tells Pilate, his servants would defend him. His kingdom surpasses the world and precisely because it does, it is an invisible principality. But this answer confuses Pilate, who asks Jesus again, more directly, if he is a king. At this point Jesus begins to discuss his mission – to testify to the truth. Now this might seem like a poor answer to Pilate's question, but, in fact, it further describes the kind of king and the kind of kingdom about which Pilate was asking. The kingship of Christ is (in Lacoste's terms) a liturgical kingship such that his visible presence in the world points towards the absolute. This kingdom of truth is not in this world, whence Jesus came to testify to it; but because it is not in this world, Pilate doesn't care about it. He doesn't stay to hear the answer to his *quid est veritas*; indeed, once he finds out that Jesus does not claim to be a worldly king, Pilate seems to lose interest in the entire proceedings. After all, if it is only an invisible kingdom (a principality imagined by a weirdo preacher in a backwater of the empire), then it is not the kind of kingdom Pilate cares about: he cares about real kingdoms with real armies, real swords, real horses, effectual truths. While it is a commonplace to mock those one beats, it is the preposterousness of an invisible kingdom to the students of Roman education that motivates the soldier's particular choices of insult. The Passion of the Christ encapsulates the historical critique of liturgy in its most radical form.

But the centurion at Golgotha testifies to the subversive power of the Passion. Just when the historical critique should be triumphant, his words suggest that there is another power in the blood. In Luke's Gospel, the centurion remarks, "Indeed, this was a just man" (Luke 24:47), and in Matthew's, he remarks, "Indeed, this was the son of God" (Matthew 27:54). How could he recognize that the crucified man is the son of God despite all the mockery, torture, and humiliation inflicted upon him? Luke suggests that it is precisely because of his proximity to those pains that recognition is possible. It is significant that, in Luke 24:47–8, everyone present for the crucifixion responds to the death of Christ with signs of either respect (the centurion) or by beating their breasts, a sign of regret and repentance for the event in which they, at least passively, participated.

The centurion was no doubt aware, however dimly, of the controversy surrounding the arrest, trial, and torture of this man; he may have suspected that the charges were trumped up, but within the Roman education one would not have thought much of it. Perhaps he thought that killing potential trouble-makers is the kind of good violence necessary for keeping peace in the colonies. But, with the shattering of that totality, our centurion is face to face with the innocence of the victim. And it is this awareness of innocence that motivates the centurion's confession; it is not merely that the crucified man is innocent of the crimes of which he was accused but that he is innocent of everything. Hamlet remarks to Polonius, "Use every man after his desert, and who should 'scape whipping?" But according to the Gospel narrative it precisely *this* scourged man that should not have been scourged. It is at this point that we can rejoin the argument Girard develops in *Things Hidden*. The complete innocence of Christ emphasized by the Gospel accounts requires traditional Christology: "The theology of the Incarnation is not just a fantastic and irrelevant invention of the theologians; it adheres rigorously to the logic implicit in the [Gospel] text … If Jesus is the only one who can fully reveal the way in which the founding murder has broadened its hold upon mankind, this is because at no point did it take hold upon him" (THSFW 216). And later: "To recognize Christ as God is to recognize him as the only being capable of rising above the violence that had, up to that point, absolutely transcended mankind. Violence is the controlling agent in every form of mythic or cultural structure and Christ is the only agent who is capable of escaping from these structures and freeing us from their dominance" (THSFW 219). If *Things Hidden* fails to develop the implications of this point – that is, if it sometimes leaves the reader wondering if the salvific events save us merely from bad sociology – this is only because of the self-imposed limits of Girard's anthropological approach (THSFW 216; OWSC 43–5). But more to our point, the passion, or perhaps more carefully, Girard's interpretation of the Passion, can be read as staging a confrontation between sacrifice and its victims.

EXHUMING SOME CORPSES

The pages of Machiavelli's texts are strewn with victims: victims of murder, of conspiracy, of riotous mobs, of scheming rulers, of invading armies, and on and on. For the most part, the presence of these victims is overlooked by both Machiavelli and Machiavelli scholars insofar as both are more interested in Machiavelli's princes, the leaders of republics and principalities who stand at the centre of his work.[24] Indeed, the parade of victims passes by almost unnoticed, as a kind of sad background procession obscured by the front-and-centre analysis of princes and captains. Nevertheless, the victims are, in fact, the most important element of this pair. If the action of a prince requires good violence then the prince requires someone to receive that violence. The prince's good violence requires victims. But, since the prince requires victims, his "principality" depends upon them: in the final analysis, the victim, not the princely founder, is the foundation of the regime. Machiavelli's use of the sacrificial distinction shows us that the foundation of a new state is always laid on the backs of victims, even as his interest in the virtues of founders obscures this fact. Both *The Prince* and *Discourses on Livy* – as well as Heidegger and Derrida in their own ways – oscillate between revealing the importance of victims and covering them up.

I cannot hope to catalogue and investigate all of the dead and abused bodies fertilizing Machiavelli's texts. I've mentioned many of them already, and in what follows (as a kind of summation) I return to two particularly well known victims. My famous victims are Remus (the victim of Romulus, as discussed in *Discourses on Livy*) and Remirro de Orco (the victim of Cesare Borgia, as discussed in *The Prince*). In the *Discourses* Romulus's murder of his brother Remus is presented as a necessary precondition for the foundation of Rome. In order to order the new city, it was necessary that Romulus have complete authority; if Remus were to be allowed to live on as Romulus's equal, as co-ruler of Rome, the kingly authority needed to found the state would be divided. If Remus had ceded his place to Romulus, he would still be a threat since he would always remain a possible rallying point for those offended by Romulus's new modes and orders. The only way to order the city is for Romulus to be alone, un solo. Killing Remus was good violence. The upshot is that Rome could only be founded over the corpse of Remus. We find a similar situation, although perhaps a bit more sordid and without the classical lustre of the Romulus story, in *The Prince*'s account of Cesare Borgia's

24 One notable exception to this tendency is found in the work of V. Sullivan.

actions in the Romagna. Upon his conquest of that region, Borgia found it to be a lawless wild place and set upon reducing it to good government. To that end he ordered his lieutenant, Remirro de Orco, to enter the Romagna and lay down the law. De Orco did this with alacrity and cruelty. The first victims were the victims of de Orco's mission. One can assume that de Orco's wrath fell upon not merely the lords of the Romagna who "despoiled their subjects" but also on any who resisted his new orders. In this way, law and order was introduced to the region, culminating with the construction of courts and a system of civil conflict resolution. The violence of de Orco was good violence. Unfortunately for de Orco, there was one last piece of good violence on order: the murder of de Orco himself. We can imagine his surprise when agents of Cesare Borgia take him by night and murder him in a spectacular manner; although we can't be sure, it is reasonable to assume that he was *at least* as surprised as the people of the Romagna were when they found his butchered remains in the piazza.

In both cases, the introduction of new modes and orders is linked to a murder. Romulus's killing of Remus precedes his ordering of Rome; while Borgia's murder of de Orco is the capstone to the (re)ordering of the Romagna. The difference between the murder-as-beginning and the murder-as-capstone is important, but it is less important than the more fundamental idea of the murder-as-required. The episodes of Borgia and Romulus both suggest that a victim is a necessary condition for the introduction or reform of modes and orders. We can find confirmation of this suggestion in the early chapters of *The Prince*. In chapter 3, Machiavelli reminds his reader that new princes (here he is focusing on mixed principalities [i.e., one in which a prince of territory A has acquired territory B]) will find it necessary to offend when he introduces new orders and that these offences must be such that the victim cannot revenge himself: "Men must be either caressed or eliminated" (P III) . Call this point (a). Further on, in chapter 6's discussion of the new prince, we find that (b) the new prince must be armed when he introduces new modes and orders because (c) he must be able to force the people to obey. Whence, Moses was forced to kill innumerable people to introduce his modes and orders to the Israelites. Implicit in (a), (b), and (c) is the further point (d) that the prince's founding or ordering of a state requires victims.

We can find other examples that circle the same point without stating it in *The Prince*. For example, Hannibal's virtues (P XVIII) require that he be cruel; his cruelty requires victims. If the good prince thinks of nothing but war (P XIV), if the prince desires to make himself feared (P XVIII), he will require victims. Indeed, even if he seeks to be merciful in the sense recommended by Machiavelli, he will require carefully selected victims (P XVIII and XIX). We can find other examples in the *Discourses.* Early in the *Discourses,* Machiavelli discusses where a founder should locate the city to be founded. Examining the options, he concludes that one should pick a good, healthy, fertile location. Even though this will reduce the immediate need for discipline on the part of citizens, one can overcome this problem by forcing them to cultivate the virtue of good citizenship (D I.1). The passages alluded to from *The Prince* will suffice to conjure up what this forcing consists in: offence, crushing, and victimization.

So far, the reader might consider that the foregoing is a kind of smear on Machiavelli, cherry-picking particularly colourful and bloody passages but ignoring his larger concerns with good government. There is something to this criticism in that I haven't really addressed good government in Machiavelli; to remedy this defect and assuage those critics, I will do so now. Despite Machiavelli's rather bloody reputation (in popular culture, if not so much among scholars anymore), it is fair to say that his overarching vision of the goals of political life is fairly attractive. All these instances of violence are good violence that is meant to protect the community. Late in *The Prince,* Machiavelli describes a city ruled by a prince who follows his advice. It sounds like a really nice place to live. The city and its citizens are secure in their possessions, fearing neither neighbour nor foreign threat; the prince rewards excellence in the arts and sciences; people are able to live their lives with little interference from the government. Occasionally, the prince visits different constituencies in the city and throws a party. One thinks of Ambrogio Lorenzetti's 1339 fresco cycle *The Allegory of Good and Bad Government,* in particular *The Effects of Good Government in the City.* This vision of civic life is as important to Machiavelli's thought as are the visions of death and murder recounted above.

But, to this we have to add another point: Machiavelli's peaceful city is built on the corpses of victims. In Lorenzetti's collection of frescos, *The Effects of Good Government in the City* is paired with another work, *The Allegory of Good Government.* This fresco presents the prince (standing for the ruling council of Sienna) as guided by the theological virtues of faith, hope, and charity. In Lorenzetti's presentation, the effects of good government are derived from these virtues. In Lorenzetti's cycle, we only find victims in the frescos concerned with bad government. Good government is basically good all the way down.

Returning to Machiavelli's vision, we can describe it as a demythologizing of Lorenzetti's (this is just a heuristic device; it is not to say that Machiavelli had Lorenzetti in mind when he wrote). Machiavelli's texts show us that even good government and good cities are built over the bodies of victims. Machiavelli's revivication of the sacrificial distinction can be taken as a kind of demythologizing of politics in precisely the sense that Girard gives to the term. For Girard, myth is the story of persecution, of victimization, told from the perspective of the victimizer. This is clearest in the oldest versions of myths; but one also sees a development in the myths as the stories are told and retold, each time in a slightly more sanitized form than the previous version. The most archaic versions of myths are the most violent: they recount the murder or persecution of the victim by the victimizers. In this telling, the victim is guilty, the victim somehow has it coming – at least as far as the victimizers are concerned. Over time, the violence is scrubbed out and the myth takes on a less disturbing shape, until initial murder is only a distant memory and perhaps ultimately forgotten. The reasons Girard gives for the process of forgetting at work in myth are not germane to our purposes; for now, it suffices to explain that, in his usage, "demythologizing" means to recall to mind, to rediscover, the hidden and forgotten victims both delivered and obscured by the myth. One unintentional effect of Machiavelli's focus on the founding violence of princes and captains is to demythologize politics by reminding his readers of the victim at the foundation of new modes and orders

Nevertheless, Machiavelli does not intentionally exhume the victim's corpse; rather, he does so inadvertently when he tells us about the virtues of the killers. The return to the Roman education he promotes is a return to the idea that founding or ordering requires victims. There is no way around it; the only trick is to pick someone whom you can victimize without blowback. Whence, in his discussion of avoiding hatred in chapter 19 of *The Prince,* Machiavelli gives criteria for determining a good victim: one should only proceed when there is manifest cause – that is, when everyone, or at least a majority, agrees that the proposed victim has it coming. In this way, one avoids the threat of vengeance. Seen in this perspective, Remus is a good choice for Romulus: in killing his brother, he ensures that no one will rise up to avenge Remus. Why? Romulus is Remus's only family; in killing his own family member, rather than someone else's family member, Romulus does not have to worry about vengeance. Similarly, Remirro de Orco was not from the Romagna and had no family or friends to speak of in the region: he was from Spain. In both cases, Remus and Remirro make good victims: one because he was so close to Romulus that no one else would avenge him, the other because he was so far from home he had no one to avenge him. Both could be safely killed.

The ability to be safely killed – if such a thing can be called an ability – is, returning to Girard, one of the key marks of the victim, one of what he calls the "stereotypes of persecution" (SG 12ff). In any social group, one can find people at the margins – the stranger from abroad, the resident minority, the widow or orphan, and so on – who, precisely because of their marginal status, make good victims. Remirro and Remus, each in his own way, were outsiders. Remus was above – a hero and potential king – while Remirro was a foreigner. The liminal status of Remirro is perhaps less confusing than that of Remus. But it should not be: history and anthropology reveal that victims can be taken from the top as easily as from the bottom. Indeed, the pairing of Remirro and Remus can be seen in figures as diverse as Oedipus and Marie Antoinette – both combine royalty with foreignness (SG 20). With this in mind, let us return to Machiavelli's advice just cited: that one should not proceed against a potential victim without *causa manifesta*. When I paraphrased the phrase in the previous paragraph I interpreted it as requiring that a majority agree that the proposed victim is deserving of punishment. Nothing in this interpretation requires the actual guilt of the victim. What is required is only the acquiescence of the people to the accusation against the victim. As we saw in our earlier discussion of calumny and accusation, the actual guilt or innocence is of less importance here than the belief in the guilt or innocence of the victim. When the victim is an outsider it is easier to acquire this belief.[25] We are more likely to believe that the outsider is deserving of punishment than we are one of our own.

Let us turn briefly to Machiavelli's *Florentine Histories*. In the second book of his history of Florence, Machiavelli describes the rise and fall of the Duke of Athens. Having tyrannized the people, they rose up against him with the aim of throwing off his yoke; the duke was forced to hide in his palace and negotiate. The people have been meeting in the church of Santa Reparata to organize a new government and choose

25 In a fascinating analysis that I believe complements my own, John McCormick argues for the connection between the religious elements of Remirro's murder and the importance of the acquiescence of the people for ruling. McCormick notes that Borgia's murder of Remirro has religious elements (e.g., it happened on St Stephen's Day) and that these elements are essential for the ordering of the Romagna. Particularly important is the following: "Formally rational institutions are not sufficient for either Machiavelli or Cesare at this point in the latter's mission to establish a state in north-central Italy. Routinized administration is not all that he provides the people; he also brings them food for their souls. Machiavelli suggests that Cesare wishes to purge the people's 'spirit' of their *hatred* more fully" (emphasis in original). The resonances of this reading with the sacrificial one that I am proposing should be apparent. See McCormick, "Prophetic Statebuilding," 9. On the other hand, I am less persuaded by McCormick's claim that "it is a Christian tenet … that one individual be sacrificed for the sake of the people" (7), if only because the Gospel texts attribute that claim to Caiaphas and can be read as, at least, pointing out the injustice of such a plan.

representatives to negotiate with the duke. As part of these proceedings, the people demand that Guiglielmo d'Assisi and his son be "put in their power" (FH II.37). The scene that follows is horrifying:

> Messer Guiglielmo and his son were placed among thousands of enemies, and the son was not yet eighteen years old; nonetheless, his age, his form, and his innocence could not save him from the fury of the multitude. Those whom they could not wound living, they wounded when dead, and not satisfied with cutting them to pieces with their swords, they tore them apart with their hands and their teeth. And so that all their senses might be satisfied in revenge, having first heard their wails, seen their wounds, and handled their torn flesh, they still wanted their taste to relish them; so as all the parts outside were sated with them, they also sated the parts within … The multitude having purged itself with the blood of these two, an accord was concluded. (FH II.37)

We find much to chew on here. The key element is the resolution of the tension via what could only be described as a kind of collective murder. The battles in the piazza are replaced by the murder of defenceless victims; in a fashion sure to interest readers of Girard, the people also eat their victims. Girard notes that communal eating of the victim often functions as a way of indicating unanimity in those situations in which not everyone is able to participate in killing the victim: in eating the victim, one indicates approval of what has transpired (VS 274–80). Machiavelli's emphasis on the youth and innocence of the son suggests a kind of scapegoating in the Girardian sense. The society that follows the scapegoating, Machiavelli continues, had prosperous results for a time, although dissension inevitably crept back in (FH II.38).

It is interesting to distinguish between the different kinds of violence we find in Machiavelli. There is the violence of war and battle; the violence of conspiracies and assassinations, the violence of riots and mobs; the list is not meant to be exhaustive. But the kind of violence we see in the case of Remus, de Orco, and, especially, Guiglielmo's son, is of a different order. In both cases, the victim is neither a soldier on the field of battle nor a hated tyrant targeted for assassination but an individual intentionally chosen for death who does not seem to deserve it. In the story of Guiglielmo's son, the tyrannical duke of Athens leaves the city in peace after the public murder of this young man. Remus did not conspire against Romulus in Machiavelli's telling, it was merely necessary that Romulus be alone; nor is there any reason to think that Remirro de Orco was anything less than a loyal lieutenant of Borgia. Remus and de Orco, whatever their failings might be, did not deserve to die, or at least deserved it no more than Romulus or Cesare Borgia deserved it. And

Machiavelli himself emphasizes the youth and innocence of Guiglielmo's unnamed son. It is not merely the case that foundations require violence: they require persecution. Persecutory violence entails (a) an indifference to truth, to guilt, and innocence in the selection of victims but (b) an interest in choosing victims that can safely be killed. Here it is worthwhile to recall Machiavelli's Germans. They maintained civic harmony and virtue, we saw earlier, by killing any "gentleman" upon whom they could lay their hands. These gentlemen are killed because they are "the *beginning* of corruption," which is to say that they are killed before they have done anything in particular (D I.55). These gentlemen are killed on principle because of whom or what they are, not because of what they have done. They are, like Remus, Remirro de Orco, and Guiglielmo's son, sufficiently different from the rest of the population that they can be safely killed.

THE PROBLEM OF FERDINAND

Founding requires persecution. This is the harsh claim that Machiavelli leaves us with, going beyond both Heidegger and Derrida: to introduce new modes and orders requires not merely violence, but the violence of a persecution. In short, the good violence of the sacrificial distinction is persecution. If this is the case, we might expect to find Machiavelli discussing modern examples of persecution somewhere. And we would expect him to tolerate the persecutions, such that, even if he finds them distasteful, he recognizes their necessity in founding a new state. And when we look to his discussion of Ferdinand the Catholic in chapter 21 of *The Prince*, we find exactly what we would expect. Machiavelli tells us that Ferdinand can be called an "almost new Prince" because, while he inherited a weak kingdom, he very quickly transformed it into a great one. As part of this transformation, he "turned to an act of pious cruelty, expelling the Marranos from his kingdom and despoiling it of them." But does Machiavelli really approve of this? He describes Ferdinand's expulsion as "wretched" (*miserabile*) and as a kind of "pious cruelty." Nathan Tarcov points out that the Italian *pietosa crudeltá* is ambiguous and could also be translated as "merciful cruelty."[26] Tarcov doesn't explore the ambiguity: in his view, the context clearly decides in favour of "pious cruelty." But his brief comments on the alternate reading are nevertheless instructive. Tarcov takes the second possible reading as

26 Tarcov, "Machiavelli's Critique of Religion," 209. Also noteworthy is the interpretation of the phrase offered by Parsons, *Machiavelli's Gospel*, 148: "a cruel action, undertaken to secure oneself, but justified by religious pretense."

indicating the kind of mercy accomplished by cruelty well used, which Machiavelli discusses elsewhere in *The Prince.* It seems obvious to many readers that *pietosa crudeltá* can't be taken in this sense insofar as it is hard to see how exiling the Marranos contributes to the common good. But things aren't that obvious: given our discussion of the sacrificial distinction in Machiavelli's thought, it seems possible to read Ferdinand's *pietosa crudeltá* as a kind of sacrifice that, by victimizing the Marranos, solidified his young state: in expelling some, he constituted those who remained as Spanish. We note, too, that the Marranos fit many of the aforementioned stereotypes of persecution. On this reading it is possible to take Machiavelli's tolerating Ferdinand's cruelty as an instance of founding violence even as he mourns the sufferings of the king's victims. Which is to say, it is plausible to read Machiavelli as including persecution among the great actions of Ferdinand. This is not, or at least should not be, entirely surprising since, earlier in the same book, Machiavelli praises cruelty well-used.

But does Machiavelli really approve of Ferdinand's activities? Erica Benner argues that, despite appearances, Machiavelli does not commend Ferdinand. In support of this view, one finds letters sent to Vettori in 1513 and 1514 that describe Ferdinand's policies as short-sighted, producing only confusion rather than lasting benefits.[27] The contrast between the evaluations of Ferdinand in the letter and in *The Prince* is fairly stark and suggests that the presentation in the latter is insincere.[28] In the letter sent in April of 1513, Machiavelli gives a long, and largely negative, evaluation of Ferdinand's actions in Italy. As Benner notes, he describes Ferdinand as "crafty and fortunate" rather than prudent.[29] This seems to be because of the great risks that he takes, but, as the letter continues, Machiavelli suggests that there might be a method to his madness: "This king from a slight and weak position has come to his present greatness, and has had always to struggle with new states and doubtful subjects. And one of the ways with which new states are held and doubtful minds are either made firm or are kept uncertain and unresolved, is to rouse about oneself great expectations ... such a necessity this king has recognized and used well" (L 128). So, Ferdinand is not always wrong. In fact, most of the errors Machiavelli points to in the letters are errors in his foreign policy; his successes, on the other hand, are found

27 See Machiavelli, *L* 128 and 145. It is only fair to mention that, whatever Machiavelli might have thought, Ferdinand did seem to lay the foundations of a secure and stable state, at least in Spain and the Americas, if not in Italy.

28 Benner, *Machiavelli's Prince*, 255–8.

29 Machiavelli, L 128.

domestically – in founding and preserving his state in Spain.[30] Although Machiavelli criticizes Ferdinand for risking all his territories in L 128, the context shows that he means only his territory in Italy, not Castile, Aragon, and other lands in Spain. Although it must pain Machiavelli to admit this, Italy is a sideshow: the point of Ferdinand's actions is to solidify his control over Spain.

In general, one may say of the letters that Machiavelli disagrees with Ferdinand's policy in Italy but finds merit in his management of domestic affairs.[31] Domestic affairs are the topic at hand in P 21. It is possible, therefore, to disengage his criticisms of Ferdinand's foreign affairs in the letters from his discussion of his domestic affairs in *The Prince*. Moreover, even if one prefers to read the letters without distinguishing between discussions of foreign policy and of domestic policy, it remains the case that the expulsion of the Marranos from Spain is not listed as one of Ferdinand's mistakes or miscalculations in either letter. If we are to take the largely negative evaluation of Ferdinand in the letters as our guide in interpreting P 21, we must take into account the fact that the mistreatment of the Marranos does not appear in the long catalogues of errors in the letters. Since *The Prince* doesn't list it as an error either, it seems to me that we have no textual evidence for attributing such a view to Machiavelli. This is not to suggest that Machiavelli rejoiced in the expulsion of the Marranos, but only that he recognized it as an act of founding sacrificial violence on the part of Ferdinand.

ACCUSATION AND CALUMNY

Despite the importance of victims, Machiavelli is more interested in princes. Ferdinand gets a paragraph in *The Prince* and a few letters; the poor Marranos only merit one sentence. This role that victimization and persecution plays, while pointed out by Machiavelli's texts, is also quickly covered over by his emphasis on the prince. Machiavelli doesn't efface the memory of violence, but he does efface the faces of the victims. Despite his own suggestions regarding the importance of victims, Machiavelli continually turns his gaze towards the opposite and places the overwhelming emphasis of his texts on the virtues of the prince.

30 Viroli, *Machiavelli*, 67–9. Viroli notes that that the King's strategy has been generally effective in holding on to new states; the apparent randomness of the rest of his actions can be explained this way.

31 But this is not to say Machiavelli entirely approves of them either. In L 128 he notes a rumour that Ferdinand has been draining the treasury to pay for his armies of disobedient conscripts.

Either he cannot bear his own insights and intentionally turns away, or he is so bedazzled by princely success he forgets his own insights into the importance of victims; he praises the cruelty of Hannibal without sparing a thought to those to whom he was cruel. The tension between the two poles is never entirely resolved in Machiavelli's thought; he continually oscillates between bedazzled admiration of successful princes and the sense that this success rests on persecution. Overall, however, it is probably fair to say that the admiration of princely success ultimately overwhelms the insight into the importance of victims.

With this in mind, let us revisit our discussion of accusation and calumny.[32] In chapter 7 of book I of the *Discourses*, Machiavelli addresses the importance of accusation in a republic. According to Machiavelli, it is important that republics are ordered such that a system of public accusation is in place. There are two chief benefits acquired by accusations: first, citizens will be afraid of attempting things against the state and second, "an outlet is given by which to vent ... the humors that grow up in cities" (D 7). Note that the first benefit assumes that, or so it seems to me, accusations are made against the guilty. Those citizens crushed subsequent to this accusation presumably deserve it. But the second benefit is more ominous: it nowhere suggests that the accused is guilty. The accused in this case is merely the unfortunate outlet for the built-up humours. When this accused is crushed, he may very well not deserve it. In short, the second benefit of accusation points to a kind of persecution, carried out not by a single prince but by the people as a whole, indifferent to the guilt or innocence of the victim. The point is to purge the humours in a kind of civic catharsis, not to punish the guilty. In chapter 8, Machiavelli oscillates again, contrasting calumny with accusation and arguing that, while calumny occurs in private without evidence, "accusations have need of true corroborations and of circumstances that show the truth of the accusation" (D 8). Machiavelli notes that Rome in her glory had systems of accusation, while Florence flounders in unregulated calumnies. Dazzled by Rome's example, Machiavelli forgets the persecutory elements of accusations. The emphasis falls on the first kind, whereby standards of evidence and legal procedures are called upon: "men are accused to magistrates, to peoples, to councils" (D 8). When these procedures are followed, one wants to rest easy in the view that the accusation was of the first forensic kind rather than of the second persecuting kind. But, stepping aside from Machiavelli's texts, we all know of cases in which magistrates, peoples, and councils have acted to vent humours

32 The previous discussion can be found in section 5 of chapter 4.

rather than to pursue justice. We readily speak of show trials, of defendants who are "railroaded by the system," of witch-hunts, and so on. Despite what Machiavelli might wish, there is nothing in the contrast between calumny and accusation that excludes the possibility of persecutory accusation. Persecution is hidden, but not gone. In the transition from chapter 7 to chapter 8, we see the two sides of Machiavelli, the awareness of persecutory violence and the reassuring turn away from it towards more palatable forms of violence (e.g., violence against the guilty). This oscillation perhaps undermines the true knowledge of histories that he promises his readers; from time to time, Machiavelli shows himself to be as credulous as his contemporaries, forgetting the victims and persecutions he points out to us.

NOT EVEN A GOD CAN SAVE US NOW

The title of this book, as is already apparent to many readers, is a play on Heidegger's famous line: "Only a god can save us now." In the 1966 interview with *Der Speigel* in which this appears, Heidegger introduces the line as a lament; the post–Second World War world, so dominated by the twin powers of communism and Americanism, each threatening the other with nuclear destruction, seems hopeless. There is nothing anyone can do to escape the pervasive and baleful influence of these phenomena on our lives: "Philosophy will be unable to effect any immediate change in the current state of the world. This is true not only of philosophy but of all purely human reflection and endeavor. Only a god can save us" (DSP 57). Heidegger seems to be holding out, on first glance, a kind of eschatological hope, whereby something from outside the modern enframing enters it, interrupts it, and rescues us. But, as with so many Heideggerian sayings, it isn't so simple or straightforward. He goes on, in the following paragraphs, to link this hope with the thinking that comes after philosophy: "Philosophy is at an end" (DSP 58). If we turn from this interview to his 1964 essay "The End of Philosophy and the Task of Thinking," his meaning becomes clearer: philosophy, by which he means the great metaphysical tradition he imbibed as a student and returned to repeatedly as a scholar – in the *Der Speigel* interview he characterizes his life's work as "only an interpretation of Western philosophy" (DSP 59) – has ended by dissolving into the various special sciences. What remains for "philosophy" is not to attempt to put Humpty-Dumpty together again, but to think, to be open, to let go, and to experience the mysteriousness of being. More precisely, it is to become aware of the strange mix of concealment and un-concealment, presence and absence, light and dark, that characterizes being. Here, Heidegger philosophizes as an old man; gone is the *destruktion* of his younger days, the dazzling critiques and attempts at overcoming metaphysics, the Sisyphean effort to reawaken the question of being or reform the university.[33] To the frustration of his interviewers, Heidegger repeatedly disclaims having any practical advice, or plan, or concrete recommendation for dealing with the problems to which he points; he seems unsure of himself. The long war against metaphysics, it seems, is over: it has all been in vain. Metaphysics in the form of technology seems triumphant. A sense of failure is intimated but never frankly admitted by Heidegger in the appeal to a "god" to save us; he and his work cannot save us. According to the *Der Spiegel* interview, the most one can do is to prepare for the coming of the god. Heidegger doesn't think that we can summon a god by means of thought but, rather, that in "thinking" (as opposed to philosophizing) one can prepare oneself to receive the god if and when it comes. All this sounds quite weird, but looking, once again, at "The End of Philosophy and the Task of Thinking" can eliminate some of the weirdness.[34] Here Heidegger describes the task of thinking, at least in part, as the cultivation of a kind of sensitivity to the interplay of *lichtung* and *dickung* (EPTT 384) in which beings appear and, ultimately, to the weirdness of appearance altogether. It is this sensitivity, or something similar to it, that Heidegger has in mind in the *Der Speigel* interview. In short, Heidegger's appeal to a god to save us is *not* an appeal to anything outside or apart from the world that could enter into it and transform either us or the world but, rather, an appeal to his readers to cultivate a certain kind of attitude, an attitude wherein the future appearance of a god – not a divinity in any traditional sense, but merely something that could transform the world – will be noticed rather than obscured in technological business.

In a certain sense, Derrida could be described as continuing and refining this task, of attempting to notice what is not ordinarily noticed, and as trying to articulate the interplay between light and dark,

33 Describing the time leading up to the writing and publishing of *Being and Time*, van Buren writes: "Heidegger was at this time a great skeptic, destroyer and demythologizer of western metaphysics, and this flurry of criticism and innovation remains perhaps unmatched in his entire corpus." See van Buren, *Young Heidegger*, 136. Caputo helpfully divides Heidegger's thought into three stages (at least as it relates to religion): first, the move from Catholicism to Protestantism around 1917–19; second, the Promethean Neopaganism of the 1930s and National Socialism; third, the mytho-poetic meditation on the holy in the later writings. See Caputo, *Demythologizing Heidegger*, 178–9.

34 One can never eliminate all the weirdness from the late Heidegger, and, indeed, one should not since the weirdness is part of the point of it insofar as what we take as "normal" is due to the technological *Gestell* characteristic of modernity.

revealing and concealing, that makes appearance possible. In Derrida's case, rather than waiting for a god to save us, we wait for the much more respectable sounding democracy-to-come. Despite the differences between Heidegger and Derrida, the basic thrust is the same: things are a mess, we are unable to fix them ourselves, so let us hope for something (impossible) to come and save us. But what does any of this have to do with Machiavelli: Why can't a god save us now? Machiavelli shows us that, in contrast to both Heidegger and Derrida, there is nothing coming from the future: no god, no messiah, and no democracy-to-come that could or would save us. El Chupacabra isn't real. This is not to say that we can't be saved but that we can't be saved now and that there is nothing coming from the future to save us. Instead of looking for a god to save us now, or a democracy-to-come, we ought to turn around, looking back at the past – the invisible principalities of the past that Heidegger and Derrida, each in his own way following Machiavelli's advice, rejected. We were already saved; but we didn't and don't want to be saved. We want to wait on the god to come rather than deal with the one that already has.

If Girard's reading of the Passion narrative is correct, then God tried to save us a long time ago; God tried to reveal to us the secret of our violent world and, with this knowledge, the world could have been transformed. But we never managed to embrace it entirely. Machiavelli holds that the Christian education rejected sacrifice but that violence still sparked up as a kind of ineffective temper tantrum, leading him to choose sacrifice as a more effective use of violence. Derrida's work suggests that there is no way of avoiding sacrifice – as we noted, as far back as "Violence and Metaphysics" he was warning us that there can be no pure peace except as an interminably deferred telos. Machiavelli shows us the vacuity of this telos. The failure of Christian education to either successfully reject violence or sacrificially manage it that Machiavelli laments is perhaps the best we can hope for: sporadic violence that is repented of rather than carefully planned persecutions that are not.

I have attempted to show that Heidegger and Derrida can be illuminated by dialogue with Machiavelli, and vice versa. Easy historical narratives that pick one moment or thinker to describe as decisive for everything that comes after often tempt so-called "continental philosophers"; Heidegger is the champion of this sort of work ("Metaphysics is Platonism"), but he is far from alone. Truth be told, we would be wrong to look for "the decisive moment" when it all went wrong, to seek a figure or epoch to blame, and correct, and condemn as at fault and surpass. Despite my focus on Machiavelli, I do not intend to blame him for reintroducing sacrifice and persecution into the world; nowhere in the text do I claim that he said these things first, although I do believe that he said these things best, and, in so doing, he enables us to better understand ourselves and our situation. We should notice both tendencies – sacrificial and non-sacrificial – at work, not only in others people, places, and times, but in ourselves. I am no stranger to sacrificial violence; I haven't done anything as dramatic as killing Remus, but I have fought with my brother over nothing. Sometimes we embrace the sacrificial distinction and sometimes we don't. Sometimes the "good violence" of sacrifice seems the only response to the pressures and depredations of the world. Sometimes we resist the temptation of sacrifice; sometimes the terror of bad violence is so unendurable that it is hard to blame anyone for embracing a good violence that promises to stop it. One may regret the violence, but one should refrain from judging too harshly those who perform sacrifices. Martin Buber, in a slightly different context, once commented: "my heart, which is acquainted with the weakness of men, refuses to condemn my neighbor for not prevailing upon himself to become a martyr."[35] It may be better to interpret resistance to the sacrificial distinction as a kind of supererogatory act and to look with understanding on people who, under intense pressure, embraced sacrifice. Not everyone can be a moral hero; one ought not to judge too harshly or to congratulate too quickly. If one has not embraced sacrifice, one might be more lucky than good. Perhaps the best one can do is muddle through, trying one's best not to kill anyone, being aware of one's own predilections – both culturally and personally – for embracing the sacrificial distinction, and attempting to resist that predilection as much as possible. The texts of Machiavelli and the others teach us – whether intentionally or not is unimportant – both the desirability of sacrifice and the necessity of resisting it, with the full knowledge that we will fail. Perhaps this knowledge will make us more understanding and forgiving of others when they fail. But the doomed attempt to resist sacrifice rather than to embrace it returns us to the incompetent violence nurtured by the Christian education.

35 Buber, "Genuine Dialogue and the Possibilities of Peace," 234–5, quoted in Mendes-Flor, "Martin Buber and Martin Heidegger in Dialogue."

Bibliography

Abbreviations used in the text:

Machiavelli, Niccolò

Cited by book and chapter number (or letter number) rather than page numbers; for translations I cite the texts listed below; when I reference the Italian I use the Italian text in Mario Bonfantini, ed., *Opere*, Naples-Milan: Ricciardi, 1954.

AW Machiavelli, Niccolò. *The Art of War.* Trans. Christopher Lynch. Chicago: University of Chicago Press, 2003.

CC – "The Life of Castruccio Castracani." Trans. Peter Constantine, in *The Essential Writings of Machiavelli.* New York: Modern Library, 2007.

DL – *Discourses on Livy.* Trans. Harvey Mansfield and Nathan Tarcov. Chicago: University of Chicago Press, 1996.

FH – *Florentine Histories.* Trans. Laura Banfield and Harvey Mansfield. Princeton: Princeton University Press, 1988.

L – *The Letters of Machiavelli.* Trans. Alan Gilbert. Chicago: University of Chicago Press, 1961.

P – *The Prince.* Trans. Harvey Mansfield. Chicago: University of Chicago Press, 1998.

Derrida, Jacques

AEL Derrida, Jacques. *Adeiu to Emmanuel Levinas.* Trans. P-A Brault and M. Nass. Palo Alto: Stanford University Press, 1999.

FK – "Faith and Knowledge: The Two Sources of 'Religion' at the Limits of Reason Alone." Trans. Samuel Webber. In Gil Anidjar, ed., *Acts of Religion.* New York: Routledge, 2002.

FOL – "Force of Law: The 'Mystical Foundation of Authority.'" Trans. Mary Quaintance. In G. Anidjar, ed., *Acts of Religion.* New York: Routledge, 2002.

GD – *The Gift of Death,* Trans. David Wills. Chicago: University of Chicago Press, 1995.

H – "Hospitality." In *Acts of Religion.* Ed. G. Anidjar. New York: Routledge, 2002. 356-420.

MC – "My Chances/*Mes Chances*: A Rendezvous with Some Epicurean Stereophonies." Trans. P. Kamuf, in *Psyche: Inventions of the Other.* Palo Alto: Stanford University Press, 2007.

OG – *Of Grammatology.* Trans. Gayatri Chakravorty Spivak. Baltimore: Johns Hopkins University Press, 1976.

VM – "Violence and Metaphysics: An Essay on the Thought of Emmanual Levinas." Trans. Alan Bass, in *Writing and Difference.* Chicago: University of Chicago Press, 1978.

Girard, René

BTTE Girard, René. *Battling to the End: Conversations with Benoît Chantre.* Trans. Mary Baker. East Lansing: Michigan State University Press, 2012.

OWSC – *The One by Whom Scandal Comes.* Trans. M.B. DeBevoise. East Lansing: Michigan State University Press, 2014.

SG – *The Scapegoat.* Trans. Yvonne Feccero. Baltimore: Johns Hopkins University Press, 1986.

THSFW – *Things Hidden since the Foundation of the World.* Trans. Stephen Bann and Michael Metteer. Palo Alto: Stanford University Press, 1987.

VS – *Violence and the Sacred.* Trans. Patrick Gregory. Baltimore: Johns Hopkins University Press, 1979.

Heidegger, Martin

BT Heidegger, Martin. *Being and Time.* Trans. John Macquarrie and Edward Robinson. San Francisco: Harper, 1962.

BDT – "Building, Dwelling, Thinking." In David Farrell Krell, ed., *Basic Writings.* San Francisco: HarperCollins, 1993.

DSp – "Only a God Can Save Us: The *Spiegel* Interview." Trans. William Richardson. In Thomas Sheehan, ed., *Heidegger: The Man and the Thinker.* Chicago: Precedent Press, 1981.

ECPA – "Essence and Concept of φύσις in Aristotle's *Physics* B, 1." Trans. Thomas Sheehan. In William McNeill, ed., *Pathmarks.* New York: Cambridge University Press, 1998.

EPTT – "The End of Philosophy and the Task of Thinking." In David Farrell Krell, ed., *Basic Writings.* San Francisco: HarperCollins, 1993.

IM – *Introduction to Metaphysics.* Trans. Gregory Fried and Richard Polt. New Haven: Yale University Press, 2000.

PDT – "Plato's Doctrine of Truth." Trans. Thomas Sheehan. In William McNeill, ed., *Pathmarks.* New York: Cambridge University Press, 1998.

PWM – "Postscript to 'What Is Metaphysics?'" Trans. William McNeill. In W. McNeill, ed., *Pathmarks*. New York: Cambridge University Press, 1998.

Lacoste, Jean-Yves

EA Lacoste, Jean-Yves. *Experience and the Absolute: Disputed Questions on the Humanity of Man*. Trans. Mark Raftery-Skehan. Bronx: Fordham University Press, 2004.

OTHER SOURCES

Althusser, Louis. *Machiavelli and Us*. Trans. Gregory Elliott. New York: Verso, 1999.

Aristotle. *The Nicomachean Ethics*. Trans. T. Irwin. Indianapolis: Hackett, 1999.

– *The Physics*. Trans. Robin Waterfield. Oxford: Oxford University Press, 2008.

– *The Rhetoric*. Trans. Hugh Lawson-Tancred. London: Penguin Classics, 1992

Augustine of Hippo. *The City of God against the Pagans*. Trans. R.W. Dyson. New York: Cambridge University Press, 1998.

– *Confessions: Text and Commentary*. Ed. James O'Donnell. Oxford: Clarendon Press, 1992.

– *Political Writings*. Trans. and ed. E.M. Atkins and R.J. Dodaro OSA. New York: Cambridge University Press, 2001.

Aquinas, Thomas. *In libros Physicorum*; Latin edition available at www.corpusthomisticum.org.

– *Summa Theologiae*; Latin edition available at www.corpusthomisticum.org.

Bambach, Charles. *Heidegger's Roots: Nietzsche, National Socialism, and the Greeks*. Ithaca: Cornell University Press, 2003.

Benner, Erica. *Machiavelli's Ethics*. Princeton: Princeton University Press, 2009.

– *Machiavelli's Prince: A New Reading*. New York: Oxford University Press, 2013.

– "*Questa Inconstante Dea:* Machiavelli's Amoral Fortune." *Spazio Filosofico* (2014): 481–99.

Bernasconi, Robert. "Useless Sacrifice." In *Between Heidegger and Levinas*, ed. John Drabinsk and Eric S. Nelson, 149–74. Albany: SUNY University Press, 2014.

Bertonneau, Thomas. "The Logic of the Undecidable: An Interview with René Girard." *Paroles Gelées* 5, 1 (1987): 1–24

Black, Robert. *Machiavelli*. London: Routledge, 2013.

Boethius. *The Consolation of Philosophy*. Trans. Joel C. Relihan. Indianapolis: Hackett, 2001.

Bondanella, Peter E. "Castruccio Castracani: Machiavelli's Archetypical Prince." *Italica* 49, 3 (1972): 302–14.

Brown, Alison. "Lucretian Naturalism and the Evolution of Machiavelli's Ethics." In *The Radical Machiavelli: Politics, Philosophy and Language*, ed.

Filippo Del Lucchese, Fabio Frosini, and Vittorio Morfino, 105–27. Leiden: Brill, 2015.

– *The Return of Lucretius to Renaissance Florence.* Cambridge: Harvard University Press, 2010.

Bruggisser, Peter. "City of Outcasts and City of the Elect: The Romulean Asylum in Augustine's *City of God* and Servius' *Commentaries on Virgil.*" In *History, Apocalypse and the Secular Imagination: New Essays on Augustine's "City of God"*, ed. Mark Vessey, Karla Pollmann, and Allan Fitzgerald OSA, 75–104. Bowling Green: Philosophy Documentation Center, 1999.

Buber, Martin. "Genuine Dialogue and the Possibilities of Peace." In *Pointing the Way: Collected Essays,* ed. and trans. Maurice Friedman, 232–9. Atlantic Highlands, NJ: Humanities Press, 1988.

Caputo, John. *Against Ethics.* Bloomington: Indiana University Press, 1993.

– *Demythologizing Heidegger.* Bloomington: Indiana University Press, 1993.

– *More Radical Hermeneutics: On Not Knowing Who We Are.* Bloomington: Indiana University Press, 2000.

– *The Prayers and Tears of Jacques Derrida.* Bloomington: Indianapolis University Press, 1997.

– "The Return of Anti-Religion: From Radical Atheism to Radical Theology." *Journal for Cultural and Religious Theory* 11, 2 (2011): 32–93. http://www.jcrt.org/archives/11.2/caputo.pdf.

Carmen, Taylor. "Heidegger on Correspondence and Correctness." *Graduate Faculty Philosophy Journal* 28, 2 (2007): 103–16.

Cicero. *De Oratore.* Trans. and ed. E.W. Sutton and H. Rackham. Loeb Classical Library 348–9. Cambridge: Harvard University Press, 1942.

– *On Duties.* Trans. and ed. E. Atkins and M. Griffin. Cambridge: Cambridge University Press, 1991.

– *On Moral Ends.* Trans. Raphael Woolf. Cambridge: Cambridge University Press, 2001

Colish, M. "Republicanism, Religion and Machiavelli's Savanarolan Moment. *Journal of the History of Ideas* 60, 4 (1999): 597–619.

Connell, William. "The Eternity of the World in Renaissance Historical Thought." *California Italian Studies* 2, 1. http://escholarship.org/uc/item/3qx3j1nb.

de Grazia, Sebastian. *Machiavelli in Hell.* New York: Vintage, 1989.

de Vries, Hent. *Religion and Violence: Philosophical Perspectives from Kant to Derrida.* Baltimore: Johns Hopkins University Press, 2002.

Diogenes Laertius. *Lives of the Philosophers,* 2 vols. Greek text with translation by R.D. Hicks. Loeb Classical Library Cambridge: Harvard University Press, 1925.

Dowden, Ken. *Zeus.* New York: Routledge, 2006.

Falque, Emmanuel. *Metamorphosis of Finitude: An Essay on Birth and Resurrection.* Trans. George Hughes. Bronx: Fordham University Press, 2013.

Fontana, Benedetto. "Love of Country and Love of God: The Political Uses of Religion in Machiavelli." *Journal of the History of Ideas* 60, 4 (1999): 639–58.

Gutting, Gary. *Pragmatic Liberalism and the Critique of Modernity.* Cambridge: Cambridge University Press, 1999.

Hadot, Pierre. "La philosophie antique: Une éthique ou une pratique?" In *Études de Philosophie Ancienne,* 207–32. Paris: Les Belles Lettres, 1998.

Hägglund, Martin. "The Necessity of Discrimination: Disjoining Derrida and Levinas." *Diacritics* 34, 1 (2004): 40–71.

Hanson, Jeff. "Returning (to) the Gift of Death: Violence and History in Derrida and Levinas." *International Journal of the Philosophy of Religion* 67, 1 (2010): 1–15.

Harding, Brian. *Augustine and Roman Virtue.* London: Continuum, 2008.

Hasse, Dag N. "Arabic Philosophy and Averroism." In *The Cambridge Companion to Renaissance Philosophy,* ed. James Hankins, 113–36. New York: Cambridge University Press, 2007.

Hochner, Nicole. "A Ritualist Approach to Machiavelli." *History of Political Thought* 30, 4 (2009): 575–95.

Johnson, Christopher. *System and Writing in the Philosophy of Jacques Derrida.* Cambridge: Cambridge University Press, 1993.

Jonas, Hans. "Heidegger and Theology." In *The Phenomenon of Life: Towards a Philosophical Biology,* 235–61. New York: Delta Books, 1966.

Jurdjevic, Mark. *Great and Wretched City: Promise and Failure in Machiavelli's Florentine Political Thought.* Cambridge: Harvard University Press, 2014.

Kierkegaard, Søren. *Fear and Trembling.* Trans. H. and E. Hong. Princeton: Princeton University Press, 1983.

Lefort, Claude. *Writing: The Political Test.* Trans. David A. Curtis. Raleigh: Duke University Press, 2000.

Livy, Titus. *Ab Urbe Condita: Books I and II.* Latin text with translation by B.O. Foster. Loeb Classical Library. Cambridge: Harvard University Press, 1988.

Macfarland, James. "Machiavelli's Imagination of Excellent Men: An Appraisal of the Lives of Cosimo de' Medici and Castruccio Castracani." *American Political Science Review* 93, 1 (1999): 133–46.

Machiavelli, Niccolo. *The Prince.* Trans. Leo Paul de Alvarez. Prospect Heights, IL: Waveland Press, 1989.

Maddox, Graham. "The Secular Reformation and the Influence of Machiavelli." *Journal of Religion* 82, 4 (2002): 539–62.

Mansfield, Harvey. *Machiavelli's New Modes and Orders.* Chicago: University of Chicago Press, 1979.

– *Machiavelli's Virtue.* Chicago: University of Chicago Press, 1996.

– "Review of *Machiavelli in Hell.*" *American Political Science Review* 87 (1993): 764–5.

Marenbon, John. *Abelard in Four Dimensions: A Twelfth-Century Philosopher in His Context and Ours.* Notre Dame: University of Notre Dame Press, 2013.

Mautner, Thomas. "Self-Sacrifice in Heidegger." *Philosophia* 38 (2010): 385–98.

McCormick, John. "The Enduring Ambiguity of Machiavellian Virtue: Cruelty, Crime and Christianity in *The Prince.*" *Social Research* 81, 1 (2014): 133–64.

– "Prophetic Statebuilding: Machiavelli and the Passion of the Duke." *Representations* 115, 1 (2011): 1–19.

McKenna, Andrew. "The Ends of Violence: Girard and Derrida." *Lebenswelt* 1 (2011): 112–26.

– *Violence and Difference: Girard, Derrida and Deconstruction.* Urbana: University of Illinois Press, 1992.

Mendes-Flor, Paul. "Martin Buber and Martin Heidegger in Dialogue." *Journal of Religion* 94, 1 (2014): 2–25.

Najemy, John. "Papirius and the Chicken-Men, or Machiavelli on the Necessity of Interpreting Religion." *Journal of the History of Ideas* 60, 4 (1999): 659–81.

Nass, Michael. *Miracle and the Machine: Jacques Derrida and the Two Sources of Religion, Science and the Media.* Bronx: Fordham University Press, 2012.

Nederman, Cary. "Amazing Grace: Fortune, God and Free Will in Machiavelli's Thought." *Journal of the History of Ideas* 60, 4 (1999): 617–38.

Ortega y Gasset, José. *Some Lessons in Metaphysics.* Trans. M. Adams. New York: Norton, 1969.

Palmer, Ada. *Reading Lucretius in the Renaissance.* Cambridge: Harvard University Press, 2014.

Parel, Anthony. "Farewell to Fortune." *Review of Politics* 75 (2013): 587–604.

– *The Machiavellian Cosmos.* New Haven: Yale University Press, 1992.

Parsons, William B. *Machiavelli's Gospel: The Critique of Christianity in "The Prince."* Rochester: University of Rochester Press, 2016.

Piercey, Robert. *The Uses of the Past from Heidegger to Rorty: Doing Philosophy Historically.* Cambridge: Cambridge University Press, 2009.

Plato. *The Republic.* Trans. G.M.A Grube, revised C.D.C. Reeve. In *Plato: The Complete Works.* Indianapolis: Hackett, 1997.

– *The Timaeus.* Trans. D.J. Zeyl, in *Plato: The Complete Works.* Indianapolis: Hackett, 1997.

Rahe, Paul. *Against Throne and Altar: Machiavelli and Political Theory under the English Republic.* Cambridge: Cambridge University Press, 2008.

– "In the Shadow of Lucretius: The Epicurean Foundations of Machiavelli's Political Thought." *History of Political Thought* 28, 1 (2007): 30–55.

Ridolfi, Roberto. *The Life of Niccolò Machiavelli.* Trans. C. Grayson. London: Routledge, 2009.

Sallis, John. *Echoes: After Heidegger.* Bloomington: Indiana University Press, 1990.

Saralegui, Miguel. "Maquiavelo y la Partitocracia: Tumulto y Mantenimiento de la Libertad." *Anuario Filosófico* 40, 1 (2007): 203–31.

Sasso, Gennaro. *Machiavelli e gli Antichi e altri Saggie.* Milan: Riccardo Ricciardi Editori, 1986.

Saussure, Ferdinand de. *Course in General Linguistics.* Trans. Wade Baskin. New York: McGraw-Hill, 1959.

Schnapp, Jeffrey. "Machiavellian Foundlings: Castruccio Castracani and the Aphorism." *Renaissance Quarterly* 45, 4 (1992): 653–76.

Schrijvers, Jori. "Jean-Yves Lacoste: A Phenomenology of Liturgy." *Heythrop Journal* 56 (2005): 314–33.

Simmons, J. Arron, and Benson Bruce. *The New Phenomenology: An Introduction.* London: Bloomsbury, 2013.

Sluga, Hans. "Conflict Is the Father of All Things: Heidegger's Polemical Conception of Politics." In *A Companion to Heidegger's "Introduction to Metaphysics,"* ed. Richard Polt and Gregory Fried, 205–25 . New Haven: Yale University Press, 2001.

Sullivan, Vickie. *Machiavelli's Three Romes: Religion, Human Liberty and Politics Reformed.* De Kalb: Northern Illinois Press, 1996.

Soll, Jacob. "The Reception of *The Prince* 1513–1700, or Why We Understand Machiavelli the Way We Do." *Social Research* 81, 1 (2014): 31–60.

Spiegl, Jakob. "Zur Universalen Theologie Augustins: Die Religionsthematic in *De Civitate Dei.*" *Augustiniana* 50, 1 (2000): 9–63.

Strauss, Leo. *Thoughts on Machiavelli.* Chicago: University of Chicago Press, 1958.

Stump, Elanore, and Norman Kretzmann. "Eternity." *Journal of Philosophy* 78 (1981): 429–58.

Tarcov, Nathan. "Belief and Opinion in Machiavelli." *Review of Politics* 75 (2013): 573–86.

– "Machiavelli's Critique of Religion." *Social Research* 81, 1 (2014): 193–216.

– "Quentin Skinner's Method and Machiavelli's *Prince.*" *Ethics* 92, 4 (1982): 692–709.

van Buren, John. *The Young Heidegger: Rumors of a Hidden King.* Bloomington: Indiana University Press, 1994.

Viroli, Maurizio. *Machiavelli.* Oxford: Oxford University Press, 1999.

– *Machiavelli's God.* Trans. Anthony Shugaar. Princeton: Princeton University Press, 2010.

– *Niccolò's Smile: A Biography of Machiavelli.* Trans. Anthony Shugaar. New York: Farrar, Straus and Giroux, 2000.

Walsh, Patrick G. "Livy and Stoicism." *American Journal of Philology* 79 (1958): 355–75.

– "Livy's Preface and the Distortion of History." *American Journal of Philology* 76, 4 (1955): 369–83.

Warner, John, and John Scott. "Sin City: Augustine and Machiavelli's Reordering of Rome." *Journal of Politics* 73, 3 (2011): 857–71.

Wright, Paul. "Machiavelli's *City of God*: Civic Humanism and Augustinian Terror." In *Augustine and Politics*, ed. John Doody, Kevin Hughes, and Kim Paffenroth, 297–336. New York: Lexington Books, 2005.

Wydra, Harald. "Human Nature and Politics: A Mimetic Reading of Crisis and Conflict in the Work of Niccoló Machiavelli." *Contagion* 7 (2000): 36–57.

Young, Julian. *Heidegger's Later Philosophy*. Cambridge: Cambridge University Press, 2002.

Index